The DLM Early Childhood EXPRESS

Teacher's Edition
Unit 1
All About Pre-K

Nell Duke • Douglas Clements • Julie Sarama • William Teale

Wright Group

The McGraw-Hill Companies

Authors

Nell K. Duke
Professor of Teacher Education and Educational Psychology and Co-Director of the Literacy Achievement Research Center Michigan State University, East Lansing, MI

Douglas H. Clements
Professor of Early Childhood and Mathematics Education University at Buffalo, State University of New York, New York

Julie Sarama
Associate Professor of Mathematics Education University at Buffalo, State University of New York, New York

William Teale
Professor of Education University of Illinois at Chicago, Chicago, IL

Contributing Authors

Kim Brenneman, PhD
Assistant Research Professor of Psychology at Rutgers University, National Institute for Early Education Research Rutgers University, New Brunswick, NJ

Peggy Cerna
Early Childhood Consultant Austin, TX

Dan Cieloha
Educator and President of the Partnership for Interactive Learning Oakland, CA

Paula Jones
Early Childhood Consultant Lubbock, TX

Bobbie Sparks
Educator and K-12 Science Consultant Houston, TX

Rita Abrams
Composer, Lyricist, Educator, Author and two-time Emmy Award winner Mill Valley, CA

The McGraw·Hill Companies

www.WrightGroup.com

Send all inquiries to:
Wright Group/McGraw-Hill
P.O. Box 812960
Chicago, IL 60681

ISBN 978-0-07-658079-8
MHID 0-07-658079-2

2 3 4 5 6 7 8 9 WEB 16 15 14 13 12 11

Acknowledgment

Building Blocks was supported in part by the National Science Foundation under Grant No. ESI-9730804, "Building Blocks— Foundations for Mathematical Thinking, Pre-Kindergarten to Grade 2: Research-based Materials Development" to Douglas H. Clements and Julie Sarama. The curriculum was also based partly upon work supported in part by the Institute of Educational Sciences (U.S. Dept. of Education, under the Interagency Education Research Initiative, or IERI, a collaboration of the IES, NSF, and NICHHD) under Grant No. R305K05157, "Scaling Trajectories and Technologies" and by the IERI through a National Science Foundation NSF Grant No. REC-0228440, "Scaling Up the Implementation of a Pre-Kindergarten Mathematics Curricula: Teaching for Understanding with Trajectories and Technologies." Any opinions, findings, and conclusions or recommendations expressed in this material are those of the authors and do not necessarily reflect the views of the funding agencies.

Reviewers

Tonda Brown, *Pre-K Specialist*, Austin ISD; Deanne Colley, *Family Involvement Facilitator*, Northwest ISD; Anita Uphaus, *Retired Early Childhood Director*, Austin ISD; Cathy Ambridge, *Reading Specialist*, Klein ISD; Margaret Jordan, *PreK Special Education Teacher*, McMullen Booth Elementary; Niki Rogers, *Adjunct Professor of Psychology/Child Development*, Concordia University Wisconsin

Table of Contents

Unit 1: All About Pre-K
Why is school important?

Week 1
What happens at School?

Week 2
What happens in our classroom?

Week 3
What makes a good friend?

Week 4
How can we play and learn together?

Getting Started

Getting Started with *The DLM Early Childhood Express*

The DLM Early Childhood Express is a holistic, child-centered program that nurtures each child by offering carefully selected and carefully sequenced learning experiences. It provides a wealth of materials and ideas to foster the social-emotional, intellectual, and physical development of children. At the same time, it nurtures the natural curiosity and sense of self that can serve as the foundation for a lifetime of learning.

The lesson format is designed to present information in a way that makes it easy for children to learn. Intelligence is, in large part, our ability to see patterns and build relationships out of those patterns, which is why *DLM* is focused on helping children see the patterns in what they are learning. It builds an understanding of how newly taught material resembles what children already know. Then it takes the differences in the new material and helps the children convert them into new understanding.

Each of the eight Teacher Edition units in *DLM* is centered on an Essential Question relating to the unit's theme. Each week has its own more specific focus question. By focusing on essential questions, children are better able to connect their existing knowledge of the world with the new concepts and ideas they are learning at school. Routines at the beginning and end of each day help children focus on the learning process, reflect on new concepts, and make important connections. The lessons are designed to allow children to apply what they have learned.

Social and Emotional Development

Social-emotional development is addressed everyday through positive reinforcement, interactive activities, and engaging songs.

Language and Communication

All lessons are focused on language acquisition, which includes oral language development and vocabulary activities.

Emergent Literacy: Reading

Children develop literacy skills for reading through exposure to multiple read-aloud selections each day and through daily phonological awareness and letter recognition activities.

Emergent Literacy: Writing

Children develop writing skills through daily writing activities and during Center Time.

Mathematics

The math strand is based on *Building Blocks,* the result of NSF-funded research, and is designed to develop children's early mathematical knowledge through various individual and group activities.

Science

Children explore scientific concepts and methods during weekly science-focused, large-group activities, and Center Time activities.

Social Studies

Children explore Social Studies concepts during weekly social studies-focused, large-group activities, and Center Time activities.

Fine Arts

Children are exposed to art, dance, and music through a variety of weekly activities and the Creativity Center.

Physical Development

DLM is designed to allow children active time for outdoor play during the day, in addition to daily and weekly movement activities.

Technology Applications

Technology is integrated throughout each week with the use of online math activities, computer time, and other digital resources.

English Language Learners

Today's classrooms are very diverse. *The DLM Early Childhood Express* addresses this diversity by providing lessons in both English and Spanish. The program also offers strategies to assist English Language Learners at multiple levels of proficiency.

Flexible Scheduling

With *The DLM Early Childhood Express*, it's easy to fit lessons into your day.

Typical Full-Day Schedule

10 min	Opening Routines
15 min	Language Time
60-90 min	Center Time
15 min	Snack Time
15 min	Literacy Time
20 min	Active Play (outdoors if possible)
30 min	Lunch
15 min	Math Time
	Rest
15 min	Circle Time: Social and Emotional Development
20 min	Circle Time: Content Connection
30 min	Center Time
25 min	Active Play (outdoors if possible)
15 min	Let's Say Good-Bye

Typical Half-Day Schedule

10 min	Opening Routines
15 min	Language Time
60 min	Center Time
15 min	Snack Time
15 min	Circle Time (Literacy, Math, or Social and Emotional Development)
30 min	Active Play (outdoors if possible)
20 min	Circle Time (Content Connection, Literacy, Math, or Social and Emotional Development)
15 min	Let's Say Good-Bye

Welcome to *The DLM Early Childhood Express.*

Add your own ideas. Mix and match activities. Our program is designed to offer you a variety of activities on which to build a full year of exciting and creative lessons.

Happy learning to you and the children in your care!

Themes and Literature

With *The DLM Early Childhood Express,* children develop concrete skills through experiences with music, art, storytelling, hands-on activities and teacher-directed lessons that, in addition to skills development, emphasize practice and reflection. Every four weeks, children are introduced to a new theme organized around an essential question.

Literature selections and cross-curricular content are linked to the theme to help children reinforce lesson concepts. Children hear and discuss an additional read-aloud selection from the *Teacher Treasure Book* at the beginning and end of each day. At the end of each unit, children take home a *My Theme Library Book* reader of their own.

Unit 1: All About Pre-K
Why is school important?

	Focus Question	Literature
Week 1	What happens at school?	Welcome to School / Bienvenidos a la escuela
Week 2	What happens in our classroom?	Yellowbelly and Plum Go to School / Barrigota y Pipón van a la escuela
Week 3	What makes a good friend?	Max and Mo's First Day at School / Max y Mo van a la escuela
Week 4	How can we play and learn together?	Amelia's Show and Tell Fiesta/Amelia y la fiesta de "muestra y cuenta"
Unit Wrap-Up	My Library Book	How Can I Learn at School? / ¿Cómo puedo aprender en la escuela?

Unit 2: All About Me
What makes me special?

	Focus Question	Literature
Week 1	Who am I?	All About Me / Todo sobre mí
Week 2	What are my feelings?	Lots of Feelings / Montones de sentimientos
Week 3	What do the parts of my body do?	Eyes, Nose, Fingers, and Toes / Ojos, nariz, dedos y pies
Week 4	What is a family?	Jonathan and His Mommy / Juan y su mamá
Unit Wrap-Up	My Library Book	What Makes Us Special? / ¿Qué nos hace especiales?

Unit 3: My Community
What is a community?

	Focus Question	Literature
Week 1	What are the parts of a community?	In the Community / En la comunidad
Week 2	How does a community help me?	Rush Hour, / Hora pico
Week 3	Who helps the community?	Quinito's Neighborhood / El vecindario de Quinito
Week 4	How can I help my community?	Flower Garden / Un jardín de flores
Unit Wrap-Up	My Library Book	In My Community / Mi comunidad

Unit 4: Let's Investigate
How can I learn more about things?

	Focus Question	Literature
Week 1	How can I learn by observing?	Let's Investigate / Soy detective
Week 2	How can I use tools to investiagte?	I Like Making Tamales / Me gusta hacer tamales
Week 3	How can I compare things?	Nature Spy / Espía de la naturaleza
Week 4	How do objects move?	What Do Wheels Do All Day? / ¿Qué hacen las ruedas todo el día?
Unit Wrap-Up	My Library Book	How Can We Investigate? / ¿Cómo podemos investigar?

Unit 5: Amazing Animals
What is amazing about animals?

	Focus Question	Literature
Week 1	What are animals like?	*Amazing Animals* *Animales asombrosos*
Week 2	Where do animals live and what do they eat?	*Castles, Caves, and Honeycombs* *Castillos, cuevas y panales*
Week 3	How are animals the same and different?	*Who Is the Beast?* *Quien es la bestia?*
Week 4	How do animals move?	*Move!* *¡A moverse!*
Unit Wrap-Up	**My Library Book**	*Hello, Animals!* *¡Hola, animales!*

Unit 6: Growing and Changing
How do living things grow and change?

	Focus Question	Literature
Week 1	How do animals grow and change?	*Growing and Changing* *Creciendo y cambiando*
Week 2	How do plants grow and change?	*I Am a Peach* *Yo soy el durazno*
Week 3	How do people grow and change?	*I'm Growing!* *Estoy creciendo!*
Week 4	How do living things grow and change?	*My Garden* *Mi jardín*
Unit Wrap-Up	**My Library Book**	*Growing Up* *Creciendo*

Unit 7: The Earth and Sky
What can I learn about the earth and the sky?

	Focus Question	Literature
Week 1	What can I learn about the earth and the sky?	*The Earth and Sky* *La Tierra y el cielo*
Week 2	What weather can I observe each day?	*Who Likes Rain?* *¿A quién le gusta la lluvia?*
Week 3	What can I learn about day and night?	*Matthew and the Color of the Sky* *Matías y el color del cielo*
Week 4	Why is caring for the earth and sky important?	*Ada, Once Again!* *¡Otra vez Ada!*
Unit Wrap-Up	**My Library Book**	*Good Morning, Earth!* *¡Buenos días, Tierra!*

Unit 8: Healthy Food/Healthy Body
Why is healthy food and exercise good for me?

	Focus Question	Literature
Week 1	What are good healthy habits?	*Staying Healthy* *Mantente sano*
Week 2	What kinds of foods are healthy?	*Growing Vegetable Soup* *A sembrar sopa de verduras*
Week 3	Why is exercise important?	*Rise and Exercise!* *A ejercitarse, ¡uno, dos, tres!*
Week 4	How can I stay healthy?	*Jamal's Busy Day* *El intenso día de Jamal*
Unit Wrap-Up	**My Library Book**	*Healthy Kids* *Niños sanos*

Tools for Teaching

The DLM Early Childhood Express is packed full of the components you'll need to teach each theme and enrich your classroom. The *Teacher Treasure Package* is the heart of the program, because it contains all the necessary materials. Plus, the *Teacher's Treasure Book* contains all the fun components that you'll love to teach. The *Literature Package* contains all the stories and books you need to support children's developing literacy. You'll find letter tiles, counters, and puppets in the *Manipulative Package* to connect hands-on learning skills with meaningful play.

Teacher Treasure Package

This package contains all the essential tools for the teacher such as the *Teacher's Treasure Book, Teacher's Editions*, technology, and other resources no teacher would want to be without!

Alphabet Wall Cards
(English and Spanish)

ABC Picture Cards
(English and Spanish)

Sequence Cards
(English and Spanish)

Oral Language Development Cards
(English and Spanish)

Photo Library
CD-ROM

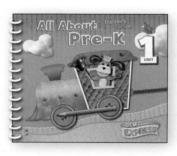

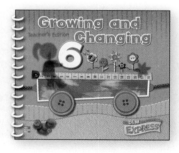
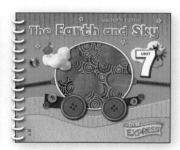

▲ Each lesson's instruction uses a variety of cards to help children learn. **Alphabet Wall Cards** and **ABC Picture Cards** help build letter recognition and phonemic awareness. **Oral Language Development Cards** teach new vocabulary, and are especially helpful when working with English Language Learners. **Sequencing Cards** help children learn how to order events and the vocabulary associated with time and sequence.

▲ There is one bilingual **Teacher's Edition** for each four-week theme. It provides the focus questions for each lesson as well as plans for centers and suggestions for classroom management.

▶ The bilingual **Teacher's Treasure Book** features 500+ pages of the things you love most about teaching Early Childhood, such as songs, traditional read alouds, folk tales, finger plays, and flannelboard stories with patterns.

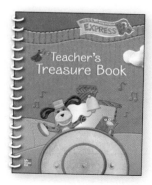

▶ An **ABC Take-Home Book** with blackline masters is provided for each letter of the English and Spanish alphabets.

ABC Take-Home Book
(English and Spanish)

▶ Flip charts and their Audio CDs support the activities in each lesson. Children practice literacy and music skills using the **Rhymes and Chants Flip Chart,** which supports oral language development and phonological awareness in both English and Spanish. An Audio CD is included and provides a recording of every rhyme or chant. The **Making Good Choices Flip Chart** provides illustrations to allow students to explore social and emotional development concepts while facilitating classroom activities and discussion. 15 lively songs recorded in both English and Spanish address key social emotional development themes such as: joining in, helping others, being fair, teasing, bullying, and much more. The **Math and Science Flip Chart** is a demonstration tool that addresses weekly math and science concepts through photos and illustrations.

▶ Other key resources include a **Research & Professional Development Guide,** and a bilingual **Home Connections Resource Guide** which provides weekly letters home and take-home story books.

Building Blocks

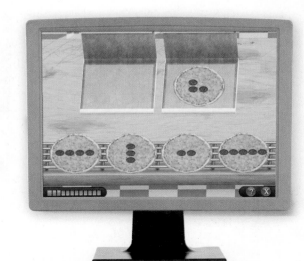

Building Blocks, the result of NSF-funded research, develops young children's mathematical thinking using their bodies, manipulatives, paper, and computers.

Building Blocks online management system guides children through research-based learning trajectories. These activities-through-trajectories connect children's informal knowledge to more formal school mathematics. The result is a mathematical curriculum that is not only motivating for children but also comprehensive.

▶ **DLMExpressOnline.com** includes the following:

● e-Books of student and teacher materials

● Audio recordings of the **My Library** and **Literature Books** (Big/Little) in English and Spanish

● Teacher planning tools and assessment support

Tools for Teaching

Literature Package

This package contains the literature referenced in the program. Packages are available in several variations so you can choose the package that best meets the needs of your classroom. The literature used in the program includes expository selections, traditional stories, and emergent readers for students. All literature is available in English or Spanish.

▶ **My Library Books** are take-home readers for children to continue their exploration of unit themes. (English and Spanish)

▶ **Concept Big Books** are nonfiction selections that introduce the essential questions for each unit and help children make connections between their background knowledge and unit themes. (English and Spanish)

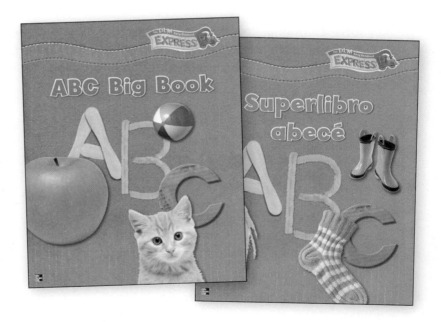

▶ The **ABC Big Book** helps children develop phonemic awareness and letter recognition. (English and Spanish)

► The **Big Books** and **Little Books** reinforce each week's theme and the unit theme. Selections include stories originally written in Spanish, as well as those written in English.

► The stories in the **Big Books and Little Books** are recorded on the **Listening Library Audio CDs**. They are available in English and Spanish.

Manipulative Package

This package contains fun tools for children to play and learn with in the classroom.

Two Puppets

Alphabet Letter Tiles (in English and Spanish)

Transportation and Farm Animal Counters

Two-Color Counters

Step-by-Step Number Line

Balance Scale

Pattern Blocks

Shape Sets

Connecting Cubes

Jumbo Hand Lenses

Magnetic Wands

A Typical Weekly Lesson Plan

Each week of **The DLM Early Childhood Express** is organized the same way to provide children with the structure and routines they crave. Each week begins with a weekly opener that introduces the focus question for the week and includes a review of the week's Learning Goals, the Materials and Resources needed for the week, a Daily Planner, and a plan for the Learning Centers children will use throughout the week.

Each day's lesson includes large-group Circle Time and small-group Center Time. Each day includes Literacy, Math, and Social and Emotional Development activities during Circle Time. On Day 1, children explore Science. On Days 2 and 4, they work on more in-depth math lessons. On Day 3, Social Studies is the focus. Fine Art or Music/Movement activities take place during Circle Time on Day 5.

You will find the **Program Materials** and **Other Materials** needed for each day on the Materials and Resources page.

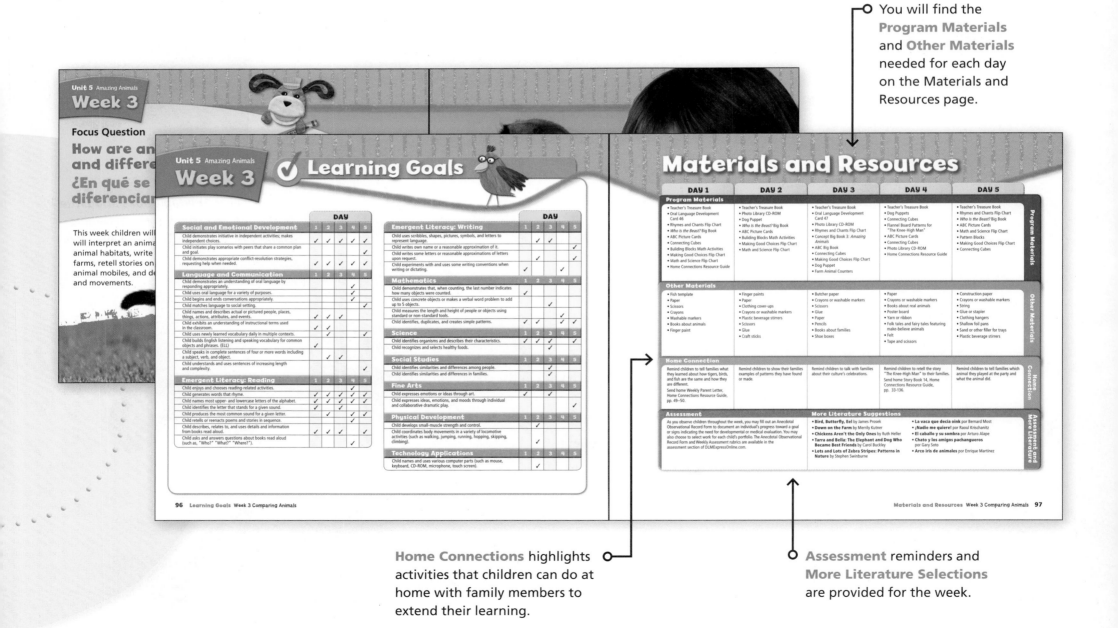

Home Connections highlights activities that children can do at home with family members to extend their learning.

Assessment reminders and **More Literature Selections** are provided for the week.

The **Daily Planner** provides a Week-at-a-Glance view of the daily structure and lesson topics for each week.

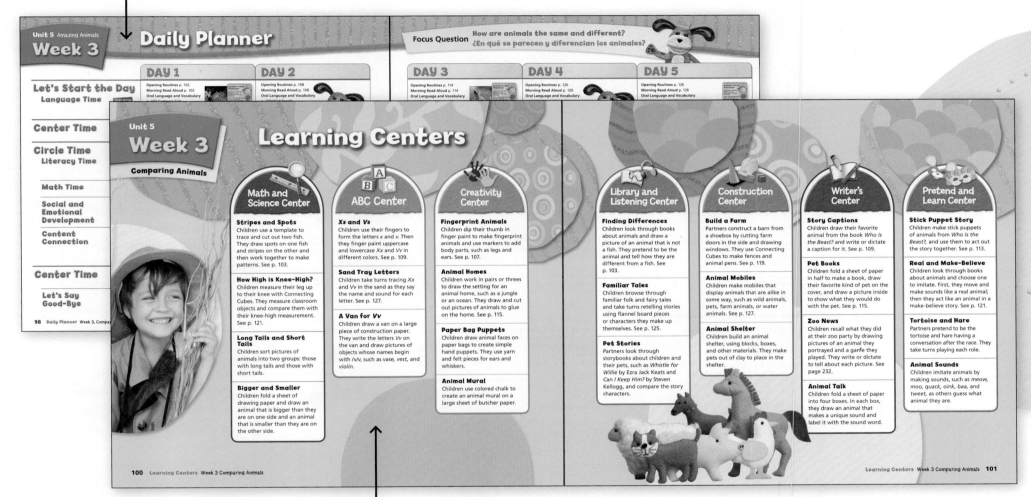

Learning Centers should be used throughout the week during Center Time. This page provides an overview of center activities to set up for children. Additional information about some center activities is provided in the daily lessons. The Learning Centers are intended to remain open for the entire week. These centers provide the opportunity for children to explore a wide range of curricular areas.

Lesson Overview

Our **Teacher's Editions** are organized by theme, week, and day. Each day's lesson is covered in six page spreads. The lessons integrate learning from the skill domain areas of: Social Emotional Development, Language and Communication, Emergent Literacy Reading and Writing, Mathematics, Science, Social Studies, Fine Arts, Physical Development, and Technology.

Each day begins with **Opening Routines** and a **Read Aloud** selection. This structured time helps children settle into their day.

The **Learning Goals** met by the lesson are listed on each page.

Observational Checks at point of use help to focus learning. These informal assessment questions help to ensure children are meeting lesson objectives.

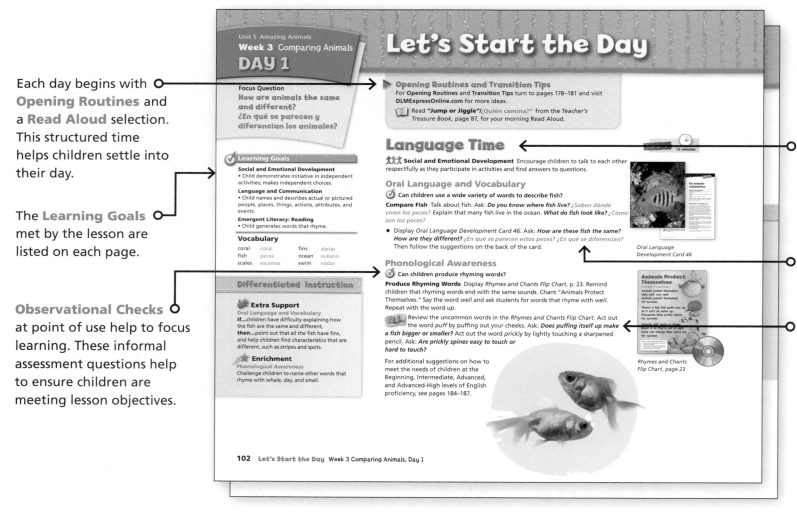

Language Time is the first large-group activity of the day. It includes Oral Language and Vocabulary Development as well as Phonological Awareness activities.

Instructional questions are provided in both **English and Spanish.**

Tips for working with **English Language Learners** are shown at point of use throughout the lessons. Teaching strategies are provided to help children of of all language backgrounds and abilities meet the lesson objectives.

Center Time provides additional information for teacher-guided small-group activities and suggestions for independent activities children will complete during weekly Center Rotation.

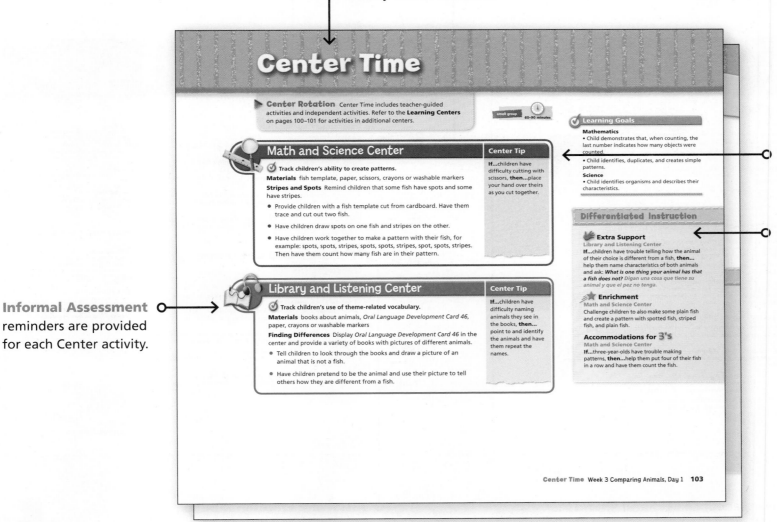

Center Time

Center Rotation Center Time includes teacher-guided activities and independent activities. Refer to the **Learning Centers** on pages 100–101 for activities in additional centers.

small group | *60–90 minutes*

Math and Science Center

✓ Track children's ability to create patterns.

Materials fish template, paper, scissors, crayons or washable markers

Stripes and Spots Remind children that some fish have spots and some have stripes.

● Provide children with a fish template cut from cardboard. Have them trace and cut out two fish.

● Have children draw spots on one fish and stripes on the other.

● Have children work together to make a pattern with their fish, for example: spots, spots, stripes, spots, spots, stripes, spot, spots, stripes. Then have them count how many fish are in their pattern.

Center Tip

If...children have difficulty cutting with scissors, **then**...place your hand over theirs as you cut together.

Library and Listening Center

✓ Track children's use of theme-related vocabulary.

Materials books about animals, *Oral Language Development Card 46*, paper, crayons or washable markers

Finding Differences Display *Oral Language Development Card 46* in the center and provide a variety of books with pictures of different animals.

● Tell children to look through the books and draw a picture of an animal that is not a fish.

● Have children pretend to be the animal and use their picture to tell others how they are different from a fish.

Center Tip

If...children have difficulty naming animals they see in the books, **then**... point to and identify the animals and have them repeat the names.

Learning Goals

Mathematics
● Child demonstrates that, when counting, the last number indicates how many objects were counted.
● Child identifies, duplicates, and creates simple patterns.

Science
● Child identifies organisms and describes their characteristics.

Differentiated Instruction

Extra Support
Library and Listening Center
If...children have trouble telling how the animal of their choice is different from a fish, **then**... help them name characteristics of both animals and ask: *What is one thing your animal has that a fish does not? Digan una cosa que tiene su animal y que el pez no tenga.*

Enrichment
Math and Science Center
Challenge children to also make some plain fish and create a pattern with spotted fish, striped fish, and plain fish.

Accommodations for 3's
Math and Science Center
If...three-year-olds have trouble making patterns, **then**...help them put four of their fish in a row and have them count the fish.

Center Time Week 3 Comparing Animals, Day 1   **103**

Center Tips are provided for center support.

Differentiated Instruction offers suggestions for modifications to activities for children who may need Extra Support or Enrichment, as well as Accommodations for 3's and Special Needs.

Informal Assessment reminders are provided for each Center activity.

Lesson Overview

Children have **Literacy Time** every day. During this time, children listen to and discuss a second Read Aloud from a nonfiction **Concept Big Book** or a **Big Book/Little Book** literature selection

Building Blocks online activities are provided each week during Math Time.

Children work in large groups on 15 minute math activities during daily **Math Time.**

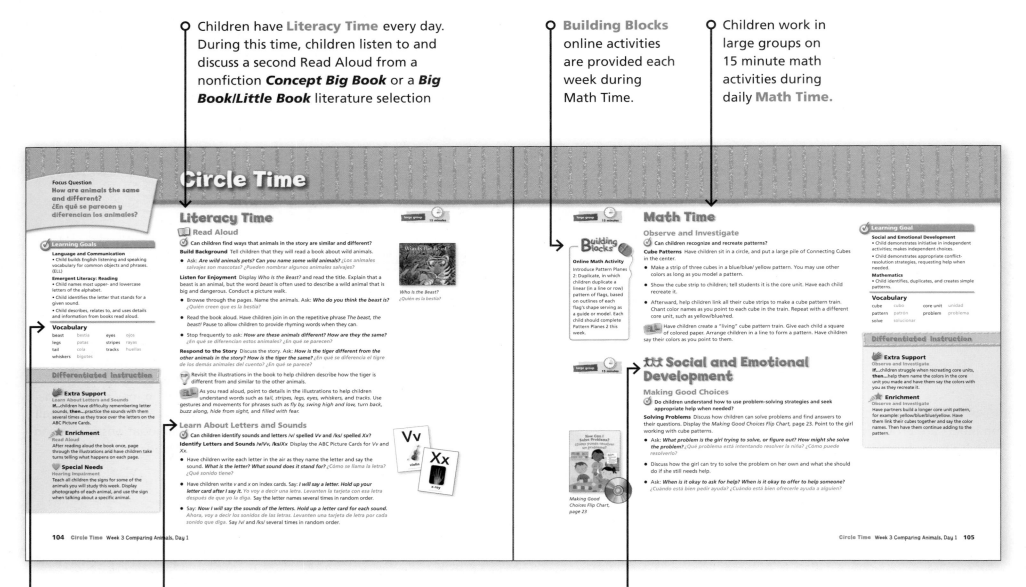

Focus Question
How are animals the same and different?
¿En qué se parecen y diferencian los animales?

Circle Time

Literacy Time

large group · 15 minutes

Read Aloud

☑ Can children find ways that animals in the story are similar and different?
Build Background Tell children that they will read a book about wild animals.

- Ask: *Are wild animals pets? Can you name some wild animals? ¿Los animales salvajes son mascotas? ¿Pueden nombrar algunos animales salvajes?*

Listen for Enjoyment Display *Who Is the Beast?* and read the title. Explain that a beast is an animal, but the word *beast* is often used to describe a wild animal that is big and dangerous. Conduct a picture walk.

- Browse through the pages. Name the animals. Ask: *Who do you think the beast is? ¿Quién creen que es la bestia?*

- Read the book aloud. Have children join in on the repetitive phrase *The beast, the beast!* Pause to allow children to provide rhyming words when they can.

- Stop frequently to ask: *How are these animals different? How are they the same? ¿En qué se diferencian estos animales? ¿En qué se parecen?*

Respond to the Story Discuss the story. Ask: *How is the tiger different from the other animals in the story? How is the tiger the same? ¿En qué se diferencia el tigre de los demás animales del cuento? ¿En qué se parece?*

TIP Revisit the illustrations in the book to help children describe how the tiger is different from and similar to the other animals.

ELL As you read aloud, point to details in the illustrations to help children understand words such as *tail, stripes, legs, eyes, whiskers,* and *tracks.* Use gestures and movements for phrases such as *fly by, swing high and low, turn back, buzz along, hide from sight,* and *filled with fear.*

Learn About Letters and Sounds

☑ Can children identify sounds and letters /v/ spelled *Vv* and /ks/ spelled *Xx*?
Identify Letters and Sounds /v/Vv, /ks/Xx Display the ABC Picture Cards for *Vv* and *Xx.*

- Have children write each letter in the air as they name the letter and say the sound. *What is the letter? What sound does it stand for? ¿Cómo se llama la letra? ¿Qué sonido tiene?*

- Have children write v and x on index cards. Say: *I will say a letter. Hold up your letter card if I say it. Yo voy a decir una letra. Levanten la tarjeta con esa letra después de que yo la diga.* Say the letter names several times in random order.

- Say: *Now I will say the sounds of the letters. Hold up a letter card for each sound. Ahora, voy a decir los sonidos de las letras. Levanten una tarjeta de letra por cada sonido que diga.* Say /v/ and /ks/ several times in random order.

Who Is the Beast?
¿Quién es la bestia?

Vv violin
Xx x-ray

Learning Goals

Language and Communication
- Child builds English listening and speaking vocabulary for common objects and phrases. (ELL)

Emergent Literacy: Reading
- Child names most upper- and lowercase letters of the alphabet.
- Child identifies the letter that stands for a given sound.
- Child describes, relates to, and uses details and information from books read aloud.

Vocabulary

beast	bestia	eyes	ojos
legs	patas	stripes	rayas
tail	cola	tracks	huellas
whiskers	bigotes		

Differentiated Instruction

Extra Support
Learn About Letters and Sounds
If...children have difficulty remembering letter sounds, then...practice the sounds with them several times as they trace over the letters on the ABC Picture Cards.

Enrichment
Read Aloud
After reading aloud the book once, page through the illustrations and have children take turns telling what happens on each page.

Special Needs
Hearing Impairment
Teach all children the signs for some of the animals you will study this week. Display photographs of each animal, and use the sign when talking about a specific animal.

Math Time

large group · 15 minutes

Observe and Investigate

☑ Can children recognize and recreate patterns?
Cube Patterns Have children sit in a circle, and put a large pile of Connecting Cubes in the center.

- Make a strip of three cubes in a blue/blue/ yellow pattern. You may use other colors as long as you model a pattern.

- Show the cube strip to children; tell students it is the core unit. Have each child recreate it.

- Afterward, help children link all their cube strips to make a cube pattern train. Chant color names as you point to each cube in the train. Repeat with a different core unit, such as yellow/blue/red.

ELL Have children create a "living" cube pattern train. Give each child a square of colored paper. Arrange children in a line to form a pattern. Have children say their colors as you point to them.

Building Blocks

Online Math Activity
Introduce Pattern Planes 2: Duplicate, in which children duplicate a linear (in a line or row) pattern of flags, based on outlines of each flag's shape serving as a guide or model. Each child should complete Pattern Planes 2 this week.

♦♦♦ Social and Emotional Development

large group · 15 minutes

Making Good Choices

☑ Do children understand how to use problem-solving strategies and seek appropriate help when needed?
Solving Problems Discuss how children can solve problems and find answers to their questions. Display the *Making Good Choices Flip Chart*, page 23. Point to the girl working with cube patterns.

- Ask: *What problem is the girl trying to solve, or figure out? How might she solve the problem? ¿Qué problema está intentando resolver la niña? ¿Cómo puede resolverlo?*

- Discuss how the girl can try to solve the problem on her own and what she should do if she still needs help.

- Ask: *When is it okay to ask for a letter. Hold up your When is it okay to offer to help someone? ¿Cuándo está bien pedir ayuda? ¿Cuándo está bien ofrecerle ayuda a alguien?*

Making Good Choices Flip Chart, page 23

Learning Goal

Social and Emotional Development
- Child demonstrates initiative in independent activities; makes independent choices.
- Child demonstrates appropriate conflict-resolution strategies, requesting help when needed.

Mathematics
- Child identifies, duplicates, and creates simple patterns.

Vocabulary

cube	cubo	core unit	unidad
pattern	patrón	problem	problema
solve	solucionar		

Differentiated Instruction

Extra Support
Observe and Investigate
If...children struggle when recreating core units, then...help them name the colors in the core unit you made and have them say the colors with you as they recreate it.

Enrichment
Observe and Investigate
Have partners build a longer core unit pattern, for example: yellow/blue/yellow/yellow. Have them link their cubes together and say the color names. Then have them continue adding to the pattern.

Vocabulary is provided in English and Spanish to help expand children's ability to use both languages.

Children learn about **Letters and Sounds** every day. The sound is introduced with the letter. Children also practice letter formation.

Social and Emotional Development concepts are addressed every day to help children better express their emotions and needs, and establish positive relationships.

Circle Time is devoted to longer activities focusing on different cross-curricular concepts each day. Day 1 is Science Time. Days 2 and 4 are Math Time. On Day 3, children have Social Studies Time. Fine arts are covered in Art Time or Music and Movement Time on Day 5.

An end-of-the-day **Writing** activity is provided each day.

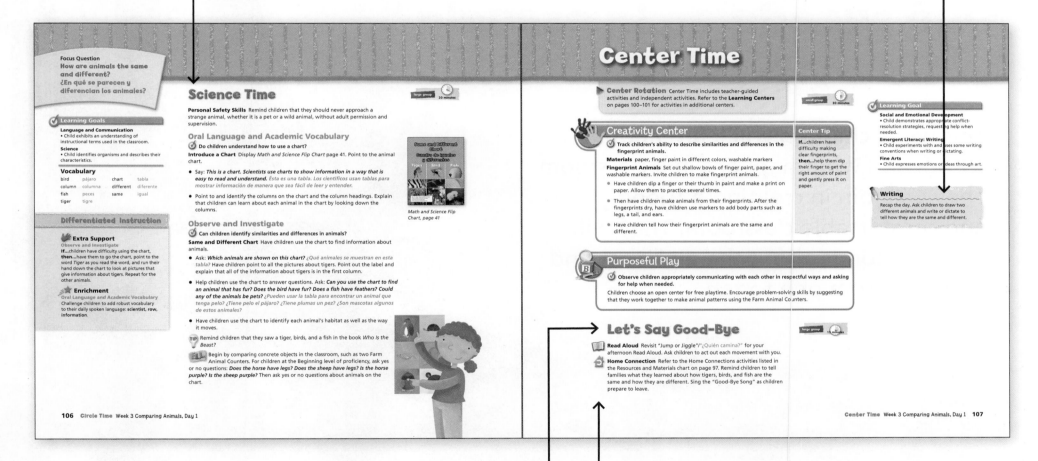

Focus Question
How are animals the same and different?
¿En qué se parecen y diferencian los animales?

Learning Goals

Language and Communication
• Child exhibits an understanding of instructional terms used in the classroom.
Science
• Child identifies organisms and describes their characteristics.

Vocabulary

bird	pájaro	chart	tabla
column	columna	different	diferente
fish	peces	same	igual
tiger	tigre		

Differentiated Instruction

Extra Support
Observe and Investigate
If...children have difficulty using the chart, then...have them go to the chart, point to the word *Tiger* as you read the word, and run their hand down the chart to look at pictures that give information about tigers. Repeat for the other animals.

Enrichment
Oral Language and Academic Vocabulary
Challenge children to add robust vocabulary to their daily spoken language: **scientist, row, information.**

Science Time

Personal Safety Skills Remind children that they should never approach a strange animal, whether it is a pet or a wild animal, without adult permission and supervision.

Oral Language and Academic Vocabulary

Do children understand how to use a chart?
Introduce a Chart Display *Math and Science Flip Chart* page 41. Point to the animal chart.

• Say: *This is a chart. Scientists use charts to show information in a way that is easy to read and understand. Ésta es una tabla. Los científicos usan tablas para mostrar información de manera que sea fácil de leer y entender.*
• Point to and identify the columns on the chart and the column headings. Explain that children can learn about each animal in the chart by looking down the columns.

Math and Science Flip Chart, page 41

Observe and Investigate

Can children identify similarities and differences in animals?
Same and Different Chart Have children use the chart to find information about animals.

• Ask: *Which animals are shown on this chart? ¿Qué animales se muestran en esta tabla?* Have children point to all the pictures about tigers. Point out the label and explain that all of the information about tigers is in the first column.
• Help children use the chart to answer questions. Ask: *Can you use the chart to find an animal that has fur? Does the bird have fur? Does a fish have feathers? Could any of the animals be pets? ¿Pueden usar la tabla para encontrar un animal que tenga pelo? ¿Tiene pelo el pájaro? ¿Tiene plumas un pez? ¿Son mascotas algunos de estos animales?*
• Have children use the chart to identify each animal's habitat as well as the way it moves.

TIP Remind children that they saw a tiger, birds, and a fish in the book *Who Is the Beast?*

ELL Begin by comparing concrete objects in the classroom, such as two Farm Animal Counters. For children at the Beginning level of proficiency, ask yes or no questions: *Does the horse have legs? Does the sheep have legs? Is the horse purple? Is the sheep purple?* Then ask yes or no questions about animals on the chart.

Center Time

Center Rotation Center Time includes teacher-guided activities and independent activities. Refer to the **Learning Centers** on pages 100–101 for activities in additional centers.

Creativity Center

Track children's ability to describe similarities and differences in the fingerprint animals.
Materials paper, finger paint in different colors, washable markers
Fingerprint Animals Set out shallow bowls of finger paint, paper, and washable markers. Invite children to make fingerprint animals.

• Have children dip a finger or their thumb in paint and make a print on paper. Allow them to practice several times.
• Then have children make animals from their fingerprints. After the fingerprints dry, have children use markers to add body parts such as legs, a tail, and ears.
• Have children tell how their fingerprint animals are the same and different.

Center Tip
If...children have difficulty making clear fingerprints, then...help them dip their finger to get the right amount of paint and gently press it on paper.

Purposeful Play

Observe children appropriately communicating with each other in respectful ways and asking for help when needed.
Children choose an open center for free playtime. Encourage problem-solving skills by suggesting that they work together to make animal patterns using the Farm Animal Counters.

Learning Goal

Social and Emotional Development
• Child demonstrates appropriate conflict-resolution strategies, requesting help when needed.
Emergent Literacy: Writing
• Child experiments with and uses some writing conventions when writing or dictating.
Fine Arts
• Child expresses emotions or ideas through art.

Writing
Recap the day. Ask children to draw two different animals and write or dictate to tell how they are the same and different.

Let's Say Good-Bye

Read Aloud Revisit "Jump or Jiggle"/"¿Quién camina?" for your afternoon Read Aloud. Ask children to act out each movement with you.
Home Connection Refer to the Home Connections activities listed in the Resources and Materials chart on page 97. Remind children to tell families what they learned about how tigers, birds, and fish are the same and how they are different. Sing the "Good-Bye Song" as children prepare to leave.

Let's Say Good-Bye includes the closing routines for each day. The Read Aloud from the beginning of the day is revisited with a focus on skills practiced during the day.

Each day provides a **Home Connection.** At the start of each week, a letter is provided to inform families of the weekly focus and offer additional literature suggestions to extend the weekly theme focus.

Week 1

Focus Question

What happens at school?
¿Qué sucede en la escuela?

This week children will learn about school and what happens in a classroom. They will join in creating a friendly and comfortable classroom. They will also sing songs about the alphabet and numbers from one to ten.

✓ Learning Goals

Social and Emotional Development	DAY 1	2	3	4	5
Child begins to show a greater ability to control intense feelings.				✓	
Child begins to be responsible for individual behavior and actions.				✓	
Child recognizes and manages feelings and impulses; increasingly maintains self-control in difficult situations (can increase or decrease intensity of emotions with guidance).			✓	✓	
Child demonstrates positive social behaviors, as modeled by the teacher.	✓	✓		✓	✓
Child initiates interactions with others in work and play situations.	✓				
Child initiates play scenarios with peers that share a common plan and goal.	✓				
Child learns how to make and keep friends.	✓				

Language and Communication	1	2	3	4	5
Child understands and uses regular and irregular plural nouns, regular past tense verbs, personal and possessive pronouns, and subject-verb agreement.			✓		
Child uses nonverbal cues to communicate with others who do not speak his or her home language. (ELL)	✓	✓			✓
Child uses individual words and short phrases to communicate. (ELL)	✓	✓			
Child tries to use newly learned vocabulary and grammar. (ELL)		✓			

Emergent Literacy: Reading	1	2	3	4	5
Child explores books and other texts to answer questions.		✓	✓		
Child listens for words (for example, hears and separates individual words within a four-word sentence).	✓				
Child names most upper- and lowercase letters of the alphabet.	✓	✓	✓	✓	✓
Child describes, relates to, and uses details and information from books read aloud.	✓	✓	✓		✓

Emergent Literacy: Writing	1	2	3	4	5
Child participates in free drawing and writing activities to deliver information.			✓		
Child uses scribbles, shapes, pictures, symbols, and letters to represent language.			✓	✓	
Child uses scribbles, shapes, pictures, symbols, and letters to represent language.					✓
Child writes some letters or reasonable approximations of letters upon request.		✓			

Mathematics	DAY 1	2	3	4	5
Child understands that objects, or parts thereof, can be counted.		✓		✓	
Child recites number words in sequence from one to thirty.	✓	✓		✓	✓
Child counts 1–10 concrete objects correctly.			✓	✓	
Child understands that objects can be counted in any order.		✓			
Child recognizes, names, describes, matches, compares, sorts common two-dimensional shapes (such as circle, square, rectangle, triangle, rhombus).				✓	
Child creates two-dimensional shapes; recreates two-dimensional shapes from memory.		✓		✓	
Child measures passage of time using standard or non-standard tools.		✓	✓		
Child sorts objects and explains how the sorting was done.	✓		✓		

Science	1	2	3	4	5
Child follows basic health and safety rules.	✓				

Social Studies	1	2	3	4	5
Child identifies common events and routines.			✓		
Child participates in voting for group decision-making.		✓			

Fine Arts	1	2	3	4	5
Child expresses emotions or ideas through art.					✓
Child participates in a variety of music activities (such as listening, singing, finger plays, musical games, performances).	✓				✓

Physical Development	1	2	3	4	5
Child develops small-muscle strength and control.		✓			

Technology Applications	1	2	3	4	5
Child names and uses various computer parts (such as mouse, keyboard, CD-ROM, microphone, touch screen).		✓			
Child uses computer software or technology to express original ideas.		✓			✓

Materials and Resources

DAY 1	DAY 2	DAY 3	DAY 4	DAY 5

Program Materials

DAY 1	DAY 2	DAY 3	DAY 4	DAY 5
• Teacher's Treasure Book • Oral Language Development Card 1 • Rhymes and Chants Flip Chart • Photo Library CD-ROM • Concept Big Book 1 • Making Good Choices Flip Chart • Math and Science Flip Chart • Home Connections Resource Guide	• Concept Big Book 1 • Teacher's Treasure Book • Dog Puppets 1 and 2 • Making Good Choices Flip Chart • Online Building Blocks Math Activities • Connecting Cubes • Two-Color Counters • Home Connections Resource Guide	• Teacher's Treasure Book • Oral Language Development Card 2 • Rhymes and Chants Flip Chart • Flannel Board Characters for "I Like School" • ABC Picture Cards • Dog Puppets 1 and 2 • Making Good Choices Flip Chart • Photo Library CD-ROM • Home Connections Resource Guide	• Teacher's Treasure Book • Flannel Board Characters for "How Two Brothers Solved a Problem" • Alphabet Wall Cards • Dog Puppets 1 and 2 • Letter Tiles • Math and Science Flip Chart • Shape Sets • Home Connections Resource Guide	• Teacher's Treasure Book • Rhymes and Chants Flip Chart • Concept Big Book 1 • Alphabet Wall Cards • Alphabet/Letter Tiles • Making Good Choices Flip Chart • Home Connections Resource Guide

Other Materials

DAY 1	DAY 2	DAY 3	DAY 4	DAY 5
• books about school • basic school supplies • dress-up clothes • index cards with images of home and school items • 3 containers with labels of house, school, house and school • scissors, pencil • symbol of circle with line through • images illustrating stop, drop, and roll procedure, fire exit chart, exit sign	• building blocks • construction paper, crayons • labeled pictures of classroom areas • name cards • stickers	• noisy and quiet labels • books about school • assorted paper • crayons, tape, pencils, markers • roll-on paint, letter stamps • name cards • classroom calendar with pictures • construction paper • images of classroom items and activities • paste	• picture books • sticky notes • play clay • paper plates	• musical instruments • construction paper • crayons • paste • collage materials, such as yarn, fabric scraps • paint, paint trays, smocks • watercolor paint brushes, pastry brushes, nail and make-up brushes • butcher paper

Home Connection

DAY 1	DAY 2	DAY 3	DAY 4	DAY 5
Encourage children to tell their families what they learned about what children do at school. Send home the following materials. Weekly Family Letter, Home Connections Resource Guide, pp. 13–14	Tell children to model their counting ability by counting their family members when they get home.	Encourage children to tell their families what they did in school today.	Remind children to sing the alphabet song and look for letters they know around their home. ABC Take-Home Book, "The ABC Song," pp. 3, 31	Have children bring paintings home and describe them to their families.

Assessment

As you observe children throughout the week, you may fill out an Anecdotal Observational Record Form to document an individual's progress toward a goal or signs indicating the need for developmental or medical evaluation. You may also choose to select work for each child's portfolio. The Anecdotal Observational Record Form and Weekly Assessment rubrics are available In the assessment section of DLMExpressOnline.com.

More Literature Suggestions

- **I Don't Want To Go To School!/No quiero ir a la escuela** by Stephanie Blake
- **How Do Dinosaurs Go to School?/¿Cómo van a la escuela los dinosaurios?** by Jane Yolen
- **Two at the Zoo** by Danna Smith
- **Chicken Chickens Go To School** by Valeri Gorbachev
- **One Little Bug** by Paola van Turennout
- **Jugando con las vocales** por Margarita Robleda

Daily Planner

	DAY 1	**DAY 2**
Let's Start the Day **Language Time** *large group*	**Opening Routines** p. 26 **Morning Read Aloud** p. 26 **Oral Language and Vocabulary** p. 26 Words for Playing and Learning **Phonological Awareness** p. 26 Concept of Word	**Opening Routines** p. 32 **Morning Read Aloud** p. 32 **Oral Language and Vocabulary** p. 32 Classroom Words **Phonological Awareness** p. 32 Name Game
Center Time *small group*	**Focus On:** **Pretend and Learn Center** p. 27 **Creativity Center** p. 27	**Focus On:** **Construction Center** p. 33 **ABC Center** p. 33
Circle Time **Literacy Time** *large group*	**Read Aloud** *Welcome to School/Bienvenidos a la escuela* p. 28 **Learn About Letters and Sounds: Names and Letters** p. 28	**Read Aloud** *Welcome to School/Bienvenidos a la escuela* p. 34 **Learn About Letters and Sounds: Names and Letters** p. 34
Math Time *large group*	**Sing "This Old Man"** p. 29	**Sing "This Old Man"** p. 35 **Counting Wand** p. 35
Social and Emotional Development *large group*	**A Friendly Classroom** p. 29	**Friendly Talk** p. 35
Content Connection *large group*	**Science:** **Oral Language and Academic Vocabulary** p. 30 Cross Safely **Observe and Investigate** p. 30 Personal Safety	**Math:** **Math Time** p. 36 Computer Time
Center Time *small group*	**Focus On:** **Math and Science Center** p. 31 **Purposeful Play** p. 31	**Focus On:** **Math and Science Center** p. 37 **Purposeful Play** p. 37
Let's Say Good-Bye *large group*	**Read Aloud** p. 31 **Writing** p. 31 **Home Connection** p. 31	**Read Aloud** p. 37 **Writing** p. 37 **Home Connection** p. 37

Building Blocks

DAY 3

Opening Routines p. 38

Morning Read Aloud p. 38

Oral Language and Vocabulary
p. 38 Quiet Times

Phonological Awareness
p. 38 School Words

Focus On:

Library and Listening Center p. 39

Writer's Center p. 39

Read Aloud
"I Like School"/"Me gusta la escuela" p. 40

**Learn About Letters and Sounds:
Learn About Lower Case Letters** p. 40

Count and Move p. 41

Let's Share p. 41

Social Studies:

Oral Language and Academic Vocabulary
p. 42 Classroom Routines

Understand and Participate
p. 42 The Daily Schedule

Focus On:

Construction Center p. 43

Purposeful Play p.43

Read Aloud p. 43

Writing p. 43

Home Connection p. 43

DAY 4

Opening Routines p. 44

Morning Read Aloud p. 44

Oral Language and Vocabulary
p. 44 Talk About Brothers and Sisters

Phonological Awareness
p. 44 Word Game

Focus On:

Library and Listening Center p. 45

ABC Center p. 45

Read Aloud
"How Two Brothers Solved a Problem"/"De cómo dos hermanos aprendieron a resolver un problema" p. 46

**Learn About Letters and Sounds:
Learn About the Alphabet** p. 46

Sing "When I Was One" p. 47

Solving Problems p. 47

Math:

Math Time
p. 48 Counting Objects

Focus On:

Math and Science Center p. 49

Purposeful Play p. 49

Read Aloud p. 49

Writing p. 49

Home Connection p. 49

DAY 5

Opening Routines p. 50

Morning Read Aloud p. 50

Oral Language and Vocabulary
p. 50 School Lessons

Phonological Awareness
p. 50 Draw a Word

Focus On:

Pretend and Learn Center p. 51

Writer's Center p. 51

Read Aloud
Welcome to School/*Bienvenidos a la escuela* p. 52

Learn About Letters and Sounds: Learn About the Alphabet p. 52

Sing "This Old Man" p. 53

Our Friendly Room p. 53

Art:

Oral Language and Academic Vocabulary
p. 54 Painters Tools

Explore and Express
p. 54 Artists at Work

Focus On:

Creativity Center p. 55

Purposeful Play p. 55

Read Aloud p. 55

Writing p. 55

Home Connection p. 55

Learning Centers

Math and Science Center

School Safety
Children review school safety, p. 31.

Explore Math Manipulatives
Children count cubes, p. 37.

Explore Shape Sets
Children use shapes to make a picture, p. 49.

Count Boys and Girls
Make picture cards of girls and boys. Place the pile on the table. Children work in pairs. One counts how many girls and the other counts the boys.

Freeze Safety
Children practice responding to school safety signals. One child rings a bell. Children "freeze" and stop what they are doing and stand up.

How Many?
Children count groups of 1–10 objects. After the last number they say, *I counted _____ crayons.*

ABC Center

Paint Your Name
Children paint their names, p. 33.

Alphabet Letters
Children make letters out of clay, p. 45.

ABC Circle
Children hold up a letter card and form an alphabet circle. Sing "The ABC Song" together. Sing again as each child "sings" her/his letter.

Line Up the Alphabet
Lay alphabet cards on the floor in a row. Children sit around the first letter of their name. Children sing "The ABC song" and stand when their letter is sung.

My Alphabet Chart
Create outline upper case letters on full-sized sheets of paper. Have children color in the letters. Laminate finished charts so children can refer to them while learning letters.

Creativity Center

School Items and Home Items
Children sort items belonging at home and at school, p. 27.

Cooperative Brush Art
Children experiment with brush strokes, p. 55.

That's My Name
Give each child a name card. Have them say, *My name is [first and last name].* Have children decorate their name card.

Classroom Creation
Children use a variety of materials to create a picture showing something they like about their classroom. Talk about textures, colors, and shapes used.

Name Collage
Prepare sheets of paper with *My name is _____.* Help children write their names. Have children use art supplies and magazine pictures to create a collage about things they like.

Library and Listening Center

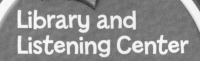

Noisy or Quiet
Children sort quiet and noisy activities, p. 39.

Book Browsing
Children look for pictures about getting along, p. 45.

Browse Pre-K Books
Pairs browse through books about going to school. Have them point out things that are like their school.

Safety Signals
Children browse through books and look for examples of children following safety signals.

All Kinds of Art
Children browse through books of different kinds of art (collage, mosaics, sculptures, and so on) and name things they know.

Listen to Big Book
Children listen in pairs to *Welcome To School/ Bienvenidos a la escuela*.

Construction Center

Create a Classroom
Children make a classroom out of blocks and paper, p. 33.

Hello and Good-Bye
Children sort pictures to show hellos and good-byes, p. 43.

My Classroom
Have pairs use blocks, boxes, and other items in the center to build a model of an item (table) or an area (book area) in their classroom.

Crossing Safely
Children build a long road with blocks. One child acts as crossing guard and helps others cross the road safely.

Outside Play
Children use blocks, boxes, and other items in the center to build something they will find outside, such as a tree or a slide.

Writer's Center

Let's Write
Children write about noisy and quiet times, p. 39.

Making Friends
Children make a collage about friendship, p. 51.

That's the Rule
Children identify classroom rules. Record the rules. Each child draws a picture representing one rule. Label their drawings and post next to the list of rules.

Yesterday, Today, Tomorrow
Children discuss routines that happen every day in school. Draw a picture of one routine. Help them label their picture.

My Name
Children draw a self-portrait. Have them state their name (first and last if possible). Help them write their names on their pictures.

Pretend and Learn Center

School Day Play
Children role-play a day in preschool, p. 27.

Sing a Song
Children use instruments to play a song, p. 51.

Playing School
Children focus on one aspect of school (morning circle) and act out what happens during that time.

Animal School
Children use stuffed animals and pretend they are outside at recess time. Have one child/animal be the teacher.

Be the Teacher
Display pictures of positive behaviors. Small groups work together. One child plays the teacher and models a good behavior. The "class" mimics the behavior.

DAY 1

Let's Start the Day

Focus Question
What happens at school?
¿Qué sucede en la escuela?

Opening Routines and Transition Tips
For **Opening Routines** and **Transition Tips** turn to pages 178–181 and visit DLMExpressOnline.com for more ideas.

Read **"Little Annie Oakley"/**"La pequeña Annie Oakley" from the *Teacher's Treasure Book,* page 253, for your morning Read Aloud.

✓ Learning Goals

Language and Communication
• Child names and describes actual or pictured people, places, things, actions, attributes, and events.

Emergent Literacy: Reading
• Child listens for words (for example, hears and separates individual words within a four-word sentence).

Fine Arts
• Child participates in a variety of music activities (such as listening, singing, finger plays, musical games, performances).

Vocabulary

act	actuar	boy	niño
clothes	vestirse	dress up	disfraz
girl	niña	playing	jugar
pretend	simular		

Differentiated Instruction

Extra Support
Phonological Awareness
If... a child has difficulty hearing his or her own name in the song, **then...** point to the child as you sing the name in an exaggerated way.

★ Enrichment
Oral Language and Vocabulary
Ask children to look around the classroom and name items they see, such as books, paints, blocks, and so on.

Accommodations for 3's
Phonological Awareness
If... three-year-olds have trouble learning the words to the song, **then...** sing one line at a time, allowing them to echo each line as you sing it.

Language Time

large group 15 minutes

👪 Social and Emotional Development Model helping children learn and remember each other's names by using first names when referring to children or responding to questions.

Oral Language and Vocabulary

✓ Can children use a wide variety of words to label and describe classroom objects and activities?

Words for Playing and Learning Welcome the children to Pre-Kindergarten. Talk about what happens at school. Say: *At school, children learn and play. What would you like to learn at school?* En la escuela los niños aprenden y juegan. ¿Qué les gustaría aprender?

● Display *Oral Language Development Card 1*. Ask: *Can you tell what these children are playing?* (dress up) ¿A qué juegan estos niños? (Juegan a disfrazarse.) Ask children if they like to play dress up, and then follow the suggestions on the back of the card.

Oral Language Development Card 1

Phonological Awareness

✓ Can children hear separate words in short sentences?

Concept of Word Display the *Rhymes and Chants Flip Chart*, page 5. Sing "This Is the Way" several times with the children until they become familiar with the tune and the words. Use a different child's name every time you sing the song.

● Say: *When we sing a song, we are singing the words in the song. The words in the first part of this song are:* This (pause) is (pause) the (pause) way (pause) we (pause) go (pause) to (pause) school. *Cuando cantamos una canción, decimos cantando las palabras de la canción. Las palabras de la primera parte de la canción son* Dame (pausa) la (pausa) Hold up a finger for each word as you say it.

● Sing each line slowly, and enunciate each word clearly. Say: *Listen for your name in this song. Stand up if you hear your name.* Presten atención y traten de escuchar su nombre en la canción. Pónganse de pie cuando escuchen su nombre.

● Repeat the song, substituting the names of the children in your class.

ELL Use the *Oral Language Development Cards* as discussion starters. Invite children to repeat and complete the sentence, *On Monday morning, I can* _____.

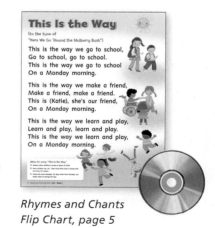

Rhymes and Chants Flip Chart, page 5

Center Time

▶ **Center Rotation** Center Time includes teacher-guided activities and independent activities. Refer to the **Learning Centers** on pages 24–25 for independent activity ideas.

 small group — 60–90 minutes

Pretend and Learn Center

✓ **Watch for examples of how children initiate interactions with others in play.**

✓ **Listen for use of the newly learned vocabulary words.**

Materials books about school, basic school supplies, dress-up clothes

School Day Play Have children browse through schoolbooks and compare what is similar to and different from their classroom. Then, invite children to dramatize their school day, using the names of classroom objects. Have children take turns being the teacher.

● Encourage the "teacher" to help children learn one another's names.

● Model the child's role by creating artwork with available supplies.

Center Tip

If... children have difficulty assuming the teacher's role, **then...** model giving simple instructions for the children to follow.

Creativity Center

✓ **Observe children as they sort and name items they find at home, items they find at school, and items they find at both places.**

Materials pictures of items found at school and items found at home (such as a bed, sofa, desk, crayons, paint) from the *Photo Library CD-ROM,* a container with a picture of a house on it, a container with a picture of a school on it, a container with pictures of both a house and a school on it

School Items and Home Items Explain that children will name the pictures and sort them into the containers.

● Identify all the pictures for the group and model placing a picture into the school container, a picture into the home container, and a picture into the container for both home and school.

● Ask children to complete the sorting activity with the pictures. Encourage them to talk with their classmates about their choices.

Center Tip

If... children have difficulty sorting, **then...** ask guiding questions to help children identify where they have seen the items.

Learning Goals

Social and Emotional Development
● Child initiates interactions with others in work and play situations.
● Child initiates play scenarios with peers that share a common plan and goal.

Language and Communication
● Child names and describes actual or pictured people, places, things, actions, attributes, and events.
● Child uses newly learned vocabulary daily in multiple contexts.

Mathematics
● Child sorts objects and explains how the sorting was done.

Differentiated Instruction

 Extra Support
Pretend and Learn Center
If... children have difficulty dramatizing classroom activities, **then...** guide them through the class day, encouraging them to remember the daily routines.

 Enrichment
Creativity Center
Challenge children to draw a picture of the things in the room where they sleep.

Accommodations for 3's
Pretend and Learn Center
If... three-year-olds have difficulty role-playing, **then...** model simple behaviors for them to follow, such as holding up a book and saying: **Let's read this together.** *Leamos este libro juntos.*

Focus Question

What happens at school?
¿Qué sucede en la escuela?

✓ Learning Goals

Language and Communication
• Child exhibits an understanding of instructional terms used in the classroom.

Emergent Literacy: Reading
• Child names most upper- and lowercase letters of the alphabet.

• Child describes, relates to, and uses details and information from books read aloud.

Vocabulary

classroom	salón de clases	circles	círculo
exercise	ejercicio	friends	amigos
habits	hábitos	healthy	saludable
learn	aprender	name	nombre
teacher	maestro		

Differentiated Instruction

🖐 Extra Support

Read Aloud
If... children have difficulty describing the story, **then...** point out specific details shown in photos and model how to describe the visual elements.

⭐ Enrichment

Read Aloud
Challenge children to look through the book and describe similarities to their own classroom.

Accommodations for 3's

Read Aloud
Guide three-year-olds to show what they learned by encouraging them to find specific links to the classroom. Ask: **Which children in the book are playing with blocks? Do you like to play with blocks in school?** *¿Qué niños del libro están jugando con bloques? ¿Les gustaría jugar con bloques en la escuela?*

Literacy Time

 🕐 large group · 15 minutes

📖 Read Aloud

✓ **Can children learn from a book about school?**

Build Background Tell children that many children their own age go to school. Explain that a classroom is a room in a school where children are taught.

● Say: *We are going to read a book about what children do and learn in Pre-K.* *Vamos a leer un libro sobre lo que los niños hacen y aprenden en Prekínder.*

● Say: *Let's learn about things that children do in school.* *Vamos a aprender lo que hacen los niños en la escuela.*

Listen for Enjoyment Display *Concept Big Book 1: Welcome to School*, and read the title. Browse through the pages, pointing out the children's activities.

● Read the book aloud, pausing to provide child-friendly explanations of vocabulary words.

● As you read individual pages, ask questions such as: **What do you see in the classroom? How is this the same as our classroom?** *¿Qué ven en el salón de clases? ¿En qué se parece a nuestro salón de clases?*

Respond to the Story Discuss the book. Encourage children to describe what they saw in the classroom scenes. Help children use vocabulary words from the book to describe what they learned.

💡 **TIP** Help children describe things from the book about school by asking questions about attributes such as color, size, amount, age, and so on.

ELL Review the book, pointing out pictures of classroom items and activities that illustrate classroom words. Say a word and have children repeat it. Guide children to find examples of the words in the classroom.

Learn About Letters and Sounds

✓ **Can children identify letters in their first names?**

Names and Letters Display a card with your first name printed on it. Say your name and explain that the word on the card is your name written down.

● Repeat your name, and slowly spell it aloud, pointing to each letter as you do so. Explain that you just named the letters in your name, and that letters work together to make names and other words. Pointing to each letter, spell your name again.

● Distribute children's name cards to them, reading each one aloud and positioning the card correctly in their hands as you do so. Then have volunteers display their name cards and name any letters they recognize. Tell every child the first letter in his or her name if the child does not know it.

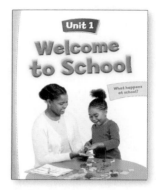

Welcome to School
Bienvenidos a la escuela

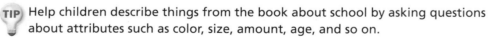

 large group 15 minutes

Math Time

Observe and Investigate

 Can children sing a counting song?

Sing "This Old Man" Sing the lyrics of the song "This Old Man" with children. As you sing, guide children in the actions listed.

> **This old man, he played one,** *(Show one finger.)*
> **He played knick-knack on his thumb.** *(Wiggle thumb.)*
> **Knick-knack paddy whack,**
> **Give the dog a bone.** *(Clap hands.)*
> **This old man came rolling home.** *(Roll arms.)*
> **This old man, he played two,** *(Show two fingers.)*
> **He played knick-knack on his shoe.** *(Wiggle fingers near shoe.)*
> **Knick-knack paddy whack,**
> **Give the dog a bone.** *(Clap hands.)*
> **This old man came rolling home.** *(Roll arms.)*

- Repeat the song until children learn the words and can count in order. Using the same verse pattern, continue to the number five: three/on his knee; four/on the floor; five/on his side.

- The Spanish version of this song is located in the *Teacher's Treasure Book*, page 24.

ELL Preview the vocabulary for this lesson: *count, move,* and *number.* Emphasize the words as you say them. Say: *I can count to the number five on my fingers. As I say each number, I move my finger up.*

 large group 15 minutes

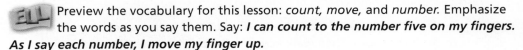 Social and Emotional Development

Making Good Choices

 Can children name friendly classroom behaviors?

A Friendly Classroom Discuss ways children can be friendly in the classroom. Help them understand they can be friendly by sharing supplies and ideas, by being helpful, and by including everyone.

Display the *Making Good Choices Flip Chart,* page 5.

- Point to the friends waving to each other. Ask: *How do you feel when a friend waves at you? What can you do if someone is not nice to you? ¿Cómo se sienten cuando un amigo los saluda? ¿Qué pueden hacer si alguien no es amable con ustedes?*

- Model the actions from the flip chart and from the class discussion for children.

Making Good Choices Flip Chart, page 5

 **Learning Goals**

Social and Emotional Development
- Child demonstrates positive social behaviors, as modeled by the teacher.
- Child learns how to make and keep friends.

Mathematics
- Child recites number words in sequence from one to thirty.

Fine Arts
- Child participates in a variety of music activities (such as listening, singing, finger plays, musical games, performances).

Vocabulary

count	contar	fair	justo
friendly	amigable	move	moverse
number	número	share	compartir

Differentiated Instruction

✋ **Extra Support**

Observe and Investigate
If... children have difficulty singing and doing the motions simultaneously, **then...** have children nod their heads instead of doing the motions.

⭐ **Enrichment**

Observe and Investigate
Challenge children to count aloud independently using their own invented motions.

Focus Question
What happens at school?
¿Qué sucede en la escuela?

✓ Learning Goals

Social and Emotional Development
• Child demonstrates positive social behaviors, as modeled by the teacher.

Language and Communication
• Child names and describes actual or pictured people, places, things, actions, attributes, and events.

Science
• Child follows basic health and safety rules.

Vocabulary

cross	cruzar	rule	regla
safe	seguro	sign	cartel
symbol	símbolo		

Differentiated Instruction

 Extra Support
Observe and Investigate
If... children need help holding scissors, **then...** properly place the scissors in a child's hand and walk along with your hand as a guide.

 Enrichment
Observe and Investigate
Encourage children to draw a picture using the symbol of a circle with a line through it to indicate a safety habit in the classroom, such as *NO running*.

 Special Needs
Cognitive Challenges
Look for opportunities to review how to cross the street as well as opportunities to practice it—on the playground, in the lunch room, and outside on a real street.

Science Time

 large group 20 minutes

Personal Safety Skills Model safety procedures by placing signs around the classroom that show proper safety skills.

Oral Language and Academic Vocabulary

✓ **Can children identify rules for crossing the street safely?**

Cross Safely Point to a child crossing the street in the *Math and Science Flip Chart*, page 5. Say: ***This child is crossing the street safely on her way to school.*** *Para ir a la escuela, este niño está cruzando la calle de manera segura.*

● Discuss where the child is crossing the street and who is crossing the street with the child. Say: ***Never cross the street without a grownup. The place where we cross the street is the crosswalk. On your way to school, always wait for the sign or crossing guard to tell you when to cross.*** *Nunca crucen la calle sin estar acompañados por una persona mayor. La calle debe cruzarse por el paso peatonal. Cuando van camino a la escuela, siempre esperen que el agente de tránsito les indique cuándo cruzar.*

Math and Science Flip Chart, page 5

● Engage children in a discussion about how to cross the street safely. Ask: ***What does it mean when the crosswalk sign shows a red X or a red* Don't Walk? *How do you cross a street where there is no crosswalk?*** *¿Qué significa la X roja en el cartel del paso peatonal? ¿Cómo cruzan la calle si no hay paso peatonal?*

ELL Explain that the word *cross* can be used to explain an action. Say: ***I am going to cross the room.*** Then walk across the room. Invite children to walk across the room as you help them say: ***I am going to cross the room.***

Observe and Investigate

✓ **Do children understand safety rules and danger symbols?**

Personal Safety Display scissors, a pencil, and symbols that show a circle with a line to indicate *NO,* such as *NO running* or *NO swimming*. Say: ***There are many things that you can do to keep yourself safe in school and out of school. Sometimes you shouldn't do things to be safe. Why might there be a* No Swimming *rule?*** *Hay muchas cosas que pueden hacer para estar seguros dentro y fuera de la escuela. Hay cosas que por seguridad no deben hacerse. ¿Por qué a veces hay una regla que dice no se puede nadar?* Display the symbols and explain to children that the circle with the line indicates *NO* and that the illustrated activity shown with that symbol means that the activity is not allowed because it would be unsafe.

● Model how to safely carry scissors in a classroom; have children practice. Then model how to safely pass scissors, and have children practice with a partner.

● Discuss other safety rules and procedures in the classroom and on the playground, such as: a fire drill; an emergency drill; and stop, drop, and roll. Lead children in practicing the procedure for stop, drop, and roll.

Center Time

▶ **Center Rotation** Center Time includes teacher-guided activities and independent activities. Refer to the **Learning Centers** on pages 24–25 for independent activity ideas.

small group 30 minutos

Math and Science Center

 Learning Goals

Language and Communication
• Child names and describes actual or pictured people, places, things, actions, attributes, and events.

• Child uses nonverbal cues to communicate with others who do not speak his or her home language. (ELL)

• Child uses individual words and short phrases to communicate. (ELL)

Science
• Child follows basic health and safety rules.

✓ **Watch for examples of children practicing school safety rules.**

Materials pictures illustrating school safety rules, fire exit chart, exit sign

School Safety Tell children that they will practice school safety procedures.

• Talk with children about how to safely exit the classroom if there is any type of emergency. Stress to students that they should be quiet and listen to directions the adults give them.

• Have children practice using the buddy system.

• For the center activity, encourage children to explore the pictures, charts, and signs and act out safety rules with a partner. Encourage communication, including non-verbal and single-word responses.

Center Tip
If... children need help remembering safety procedures, **then...** post charts with pictures of the appropriate actions.

Writing
Have children draw a picture showing themselves being fair at school. Ask each child to describe what the picture is showing. To demonstrate respect for other's work, ask permission to write the dictated sentence on paper. Model how to hold a pen or pencil as you transcribe what they say onto the bottom on the page.

Purposeful Play

✓ **Observe how children work together, talk, and plan their play.**

Children choose an open center for free playtime. Encourage them to act out safety skills as they play together.

Let's Say Good-Bye

large group 15 minutes

 Read Aloud Revisit "Little Annie Oakley"/"La pequeña Annie Oakley" for your afternoon Read Aloud. Ask if any of the words have some of the letters in their names.

 Home Connection Refer to the Home Connections activities listed in the Resources and Materials chart on page 21. Encourage children to tell their families what children do in Pre-K. Sing the "Good-Bye Song"/"Hora de ir a casa" (*Teacher's Treasure Book,* page 68) as children prepare to leave.

DAY 2

Focus Question

What happens at school?
¿Qué sucede en la escuela?

Learning Goals

Language and Communication
• Child tries to use newly learned vocabulary and grammar. (ELL)

Social Studies
• Child participates in voting for group decision-making.

Vocabulary

classroom	salón de clases
exercise	ejercicio
friends	amigos
habits	hábitos
healthy	saludable
learn	aprender
teacher	maestro

Differentiated Instruction

Extra Support
Oral Language and Vocabulary
If...children have difficulty naming an activity they enjoy, **then...**use *Concept Big Book 1: Welcome to School* to prompt them. As you page through, point to the various pictures. Ask: *What do you like about circle time? What is your favorite type of exercise? ¿Qué les gusta de la hora del círculo? ¿Cuál es su tipo de ejercicio favorito?*

Enrichment
Oral Language and Vocabulary
Challenge children to pantomime something they learned to do in school, and encourage other children to guess what it is.

Let's Start the Day

Opening Routines and Transition Tips
For **Opening Routines** and **Transition Tips** turn to pages 178–181 and visit DLMExpressOnline.com for more ideas.

📖 Read **"Dress Me Bears for School"/"¡A vestirse para la escuela!"** from the *Teacher's Treasure Book*, page 233, for your morning Read Aloud.

Language Time

large group 🕐 15 minutes

👫👤 **Social and Emotional Development** Help children to feel comfortable expressing their own unique ideas and opinions in group discussions and at play.

Oral Language and Vocabulary
✓ **Can children use new vocabulary words as they discuss classroom experiences?**
Classroom Words Talk about the day at school. Ask: *What are some of the things we do in Pre-K? Which is your favorite? Why? ¿Qué cosas hacemos en Prekínder? ¿Cuál es su actividad favorita? ¿Por qué?*

● Display *Concept Big Book 1: Welcome to School*. Review the activities displayed as you page through the book. Invite children to give examples of similar activities.

● Guide children to understand that each activity named helps them learn something. Ask: *What did you learn at school yesterday? What would you like to learn? ¿Qué aprendieron ayer en la escuela? ¿Qué les gustaría aprender?*

Phonological Awareness
✓ **Can children vote to decide on names for the Dog Puppets? Can they listen for words and use each other's names in spoken sentences?**
Name Game Display the Dog Puppets. Ask children for suggestions on what to name the puppets and have the class vote on the names. Then have the two Dog Puppets introduce themselves to the children. Say: *My name is [Miguel]. My name starts with [/m/]. My name is [Anne]. My name starts with [/a/]. Mi nombre es Miguel. Me gusta pintar; mi nombre es Anne. Me gusta cantar.* Have the puppets ask: *What is my name? What sound does it start with?* Encourage children to answer in complete sentences, using the puppets' names.

Continue by having one puppet ask several children to tell his or her name and the sound it starts with. The other puppet can then point to one of the children and ask: *What is her name? What sound does it start with? ¿Quién sabe el nombre de esta niña? ¿Cón qué sonido empieza su nombre?* Extend by having children take turns asking one another questions with the Dog Puppets.

ELL Use one of the Dog Puppets to give children additional opportunities to use their names in sentences about classroom activities. The Dog Puppet can point out the activities children in the class enjoy, while playing the name game with children.

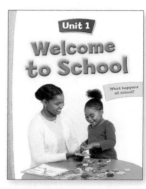

Welcome to School
Bienvenidos a la escuela

Center Time

 small group 60–90 minutes

Construction Center

	Center Tip

☑ Track the use of classroom vocabulary as children plan and create a classroom.

☑ Watch for examples of children recognizing and respecting the needs of others as they build together.

Materials building blocks, construction paper, crayons, labeled pictures of areas of the room

Create a Classroom Have children work together to plan a classroom. Ask: *What areas will you need in your room? ¿Qué áreas serán necesarias en el salón de clases?* Make a large map identifying walls, windows, and doors. Encourage children to add other "landmarks."

• Invite children to use blocks to create areas for different classroom activities. Show children how to use folded paper to draw pictures of themselves or friends and place them standing up in the classroom.

Center Tip
If...children have difficulty making stand-up pictures, **then**...fold paper for them, and show them where to draw the picture.

ABC Center

	Center Tip

☑ Note children's control of materials that require eye-hand coordination.

☑ Listen for children talking together as they decorate name cards.

Materials name cards, crayons, stickers

Paint Your Name Provide children with name cards, and invite them to use crayons and stickers to decorate their cards.

• Model decorating your own name card with crayons and stickers.

• Say your name aloud as you decorate your card: *My name is [name]. I am going to use red and blue crayons to decorate my name card. Mi nombre es [nombre]. Voy a usar crayones rojos y azules para decorar la tarjeta con mi nombre.*

• Have children recite their names as you hand them their name cards.

• Ask children to listen for other children's names as they work.

Center Tip
If...children show an interest in writing their name, **then**... provide additional cards for practice.

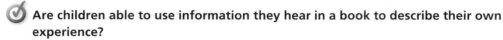
 Learning Goals

Emergent Literacy: Reading
- Child explores books and other texts to answer questions.
- Child describes, relates to, and uses details and information from books read aloud.

Vocabulary

classroom	salón de clases
exercise	ejercicio
friends	amigos
habits	hábitos
healthy	saludable
learn	aprender
teacher	maestro

Differentiated Instruction

Extra Support

Read Aloud

If...children have difficulty understanding that the print on the page is related to the words you are reading, **then...**have them review the pictures of children learning, and point to a specific word or phrase pictured. Say the word or phrase as you underline the text with your finger. Have children repeat the procedure.

⭐ Enrichment

Learn About Letters and Sounds
Invite children to go on a letter hunt in the room to find an example of a word on a classroom label or book that starts with the same letter as their names.

Accommodations for 3's

Learn About Letters and Sounds
If...three-year-olds have difficulty matching the first letter of their name to the letter on the alphabet chart, **then...**write the letter by itself on a larger piece of paper for the children to use for the match.

Literacy Time

 **large group   15 minutes**

📖 Read Aloud

 Are children able to use information they hear in a book to describe their own experience?

Build Background Remind children that there are many different things they can learn at school.

- Ask children to share some of the things they have already learned in school. Ask children to remember some of the things they read about yesterday in the book about what Pre-K children learn and do in school.

- Ask: **Have you ever asked to be read to? In school, it's okay to ask someone to read to you or to ask questions about the book.** *¿Le pidieron a alguien que les leyera este libro? En la escuela, pueden pedirle a alguien que lo lea o pueden hacerle preguntas sobre el libro.*

Listen for Understanding Display *Concept Big Book 1: Welcome to School*, and read the title. Say: **The author of the book is writing about children who go to school, what they learn, and how they stay safe and healthy.** *El autor de este libro escribe sobre niños que van a la escuela, sobre lo que aprenden y sobre cómo se cuidan y se mantienen saludables.*

- Say: **This book helps us learn about our own classroom.** *Este cuento nos ayuda a aprender sobre nuestro propio salón de clases.*

- Track with your finger as you read. Pause while reading and use the questions to prompt children to describe similarities between their own classroom activities and those portrayed in the book.

Respond to the Book Discuss by encouraging children to describe things children do at school. Ask why these are important and why they think school is important.

ELL To support comprehension, use gestures and pantomime to support feeling and action words such as *sad, happy, laugh, exercise, paint,* and *sing.* Reinforce them during the day. For example, ask: **You look happy running. Do you like to exercise?**

Learn About Letters and Sounds

 Can children identify upper case letters in their names?

Names and Letters Print upper case letters of the children's first names on chart paper or an interactive whiteboard, naming each letter. Explain that upper case letters are used at the beginning of names and special words.

- Display your name and point to the upper case letter it begins with.

- Demonstrate for children proper letter formation for the first letter in their names.

- Conclude by singing "The ABC Song" together, pointing to any upper case letters displayed in the room as you do so.

Welcome to School
Bienvenidos a la escuela

Math Time

Observe and Investigate

 Can children demonstrate that the last number counted tells how many?

Sing "This Old Man" Say: *Yesterday we sang the song "This Old Man." Today we will sing it again! Tomorrow we will learn a new song.* Sing "This Old Man" with children, guiding them in the actions.

Counting Wand Use a Magnetic Wand to count each child in the classroom.

● Say: *Numbers tell us how many of something there are. We can find out how many children are in our classroom today.* *Los números nos dicen cuánto hay de algo. Podemos saber, por ejemplo, cuántos niños hay en el salón de clases hoy.*

● Using the Magnetic Wand, count each child with a gentle tap on the shoulder. As children listen to you count, encourage them to count along with you.

● Once you have counted the last child, repeat the last number word. Emphasize that this number tells how many children are in the classroom. Ask: *What number tells how many children are in the classroom? ¿Qué número dice la cantidad de niños que hay en el salón de clases?*

✗✗✗ Social and Emotional Development

Making Good Choices

 Can children engage in friendly greetings and discussions with teachers?

Friendly Talk Discuss friendly greetings with the children. Display the *Making Good Choices Flip Chart*, page 5.

● Have the first Dog Puppet point to the teacher asking questions about painting and ask: *What could the child tell the teacher about the painting? ¿Qué le podría estar diciendo el niño al maestro sobre su pintura?*

● Have the second Dog Puppet point to the child waving and ask: *Why does the child wave when coming into the room? What are some of the best ways to greet children and teachers? ¿Por qué el niño saluda cuando entra al salón de clases? ¿Cuál es la mejor manera de saludar a los niños y a los maestros?*

Making Good Choices Flip Chart, page 5

● Have the first Dog Puppet ask: *Why do you think the child is looking at the teacher when they are talking? ¿Por qué creen que el niño mira al maestro cuando el maestro habla?*

ELL Greet the children using a variety of words and gestures, such as *hello, hi, wassup, hola,* waves, fist bumps, thumbs up, and smiles. Explain that these are all ways to greet each other.

Learning Goals

Social and Emotional Development
• Child demonstrates positive social behaviors, as modeled by the teacher.

Language and Communication
• Child uses nonverbal cues to communicate with others who do not speak his or her home language. (ELL)

• Child uses individual words and short phrases to communicate. (ELL)

Mathematics
• Child understands that objects, or parts thereof, can be counted.

• Child demonstrates that, when counting, the last number indicates how many objects were counted.

• Child measures passage of time using standard or non-standard tools.

Vocabulary

friendly	amigable
good-bye	adiós
greeting	saludo
hello	hola
today	hoy
tomorrow	mañana
yesterday	ayer

Differentiated Instruction

 Extra Support

Making Good Choices
If...children have difficulty relating their explanations of the flip chart to their own experiences, then...have the Dog Puppets ask them to explain how each behavior would make the classroom a friendlier place.

Enrichment

Observe and Investigate
Challenge children to think of a word that rhymes with the number word *six* to be used in the next verse of the song.

Focus Question
What happens at school?
¿Qué sucede en la escuela?

Learning Goals

Technology Applications
• Child opens and correctly uses age-appropriate software programs.

• Child names and uses various computer parts (such as mouse, keyboard, CD-ROM, microphone, touch screen).

• Child uses computer software or technology to express original ideas.

Vocabulary

click	clic	icon	ícono
keyboard	teclado	monitor	monitor
mouse	mouse	name	nombre
parts	partes	password	contraseña

Differentiated Instruction

Extra Support
Math Time
Help children use the parts of the computer. Children may especially need help positioning and clicking the mouse.

Enrichment
Math Time
Challenge children to add more technology vocabulary to their spoken language repertoire: *input devices, touch screen,* and *CD-ROM.*

Special Needs
Delayed Motor Development
One of the most important tools for helping children with delayed motor skills use a computer is an adaptive keyboard. There are also adaptive mouse devices available. A speech pathologist or occupational therapist can help you decide which tools work best for the child.

Math Time

  large group 20 minutes

Can children name the parts of a computer?

Computer Time

● With children gathered around the computer, discuss its parts, focusing especially on the monitor, keyboard, and mouse. Review how to use a computer, modeling how to be gentle with it and its parts. Say: *A computer is a fragile machine. You must be gentle with it. If you need help using the computer, [assistant's name] or I will help you. Una computadora es una máquina frágil. Deben ser cuidadosos con ella. Si necesitan ayuda para usarla, los ayudaré.*

● Demonstrate how to choose an icon, name, and password in the *Building Blocks* software. Then show how to complete Count and Race. Click on the garage to add cars, and then click on the flag to make the cars race. As you do so, have children count aloud.

● Tell children they will have a chance to work on computer activities during computer time or Center Time each week. Provide opportunities for children to use software applications to create their own stories and artwork, to express and record their feelings and ideas, to listen to music or books, and to explore images.

Center Time

Center Rotation Center Time includes teacher-guided activities and independent activities. Refer to the **Learning Centers** on pages 24–25 for independent activity ideas.

small group   30 minutes

Refer to the **Learning Centers** on pages 24–25 for independent activity ideas.

Math and Science Center

	Center Tip

☑ **Encourage children to count using math manipulatives.**

Materials various math manipulatives, such as cubes and counters

Explore Math Manipulatives Have children explore counting using math manipulatives.

- Give children a chance to explore the math manipulatives.

- Ask children to group the manipulatives together into designs.

- Ask: *How many cubes are in your design?* ¿Cuántos cubos hay en la figura que formaron?

Center Tip

If...children have difficulty counting the manipulatives independently, **then...**count with them.

Learning Goals

Emergent Literacy: Writing
• Child writes some letters or reasonable approximations of letters upon request.

Mathematics
• Child demonstrates that, when counting, the last number indicates how many objects were counted.

• Child creates two-dimensional shapes; recreates two-dimensional shapes from memory.

Purposeful Play

☑ **Observe as children make designs or shapes with math manipulatives.**

Children choose an open center for free playtime. Encourage children to create shapes or suggest classroom objects that children can mimic with the manipulatives.

Writing

Provide assorted writing implements and paper in a variety of colors. Invite children to practice writing the first letters in their names. Reinforce proper letter formation. Make children's name cards available as well as the *ABC Big Book* to use as a resource.

Let's Say Good-Bye

large group   15 minutes

 Read Aloud Revisit "Dress Me Bears for School"/"¡A vestirse para la escuela!" for your afternoon Read Aloud. Remind children that part of being friendly is being quiet at story time so that everyone is able to hear the story.

Home Connection Refer to the Home Connections activities listed in the Resources and Materials chart on page 21. Remind children to say good-bye before they go home. Sing the "Good-Bye Song"/"Hora de ir a casa" (*Teacher's Treasure Book,* page 68) as children prepare to leave.

Let's Start the Day

Focus Question
What happens at school?
¿Qué sucede en la escuela?

▶ Opening Routines and Transition Tips
For **Opening Routines** and **Transition Tips** turn to pages 178–181 and visit
DLMExpressOnline.com for more ideas.

 Read **"Fish Games"/**"Juegos de peces" from the *Teacher's Treasure Book,* page 275, for your morning Read Aloud.

✓ Learning Goals

Social and Emotional Development
• Child follows simple classroom rules and routines.

Language and Communication
• Child names and describes actual or pictured people, places, things, actions, attributes, and events.

Vocabulary

friend	amigo	group	grupo
listen	escuchar	Monday	lunes
noisy	ruidoso	quiet	silencio

Differentiated Instruction

 Extra Support
Phonological Awareness
If...children have difficulty hearing individual words, **then...**give each focus word more emphasis as you sing it.

Enrichment
Phonological Awareness
Challenge children to listen for the focus words while singing the song in different tempos (fast, slow) and different voices (happy, sad, quiet).

Language Time

 large group | 15 minutes

👪👪👪 Social and Emotional Development Encourage children to take turns offering ideas and listening to other children's ideas during group discussion about quiet times at school.

Oral Language and Vocabulary

✓ **Can children use the information on the card to describe their own classroom routines?**

Quiet Times Talk about school times and routines when children are noisy and when they are quiet. Ask: *When is it okay to be noisy? When is it important to be quiet?*
¿Cuándo es divertido ser ruidoso? ¿Cuándo es importante estar en silencio?

● Display *Oral Language Development Card 2.* Point out the group of children. Discuss what they are doing and why they might be sitting quietly. Then follow the suggestions on the back of the card.

Oral Language Development Card 2

Phonological Awareness

✓ **Are children able to hear and identify individual words in a song?**

School Words Explain to children that songs, like stories, are made up of words. Say: *When we sing a song, we sing words.* *Cuando cantamos una canción, cantamos palabras.* Display the *Rhymes and Chants Flip Chart,* page 5. Sing: "This Is the Way." Hold up a finger for each word as you say it. Choose one word and sing the song again, having children stand each time they hear the word.

ELL Review one of the verses and then ask children questions to engage them in simple conversation using the classroom words focused on in the song. Ask: *Did you make a friend? Who is your friend?* *¿Hiciste un amigo? ¿Quién es tu amigo?* If children answer with one or two word answers, help them expand their sentences. For example, if a child answers Maria, ask: *Oh, Maria is your friend? Did you make friends with Maria? Tell me about her.* *¡Ah! ¿María es tu amiga? ¿Se hicieron amigos? Cuéntame algo sobre ella.*

This Is the Way
(to the tune of
"Here We Go 'Round the Mulberry Bush")

This is the way we go to school,
Go to school, go to school.
This is the way we go to school
On a Monday morning.

This is the way we make a friend,
Make a friend, make a friend.
This is (Katie) she's our friend,
On a Monday morning.

This is the way we learn and play,
Learn and play, learn and play.
This is the way we learn and play,
On a Monday morning.

Rhymes and Chants Flip Chart, page 5

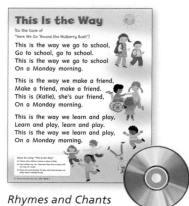

Center Time

▶ **Center Rotation** Center Time includes teacher-guided activities and independent activities. Refer to the **Learning Centers** on pages 24–25 for independent activity ideas.

Learning Goals

Language and Communication
• Child names and describes actual or pictured people, places, things, actions, attributes, and events.

Emergent Literacy: Writing
• Child participates in free drawing and writing activities to deliver information.

Library and Listening Center

Center Tip

☑ **Observe the ways children use words to label things and activities.**

Materials noisy and quiet labels, books about school, paper, crayons, tape

Noisy or Quiet Have children browse through books about school. Ask them to search for pictures of children doing noisy and quiet activities. Encourage them to describe the activities.

● Have children draw a noisy or quiet activity they like to do.

● Have children tape their drawings under the appropriate label.

If...children have difficulty staying focused as they look through books, **then...**allow them to pick an activity they observe in their own classroom and label the location.

Differentiated Instruction

 Extra Support

Writer's Center
If...children are unsure about what to write, **then...**suggest they revisit *Oral Language Card 2* to give them some ideas.

⭐ **Enrichment**

Library and Listening Center
Challenge children to look through the classroom books and hunt for examples of other types of school activities, such as painting, singing, or exercising.

Accommodations for 3's

Library and Listening Center
If...three-year-olds have difficulty determining if an activity would be noisy or quiet, **then...**ask a guiding question, such as: *Would you use a loud voice or whispering voice when you do that?*
¿Usarían un tono de voz alto o susurrarían al hacer eso?

Writer's Center

Center Tip

☑ **Listen for the ways in which children incorporate new vocabulary into their stories as they draw and/or write.**

Materials assorted paper, pencils, markers, crayons, roll-on paint, letter stamps

Let's Write Provide children with a variety of writing supplies and invite them to draw and/or write. Encourage exploration and experimentation, allowing random drawing and scribbling along with experimental letter formation. Ask children to compose stories about noisy and quiet classroom times.

● Encourage children to use vocabulary words by asking questions such as: *Are the children in your picture quiet? What can they hear? ¿Están en silencio los niños del dibujo? ¿Qué están escuchando?*

● Support children's emergent writing by encouraging them to share what they have created with you and with each other.

If...children have difficulty holding writing supplies properly, **then...**demonstrate proper pencil grip.

Focus Question
What happens at school?
¿Qué sucede en la escuela?

Literacy Time

large group · 15 minutes

 Read Aloud

✓ **Can children use the information from the poem to describe the activities in their own classroom?**

Build Background Tell children you will be reading a poem about a Pre-K child who likes going to school.

- Ask: *What are some things you like about going to school?* ¿Qué cosas les gustan de ir a la escuela?

Listen for Understanding Display the flannel board pieces for "I Like School"/"Me gusta la escuela" (*Teacher's Treasure Book*, page 274), and share the title with children.

- Say: *Let's see if you like any of the same things about school that the child in the poem likes.* Vamos a ver si les gustan las mismas cosas de la escuela que al niño del poema.

- Read the poem aloud, using the flannel board characters to act out events. Provide child-friendly explanations of vocabulary.

Respond to the Poem Discuss the poem.

- Ask: *What does the child in the poem do at school? What does the child like about school?* ¿Qué hace el niño del poema en la escuela? ¿Qué le gusta de la escuela? Help children describe information from the poem.

- Ask children to describe school day activities they like. Remind children that they can always ask to be read to or ask questions about whatever is being read.

ELL Reinforce comprehension by asking children to act out something they like about school. Encourage children to tell you why they like a particular activity and who they work with when they do it.

Learn About Letters and Sounds

✓ **Can children identify lower case letters in their names?**

Learn About Lower Case Letters Introduce lower case letters by displaying the *ABC Picture Cards.* Say: *The first letter in a name is upper case, but the rest of the letters are usually lower case. Lower case letters are used in other words too.* La primera letra de un nombre se escribe con mayúscula, pero el resto de las letras en general se escriben en minúscula. Las mayúsculas y minúsculas también se usan en otras palabras. Display your name. Point to lower case letters and name them.

- Distribute children's name cards to them and have them repeat the procedure. Try to name at least one letter for each child.

- Conclude by singing "The ABC Song" together, pointing to the lower case letters on the cards as you sing.

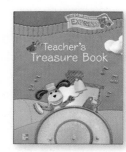

Teacher's Treasure Book, page 274

Learning Goals

Emergent Literacy: Reading
- Child explores books and other texts to answer questions.
- Child names most upper- and lowercase letters of the alphabet.
- Child describes, relates to, and uses details and information from books read aloud.

Vocabulary

favorite	favorito	home	hogar
love	amor	school	escuela

Differentiated Instruction

 Extra Support
Learn about Letters and Sounds
If...children have difficulty finding the letters on the chart, **then...**simplify the search by pointing to a letter on the chart, naming it, and then having children look at their cards to see if they have that letter in their name.

 Enrichment
Learn about Letters and Sounds
Encourage children to compare name cards to see if they have any of the same letters in them.

Accommodations for 3's
Read Aloud
If...three-year-olds have difficulty answering the questions, **then...**point to one of the flannel board scenes and have a child describe it. Then ask the child to describe a time he or she has done the same activity at school.

Math Time

Observe and Investigate

 Can children count 1 to 10 actions one at a time?

Count and Move Clap with children as they count aloud to the number 10.

- Have all children count from 1 to 10, clapping their hands as they say each number.

- Repeat throughout the day, using various motions, such as marching or hopping. Say: *You can clap, hop, or march as you say each number. You choose!* *Aplaudan, salten o marchen cuando digan cada número. ¡Ustedes eligen qué van a hacer!*

👥 Social and Emotional Development

Making Good Choices

 Do children use positive social behaviors to demonstrate a friendly classroom to the Dog Puppets?

Let's Share Discuss the ways children can talk with each other and adults, such as sharing their thoughts and ideas in a conversation, making eye contact, and using greetings. Have the first Dog Puppet tell children that he is still very new at school and doesn't know how to meet or leave people or how to talk with them. Have the puppet ask children what he should do. Invite children to encourage the Dog Puppets by giving them some friendly tips about getting along with teachers and other children. Display the *Making Good Choices* flip chart, page 5. Have children role play with the puppets, inviting children to take on the role of the teacher and the Dog Puppets the role of children.

- Have a child/teacher encourage the first Dog Puppet to chat with the teacher about an activity at school.

- Have the children/teachers discuss appropriate attitudes and behaviors with the Dog Puppets, including ideas for increasing happiness or decreasing the intensity of feelings such as fear and anger.

- After children portray an encouraging teacher, turn the roles around and have children dramatize for Dog Puppets the behaviors they were encouraging.

 Have students share first language greetings and good-byes.

Building Blocks

Online Math Activity

Children can complete Count and Race during computer time or Center Time.

Making Good Choices Flip Chart, page 5

Focus Question
What happens at school?
¿Qué sucede en la escuela?

Learning Goals

Social and Emotional Development
• Child follows simple classroom rules and routines.

Language and Communication
• Child understands and uses regular and irregular plural nouns, regular past tense verbs, personal and possessive pronouns, and subject-verb agreement.

Mathematics
• Child measures passage of time using standard or non-standard tools.

Social Studies
• Child identifies common events and routines.

Vocabulary

calendar	calendario	routine	rutina
schedule	cronograma	today	hoy
tomorrow	mañana	yesterday	ayer

Differentiated Instruction

Extra Support
Oral Language and Academic Vocabulary
If...children have difficulty understanding how all the day's activities fit into a schedule, **then...** talk about arriving and departing routines. Ask children what they do every day when they first get to school and what they do every day just before they go home.

Enrichment
Understand and Participate
Challenge children to name something they did at home yesterday and today that they will also do at home tomorrow.

Special Needs
Speech/Language Delays
Remind the child that if s/he doesn't know what happens next in the daily routine s/he can look at the picture cues. Use simple one-word descriptions for each center.

Social Studies Time

large group · 20 minutes

Social and Emotional Skills Model classroom rules by placing signs around the room that show the rules and by pointing out when children are following them.

Oral Language and Academic Vocabulary

Can children organize their day around predictable routines?

Classroom Routines Talk to children about the things they do everyday in the classroom. Explain that each day children come to school there is a schedule for them to follow that tells them what happens next. Explain that some things are different each day, but many things are the same every day. These are called *routines*.

● Ask: *What did we do yesterday that we also did today? What did we do today that we will do tomorrow? What are the routines that we do every day at school?* *¿Qué cosa hicimos ayer y también hicimos hoy? ¿Qué cosa hicimos hoy y también haremos mañana? ¿Qué rutinas tenemos todos los días en la escuela?*

● Introduce and practice classroom transition routines. Refer to Transition Tips on pages 180–181.

● Encourage children to think about, talk together, and help construct the rule for cleaning up. Ask: *Have you ever gone to use something and somebody had left a mess? How did you feel? What did you do? What could you do so that there wouldn't be a mess?* *¿Alguna vez han querido usar un rincón del salón o de su casa y descubrieron que otra persona lo había desordenado? ¿Cómo se sintieron? ¿Qué hicieron? ¿Qué podemos hacer para que no esté todo desordenado?*

Understand and Participate

Can child identify common daily routines such as snack time and story time?

The Daily Schedule Display an illustrated classroom schedule, or *calendar*, and review each of the day's activities with the children. Point to each picture and word label as you identify them.

● Ask: *What activities on the schedule did we do today? ¿Qué actividades del cronograma hicimos hoy?*

● Invite children to point to the pictures on the schedule and discuss which activities they did yesterday, which they will do today, and which they will do tomorrow.

ELL Model sentences for children to echo to help them learn about tenses. Say: *Yesterday we played outside. Tomorrow we will play outside; Yesterday we had computer center. Today we are having social studies time. Tomorrow we will have math time.*

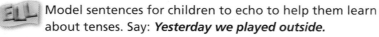

Center Time

Center Rotation Center Time includes teacher-guided activities and independent activities. Refer to the **Learning Centers** on pages 24–25 for independent activity ideas.

 small group · 30 minutes

Refer to the **Learning Centers** on pages 24–25 for independent activity ideas.

Construction Center

	Center Tip

☑ **Can children identify daily morning and afternoon classroom routines?**

Materials construction paper; pictures of classroom items and activities from the *Photo Library CD-ROM,* magazines, or digital camera printouts; paste

Hello and Good-Bye Have children sort pictures into routine activities children do when they first arrive at school and routine activities children do at the end of the day.

- Have children paste their sorted pictures onto two pieces of construction paper, a *Hello* paper for arrival time, and a *Good-bye* paper for going home activities.

- Ask children to share and talk about their choices.

Center Tip

If...children have difficulty categorizing an activity, **then**...review the illustrated daily schedule with the child to help them determine the category.

Learning Goals

Emergent Literacy: Writing
- Child participates in free drawing and writing activities to deliver information.
- Child uses scribbles, shapes, pictures, symbols, and letters to represent language.

Mathematics
- Child sorts objects and explains how the sorting was done.

Social Studies
- Child identifies common events and routines.

Writing

Review the day. Have children share what they learned about classroom routines. Provide booklets in which children can record their thoughts and ideas. Encourage exploration and experimentation, allowing random drawing and scribbling along with experimental letter formation to make words or parts of words.

Purposeful Play

☑ **Can children recognize one or more of the letters in their names?**

Children choose an open center for free playtime. Encourage children to be letter detectives and locate letters in their names on labels or signs posted around the classroom. Name the letters for children. You may also do this as a partnered activity.

Let's Say Good-Bye

 large group · 15 minutes

 Read Aloud Revisit the story "Fish Games"/"Juegos de peces" for your afternoon Read Aloud. Ask children to raise their hands when they hear any of the new words they have learned today.

 Home Connection Refer to the Home Connections activities in the Resources and Materials chart on page 21. Encourage children to share what they did in school today. Sing the "Good-Bye Song"/ "Hora de ir a casa" (*Teacher's Treasure Book,* page 68) as children prepare to leave.

Focus Question
What happens at school?
¿Qué sucede en la escuela?

 **Learning Goals**

Social and Emotional Development
• Child begins to show a greater ability to control intense feelings.

• Child begins to be responsible for individual behavior and actions.

• Child recognizes and manages feelings and impulses; increasingly maintains self-control in difficult situations (can increase or decrease intensity of emotions with guidance).

Vocabulary

angry	enojado	problem	problema
mad	furioso	quarrel	riña
together	juntos		

Differentiated Instruction

 Extra Support
Phonological Awareness
If…children have difficulty thinking of classroom items to name, **then…**encourage them to name things pictured on the *Alphabet Wall Cards*.

 Enrichment
Phonological Awareness
Have a Dog Puppet name something it can see without pointing to it, and challenge children to point out where it is as they say the beginning sound.

 Special Needs
Behavioral Social/Emotional
Recognize that if the child laughs when someone falls down and gets hurt it is because children with behavior issues may not understand the feelings of others. Consistently model the appropriate way to respond when someone is hurt or unhappy.

Let's Start the Day

 Opening Routines and Transition Tips
For **Opening Routines** and **Transition Tips** turn to pages 178–181 and visit **DLMExpressOnline.com** for more ideas.

Read **"Smart Cookie's Best Friend, Gabby Graham"/**"Gaby Graham, la mejor amiga de Smart Cookie" from the *Teacher's Treasure Book,* page 226, for your morning Read Aloud.

Language Time

Social and Emotional Development Encourage each child to treat everyone else in the group the way he or she wants to be treated, inviting others to join the group using phrases such as *play with us.*

Oral Language and Vocabulary

Are children able to understand and control their feelings?

Talk About Brothers and Sisters Ask children whether they have brothers or sisters. Invite children to talk about how they get along with their brothers, sisters, and other children.

● Ask: *What do you like about playing with other children? What makes you happy when you are playing together?* ¿Qué les gusta hacer con otros niños? ¿Qué los pone contentos cuando juegan juntos?

● Ask: *What makes you mad or angry when you're playing with other children? Are there things that make you angrier? How do you get to be less angry?* ¿Qué los enoja o los pone furiosos cuando juegan con otros niños? ¿Hay cosas que los enojan aun más? ¿Cómo logran tranquilizarse?

● Invite children to share stories about siblings or friends. Ask: *Do you stay mad after a quarrel, or fight? What usually happens? What do you do?* ¿Se quedan enojados después de una riña? ¿Qué ocurre normalmente? ¿Qué hacen en esa situación?

ELL Explain that a *quarrel* is an argument or a disagreement. Use gestures and facial expressions to help children understand the concept.

Phonological Awareness

Can children listen for individual words and names in short sentences?

Word Game Remind children they are learning the names of many new things at school, including the names of other children. Tell them you are going to play a word game taking turns to name things you can see in the room and saying the beginning sound. Start by pointing to a book and saying: *I see a book. Book starts with /b/. Veo un book. Book empieza con /b/.* Pick a child to go next, and take turns, making sure that each child has a turn. Encourage children to point to what they see, and to try not to name anything that has already been named.

Center Time

Center Rotation Center Time includes teacher-guided activities and independent activities. Refer to the **Learning Centers** on pages 24–25 for independent activity ideas.

 small group · 60–90 minutes

Library and Listening Center

Center Tip

✓ Listen for the use of oral vocabulary you focused on.

Materials picture books, sticky notes

Book Browsing Invite children to browse through books together. Have them look for examples of children playing together nicely and fairly and examples that show children who might be angry with each other.

● Have children mark the pictures of children playing nicely with green sticky notes and the pictures of children who are angry with red sticky notes.

● Invite children to make up their own stories about the pictures they marked with sticky notes.

Center Tip

If...children have difficulty making up a story, **then...**ask: *What do you think the children are playing? ¿A qué crees que están jugando juntos?* or *What do you think the problem is? ¿Cuál crees que es el problema?*

ABC Center

Center Tip

✓ Track which letters children recognize and can identify in their own names and around the room.

✓ Notice ways in which children demonstrate an understanding and respect for personal boundaries as they work.

Materials name cards, play clay, paper plates

Alphabet Letters Remind children that every word is made up of the letters in the alphabet, and that each letter has a different shape. Give each child a paper plate and a ball of play clay.

● Model forming the play clay into the shape of the first letter in their name.

● Encourage children to name the letter they are forming. Name the letter for children as needed.

Center Tip

If...children have difficulty manipulating clay into a letter shape, **then...**help them roll it into a snake shape so the letter can more easily be formed.

Learning Goals

Language and Communication
• Child names and describes actual or pictured people, places, things, actions, attributes, and events.

Emergent Literacy: Reading
• Child names most upper- and lowercase letters of the alphabet.

Differentiated Instruction

✋ **Extra Support**
ABC Center
If...children have difficulty remembering the shape of the first letters in their names, **then...** provide them with name cards.

⭐ **Enrichment**
Library and Listening Center
Challenge children to make up a beginning, middle, and end to a picture they have marked.

Accommodations for 3's
ABC Center
If...three-year-olds have difficulty making clay match a letter shape, **then...**mark a thick letter shape onto the paper plate for children to trace with a clay snake.

💜 **Special Needs**
Delayed Motor Development
If necessary, a peer can roll the clay into a snake shape. Then the child can use a tongue depressor or other object to push the clay into a letter shape.

Focus Question
What happens at school?
¿Qué sucede en la escuela?

 Learning Goals

Language and Communication
• Child demonstrates an understanding of oral language by responding appropriately.

Emergent Literacy: Reading
• Child names most upper- and lowercase letters of the alphabet.

Vocabulary

Iroquois	iroqués	problem	problema
quarrel	riña	solve	resolver

Differentiated Instruction

 Extra Support

Learn About Letters and Sounds
If...children are unable to locate a letter on the wall cards, **then...**encourage them to sing "The ABC Song" as they point to each letter.

Enrichment
Read Aloud
Encourage children to recall a time when the three-stick solution might have helped them.

Accommodations for 3's
Read Aloud
If...three-year-olds have difficulty focusing on the story, **then...**pause throughout to relate the story experience to their own.

Literacy Time

large group 15 minutes

📖 Read Aloud

✓ **Can children respond appropriately to questions about the story?**

Build Background Tell children you will be sharing a story about two Iroquois brothers who have a quarrel. Explain that *Iroquois* is the name for a particular group of Native American people, and that a *quarrel* is an argument between two or more people. Quarrels happen when people get mad at each other.

• Say: *Sometimes, when you have a problem with someone, it can turn into a quarrel, or fight.* A veces, cuando se tiene un problema con una persona, ese problema puede transformarse en una riña.

• Ask: *Have you ever had a quarrel with a brother, sister, or friend? What happened?* ¿Alguna vez tuvieron una riña con un hermano o con un amigo? ¿Por qué?

Listen for Enjoyment Display the flannel board pieces for "How Two Brothers Solved a Problem"/"De cómo dos hermanos aprendieron a resolver un problema" (*Teacher's Treasure Book,* page 308), and share the title with children. Explain that *solve* means "to find an answer."

• Say: *In this story, the two brothers learn how to solve their problem together. Let's see how they do it.* En este cuento, los dos hermanos aprenden a resolver juntos su problema. Veamos cómo lo hacen.

• Read the story. Use the flannel board characters to act out story events.

Respond to the Story Discuss the story.

• Ask children what the brothers learned about quarreling and fighting.

• Ask children how the three sticks helped the brothers solve their problem.

ELL Point out how the words *problem* and *solve* are closely related to their Spanish equivalents, *problema* and *resolver*.

Learn About Letters and Sounds

✓ **Can children match upper and lower case letters of the alphabet?**

Learn About The Alphabet Display and identify each *Alphabet Wall Card,* explaining that each one shows the upper and lower case version of the letter.

• Display the Alphabet/Letter Tiles, and hold up the upper case *A,* asking for help to identify it.

• Model using the *Alphabet Wall Cards* for reference to match the upper case *A* and to help you find the lower case Alphabet/Letter Tile *a.*

• Repeat the procedure having children find and match additional pairs. Name each letter as children match pairs.

• Conclude by singing "The ABC Song" together, as you point to each card.

Teacher's Treasure Book, page 308

Alphabet Wall Cards

Math Time

Observe and Investigate

 Can children use words to rote count?

Sing "When I Was One" Sing with children the lyrics of the song "When I Was One" below. As you sing, guide children in the actions listed.

> **When I was one, I was so small,** *(Show one finger.)*
>
> **I could not speak a word at all.**
>
> *(Move head left to right indicating "no.")*
>
> **When I was two, I learned to talk,** *(Show two fingers.)*
>
> **I learned to sing. I learned to walk.** *(Point to mouth and feet.)*
>
> **When I was three, I grew and grew,** *(Show three fingers.)*
>
> **Now I am four and so are you!** *(Show four fingers.)*

- If most children in the class are three years old, change the last line to: *Soon I'll be four and so will you!* If there is a mixture, say: *Soon we'll all be four, it's true!* If some children are five, have five-year-olds say "I'm five," showing five fingers. Then all children say "How old are you?"

- The Spanish version of the song is located in the *Teacher's Treasure Book,* page 128.

Online Math Activity
Children can complete Count and Race during computer time or Center Time.

large group 15 minutes

𝍆 Social and Emotional Development

Making Good Choices

 Can children give the Dog Puppets advice about friendly greetings and conversations?

Solving Problems Remind children of all the ideas they have discussed about greeting each other, talking to each other, and including each other in order to have a friendly classroom. Have the Dog Puppets tell children they have forgotten what the class learned about friendly greetings and conversations. Have them ask the children for advice.

- Have the first puppet dramatize improper morning greetings, such as talking loudly or shouting. Have children show the puppet a better way to greet them. Then have the children improvise other friendly interactions.

- Have the second puppet ask children to name the most important things they have learned this week about how to greet, talk to, and leave each other.

 Learning Goals

Social and Emotional Development
- Child demonstrates positive social behaviors, as modeled by the teacher.

Mathematics
- Child recites number words in sequence from one to thirty.

Vocabulary

advice	consejo	counting	contar
discussion	conversación	old	viejo
shout	grito	years	años

Differentiated Instruction

✋ **Extra Support**
Observe and Investigate
If...children are having difficulty with the actions of the song, **then...**go slowly to allow children time to move their fingers.

⭐ **Enrichment**
Making Good Choices
Ask pairs of children to role play talking to each other, one as the teacher and the other as a child.

Focus Question
What happens at school?
¿Qué sucede en la escuela?

large group — 20 minutes

Math Time

 Can children count items in the classroom using one count per item?

Counting Objects Lead children in counting aloud. Choose something large in the classroom such as desks, tables, or chairs, and practice counting aloud.

- Display the *Math and Science Flip Chart,* page 6. Say: **Look at the picture. Do you see anything we can count?** *Observen este dibujo. ¿Ven algo que podamos contar?*

- Help children in counting aloud. Point to a shelf and say: **Let's count the books on this shelf. 1, 2, 3, 4. There are 4 books.** *Contemos los libros que hay en este estante. 1, 2, 3, 4.*

- Repeat with the other shelves on the chart.

- Next, choose a classroom book that has many visuals that will allow for counting. A counting book with big, bright objects would be best.

- Read the book aloud to children.

- As you read, stop and draw children's attention to a particular object. Name the object. Say: **How many of these are on this page?** *¿Cuántos de éstos hay en esta página?*

ELL Ask children questions about the chart that involve number questions, such as: **Can you find the shelf with two books on it?**

Counting Books
Contar libros

Math and Science Flip Chart, page 6

Learning Goals

Mathematics
- Child recites number words in sequence from one to thirty.

Vocabulary

books	libros	chairs	sillas
desk	escritorio	shelf	estante
table	mesa		

Differentiated Instruction

 Extra Support

Math Time
If...children need help children focusing on the objects in the book they are counting, **then...** point clearly to the objects on the page, so that all children can see them.

 Enrichment

Math Time
Challenge children to add object vocabulary to their spoken-language repertoire.

Center Time

 small group 30 minutes

Learning Goals

Social and Emotional Development
• Child demonstrates positive social behaviors, as modeled by the teacher.

Emergent Literacy: Writing
• Child uses scribbles, shapes, pictures, symbols, and letters to represent language.

Mathematics
• Child understands that objects, or parts thereof, can be counted.

• Child counts 1–10 concrete objects correctly.

• Child recognizes, names, describes, matches, compares, sorts common two-dimensional shapes (such as circle, square, rectangle, triangle, rhombus).

• Child creates two-dimensional shapes; recreates two-dimensional shapes from memory.

Math and Science Center

☑ **Encourage children to count and explore different Shape Sets.**

Materials Shape Sets

Explore Shape Sets Prepare two complete Shape Sets for children. Observe what children do and say with the shapes as they work freely with them.

● Encourage children to name and count the shapes.

● Say: *Can you put shapes together to make a picture?* *¿Pueden unir las figuras para formar una imagen?*

● Ask children to count how many of each shape they used in their picture. Note when the pictures form other shapes.

Center Tip

If...children have difficulty making a picture, **then...** demonstrate by building the beginning of a picture.

Purposeful Play

☑ **Observe children showing willingness to learn and follow classroom rules.**

Children choose an open center for free playtime. Have children practice greeting one another as they move around the room. Challenge them to find different ways to give one another friendly greetings.

Writing

Review the lessons the children helped the Dog Puppets learn. Write a letter together to the dogs to help the dogs remember the lessons, too. Reread the letter, emphasizing the individual words that work together to make up the children's message. Allow each child to sign their name by making a mark at the bottom.

Let's Say Good-Bye

 large group 15 minutes

 Read Aloud Revisit "Smart Cookie's Best Friend, Gabby Graham"/"*Gabby Graham, la mejor amiga de Smart Cookie*" for your afternoon Read Aloud. Invite children to give tips they learned about what children can do to solve a problem if they have a quarrel.

 Home Connection Refer to the Home Connections activities listed in the Resources and Materials chart on page 21. Remind children to look for letters they know at home. Sing the "Good-Bye Song"/"*Hora de ir a casa*" (*Teacher's Treasure Book,* page 68) as children prepare to leave.

DAY 5

Focus Question
What happens at school?
¿Qué sucede en la escuela?

 Learning Goals

Technology Applications
• Child opens and correctly uses age-appropriate software programs.

Vocabulary

Friday	viernes	friend	amigo
go	ir	learn	aprender
morning	mañana	play	jugar

Differentiated Instruction

 Extra Support

Oral Language and Vocabulary
If...children have difficulty telling what they learned about what happens at school, **then...** give one example to initiate discussion.

 Enrichment

Phonological Awareness
Have children take turns leading each other in the sing along.

Accommodations for 3's

Phonological Awareness
If...three-year-olds have trouble with the song, **then...**invite them to clap along and sing the words they know.

 Special Needs

Vision Loss
Since drawing may be difficult, find an alternative activity, such as letting the child make an audio recording about the word.

Let's Start the Day

▶ **Opening Routines and Transition Tips**
For **Opening Routines** and **Transition Tips** turn to pages 178–181 and visit DLMExpressOnline.com for more ideas.

📖 Read **"Weather/**"El tiempo" from the *Teacher's Treasure Book*, page 234, for your morning Read Aloud.

Language Time

 large group 15 minutes

 Social and Emotional Development Encourage and support children in learning and following the common events and routines of the day.

Oral Language and Vocabulary

✓ **Can children use information learned in chants to describe their classroom day?**

School Lessons Remind children that this week they have sung songs about school, read stories about school, learned words about school, and they have gone to school themselves. Say: **You are school experts!** *¡Son expertos en escuela!*

● Display the *Rhymes and Chants Flip Chart*, page 5, to review a song about school. Sing "This Is the Way."

● Say: **Today is Friday. It is the last day of the school week. What did you learn this week about what happens at school?** *Hoy es viernes. Es el último día de clases de la semana. ¿Qué aprendieron esta semana sobre lo que sucede en la escuela?*

● Ask: **What did you learn about school this week that you did not know before?** *¿Aprendieron algo esta semana que antes no supieran?*

Phonological Awareness

✓ **Can children draw illustrations of an isolated word?**

Draw a Word Sing "This Is the Way" with the children again. Say: **Let's draw pictures of some of the words from the song.** *Dibujemos algunas de las palabras de la canción.* Sing the first line of the song slowly. Invite children to listen for a word that can be drawn in a picture, such as *school*. Have children identify the word they isolated, then create pictures that represent the words from the song on chart paper or an interactive whiteboard. After they have represented their ideas in pictures, sing the song again and have the children point to the pictures they created when they hear the word.

 Use the chart to extend conversation about school, friends, and play. Ask children to tell you how they get to school, and what they like to play at school or at home.

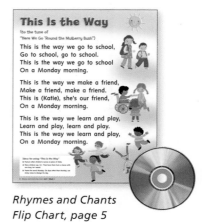

This Is the Way
(to the tune of
"Here We Go 'Round the Mulberry Bush")

This is the way we go to school,
Go to school, go to school.
This is the way we go to school
On a Monday morning.

This is the way we make a friend,
Make a friend, make a friend.
This is (Katie), she's our friend,
On a Monday morning.

This is the way we learn and play,
Learn and play, learn and play.
This is the way we learn and play,
On a Monday morning.

Rhymes and Chants
Flip Chart, page 5

Center Time

► **Center Rotation** Center Time includes teacher-guided activities and independent activities. Refer to the **Learning Centers** on pages 24–25 for independent activity ideas.

Pretend and Learn Center

☑ **Listen as children emphasize an individual word within a song.**

Materials *Rhymes and Chants Flip Chart,* musical instruments

Sing a Song Have children choose musical instruments to add accompaniments to the song "This Is the Way." Remind children that music can be used for emphasis.

- Model using an instrument to give emphasis each time you sing a focus word.

- Encourage children to take turns choosing a word from the song to listen for. Point out its illustration in the *Rhymes and Chants Flip Chart,* and then help children emphasize their chosen word as the band plays along.

Center Tip

If...children have difficulty listening for a word, **then...**designate a leader to stamp, or clap, when they sing the chosen word.

Writer's Center

☑ **Notice how children incorporate information learned in stories, books, and chants into their own story descriptions.**

Materials construction paper; crayons; paste; collage materials, such as yarn and fabric scraps

Making Friends Ask children to think of a new friend they have made at school. Encourage them to think about how they became friends.

- Have children use collage and drawing materials to make a picture of themselves and their new friend.

- Ask children about their drawings, and write down something each child says, such as *Ahbi is my friend.*

Center Tip

If...children have difficulty naming a friend, **then...**name classmates until each child is able to select one name. Children may also select friends from outside the class.

 Learning Goals

Fine Arts
- Child expresses emotions or ideas through art.
- Child participates in a variety of music activities (such as listening, singing, finger plays, musical games, performances).

Differentiated Instruction

 Extra Support

Writer's Center
If...children have difficulty using collage materials to represent a friend, **then...**have them observe their friend and describe the clothing she or he is wearing.

Enrichment

Writer's Center
Challenge children to listen for their friend's name when you read their dictated sentence back to them.

Accommodations for 3's

Pretend and Learn Center
If...three-year-olds have difficulty playing an instrument and listening at the same time, **then...**ask musicians to play their instruments only when they hear the focus word.

Focus Question
What happens at school?
¿Qué sucede en la escuela?

 ## Learning Goals

Language and Communication
• Child exhibits an understanding of instructional terms used in the classroom.

Emergent Literacy: Reading
• Child names most upper- and lowercase letters of the alphabet.

• Child describes, relates to, and uses details and information from books read aloud.

Vocabulary

circle	círculo	exercise	ejercicio
habits	hábitos	healthy	saludable
learn	aprender		

 ## Differentiated Instruction

👋 Extra Support
Learn About Letters and Sounds
If...children have difficulty matching letters, **then...**remind them to note letter shapes. Have them note whether the letter is round or straight, short or tall.

⭐ Enrichment
Learn About Letters and Sound
Have a small group of children sing "The ABC Song" together as they browse through the *ABC Big Book*, pointing to each letter as they sing.

Accommodations for 3's
Read Aloud
If...three-year-olds have difficulty with the vocabulary words, **then...**provide extra support by pointing them out in the illustrations as you read.

Literacy Time

 large group 15 minutes

📖 Read Aloud

✓ **Can children use information learned from the book to understand and discuss their own experiences?**

Build Background Remind children that they have now had many of the same experiences as the children in the book, and have learned many things about school.

● Ask: *What would you tell someone who was about to start Pre-K?* ¿Qué le dirían a alguien que está por comenzar Prekínder?

Listen for Understanding Display *Concept Big Book 1: Welcome to School,* and read the title. As you read aloud, point to the illustrations and help children identify classroom words they have learned during the week.

● Read the book aloud, providing child-friendly explanations of vocabulary words as you read.

● Encourage children to point to the illustrations as they describe similar things that have happened this week in their classroom.

Respond and Connect Point out how the book highlights things children might learn in Pre-K.

● Invite children to describe their own experiences in the classroom.

● Ask: *Did you do any of the same things as the children in the book? What else did you do?* ¿Hicieron algunas de las cosas que hacen los niños del cuento? ¿Qué otra cosa hicieron?

● Ask: *What do children learn from doing these things?* ¿Qué aprenden los niños cuando hacen estas cosas?

ELL Take a picture walk through *Concept Big Book 1: Welcome to School,* discussing selected pictures with children. Help children point out examples of vocabulary words. Label additional classroom words.

Learn About Letters and Sounds

✓ **Can children recite the letters of the alphabet in sequence?**

Learn About The Alphabet Point to the *Alphabet Wall Cards,* one by one, naming each pair. Repeat, saying: *Can you name the letters with me this time?* ¿Pueden esta vez nombrar conmigo las letras?

● Display the Alphabet/Letter Tiles, and model finding upper and lower case *Aa*. Place them under the corresponding wall card.

● Have partners repeat the task with the letters *Bb–Zz*. Together, recite the alphabet.

● Conclude by singing "The ABC Song" together, pointing to each letter as you sing.

Welcome to School
Bienvenidos a la escuela

Alphabet Wall Cards

Math Time

Observe and Investigate

✓ **Can children count items one at a time?**

Sing "This Old Man" Sing with children the lyrics of the song "This Old Man." As you sing, guide children in the actions from the song.

● This activity is an extension of the activity introduced on Day 1.

● Using the same verse pattern, continue to the number ten: three/on his knee; four/on the floor; five/on his side; six/with some sticks; seven/under the heavens; eight/on his plate; nine/all the time; ten/once again.

uilding Blocks

Online Math Activity
Children can complete Count and Race during computer time or Center Time.

✗✗✗ Social and Emotional Development

Making Good Choices

✓ **Can children talk about positive behaviors modeled on the flip chart?**

Our Friendly Room Discuss how children have helped create a friendly classroom this week that makes them feel welcome. Ask children how they have been helpful and kind. Remind them how they shared ideas, looked at one another when chatting, and greeted each other. Display the *Making Good Choices Flip Chart, page 5*.

● Ask: *What is the child who is painting doing to help make a friendly classroom?*
¿Cómo ayuda el niño de la ilustración a crear una clase amistosa?

● Ask: *What is the child who is arriving at school doing to help make a friendly classroom?* *¿Cómo ayuda el niño que llega a la escuela a crear una clase amistosa?*

ELL Help children understand the word *welcome* by pantomiming welcoming behavior. Encourage children to pantomime welcoming behaviors such as waving hello, smiling, and looking at one another when they talk. You may also make individual placards each with the word *Welcome* in English and other languages spoken by children in the class and their families.

Making Good Choices Flip Chart, page 5

Social and Emotional Development
● Child demonstrates positive social behaviors, as modeled by the teacher.

Language and Communication
● Child uses nonverbal cues to communicate with others who do not speak his or her home language. (ELL)

Mathematics
● Child recites number words in sequence from one to thirty.

Vocabulary

computer	computadora
count	contar
helpful	útil
kind	amable
race	carrera
welcome	bienvenido

Differentiated Instruction

✋ Extra Support
Making Good Choices
If...children have difficulty explaining why the behaviors pictured are friendly, **then**...have children describe how they felt when someone greeted them in a friendly or kind way or when they greeted someone in a friendly or kind way.

⭐ Enrichment
Observe and Investigate
Ask children to tell how high they counted on the computer with Count and Race, and then count to that number aloud.

Accommodations for 3's
Making Good Choices
If...children have difficulty explaining how a child in the flip chart picture is helping to create a friendly classroom, **then**...ask the child to describe what the child in the illustration is doing. Provide prompts to help identify the friendly behavior.

Focus Question
What happens at school?
¿Qué sucede en la escuela?

Learning Goals

Social and Emotional Development
• Child recites number words in sequence from one to thirty.

Fine Arts
• Child recites number words in sequence from one to thirty.

Vocabulary

artist	artista	blue	azul
color	color	paintbrush	pincel
red	rojo	yellow	amarillo

Differentiated Instruction

✋ Extra Support

Explore and Express
If...children are hesitant or don't know know how to start, then...provide a prompt such as *Can you paint a thick, wavy line? ¿Pueden pintar una línea gruesa y ondulada?*

⭐ Enrichment

Explore and Express
Challenge children to fill the paper with color by making thick, thin, wavy, and straight lines, and big and small dots.

Accommodations for 3's

Explore and Express
If...children have difficulty holding paintbrushes, then...provide a variety of alternatives in different sizes and handle types, such as pastry brushes and cotton swabs.

Art Time

large group 20 minutes

Social Emotional Skills Help children find a workplace at the table with enough room so they can paint comfortably without getting in the way of other painters. Alternatively, encourage pairs or small groups of children to lay out a shared space and talk about how they'll use it.

Oral Language and Academic Vocabulary

✓ **Can children talk about artists and their tools?**

Painter's Tools Name the different colors of paint. Point out the various sizes and kinds of brushes, and ask children to describe them.

● Ask: **Do you know who uses these kinds of tools?** *¿Saben quién usa estas herramientas?*

● Say: **Some artists use paintbrushes to make paintings.** *Algunos artistas usan pinceles para hacer pinturas hermosas.*

● Explain that the children will be artists today. Have children identify and name the tools. Encourage children to create rules for taking care of the tools and discuss why they should be cared for.

Explore and Express

✓ **Are children able to create original art with color?**

Materials several colors of paint in shallow trays; a variety of brushes, such as watercolor brushes, pastry brushes, nail brushes, and make-up brushes

Artists at Work Model exploring by observing and touching the different brushes before choosing one to work with. Show children how to dip the brush in paint. Then brush it across the paper.

● Let children choose one brush to begin. Let children know they can experiment with different brushes.

● Encourage children to explore the variety of effects they can make using different brushes and different colors of paint.

ELL Use children's paintings to talk about color names and to compare the paint colors to other objects in the room. For example, say: **The yellow in your painting is like the yellow on the calendar picture.** Then encourage children to point out other yellow items in the room to check for understanding.

Circle Time

 Center Rotation Center Time includes teacher-guided activities and independent activities. Refer to the **Learning Centers** on pages 24–25 for independent activity ideas.

small group · 30 minutes

Creativity Center

 ✓ Encourage children to explore different brushes and explore the different shapes and textures they can make with them.

Materials table covered with butcher paper, smocks, paints in shallow trays, assorted brushes

Cooperative Brush Art Invite children to continue the exploration of textures and shapes they can make with different brushes. Have children work together around a table covered with butcher paper. Have them describe the designs they make.

Center Tip

If...children have difficulty finding different ways to use a brush, **then...**guide them to notice the effect of gliding the brush over the paper or tapping it on the paper.

✓ Learning Goals

Social and Emotional Development
• Child demonstrates positive social behaviors, as modeled by the teacher.

Emergent Literacy: Writing
• Child writes own name or a reasonable approximation of it.

Fine Arts
• Child expresses emotions or ideas through art.

 Writing

Have children describe what they liked most about their day. Write down their ideas and read back their dictated words about the day. Then ask children to write their names next to the activity they like best. If children are not yet able to write their names, write their names in dotted letters and allow children to trace over them. Have children describe why they selected that activity.

Purposeful Play

✓ Do children identify common routines of the day?

Children choose an open center for free playtime. Encourage children to create a friendly classroom by finding ways to take turns and solve problems as they work and play.

Let's Say Good-Bye

large group · 15 minutes

 Read Aloud Revisit "Weather"/"El tiempo" for your afternoon Read Aloud. Invite children to share examples of experiences they have had with different types of weather.

 Home Connection Refer to the Home Connections activities listed in the Resources and Materials chart on page 21. Remind children to tell their families about the work they did as artists today. Sing the "Good-Bye Song"/"Hora de ir a casa" (*Teacher's Treasure Book,* page 68) as children prepare to leave.

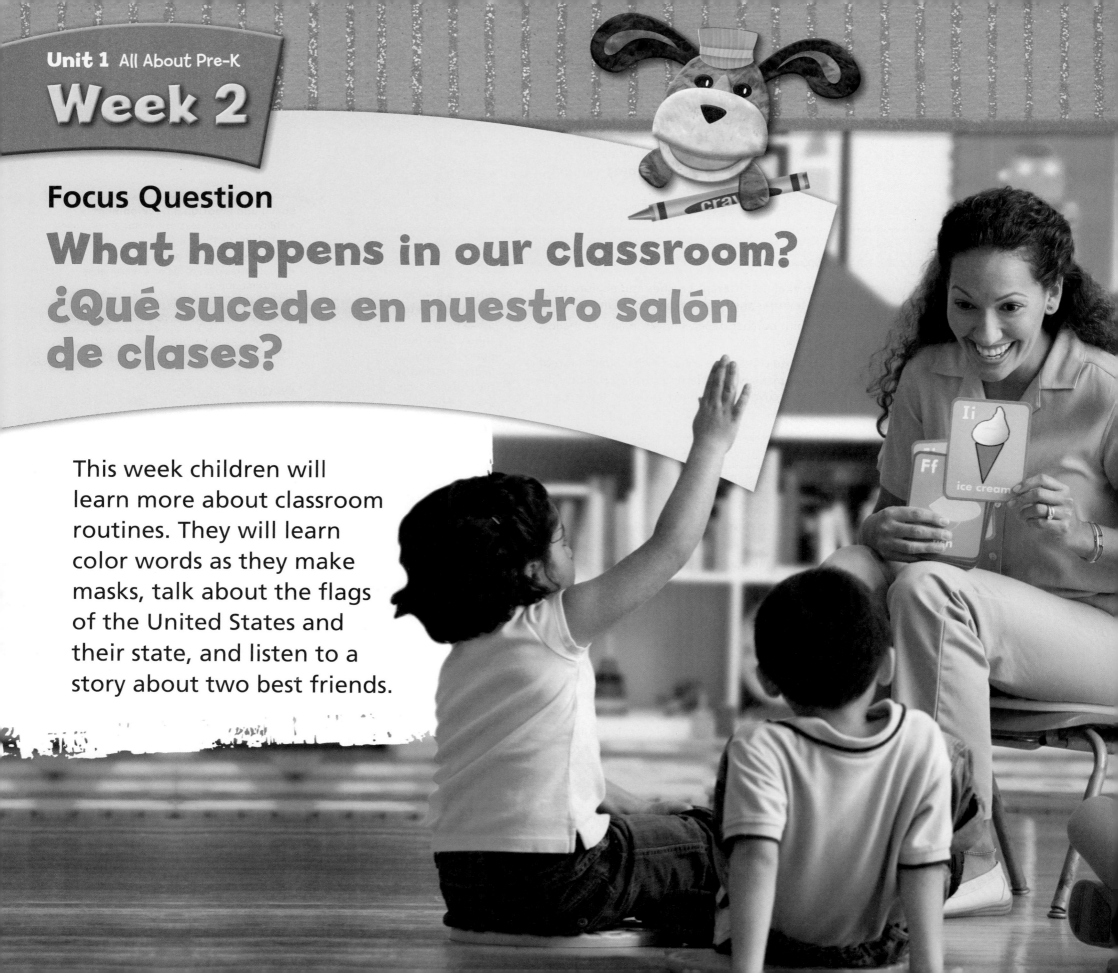

Focus Question

What happens in our classroom?
¿Qué sucede en nuestro salón de clases?

This week children will learn more about classroom routines. They will learn color words as they make masks, talk about the flags of the United States and their state, and listen to a story about two best friends.

Social and Emotional Development	Day 1	2	3	4	5
Child is aware of self in terms of abilities, characteristics and preferences, and respects personal boundaries.				✓	✓
Child follows simple classroom rules and routines.	✓	✓	✓	✓	✓
Child uses classroom materials carefully.	✓				
Child accepts responsibility for and regulates own behavior.	✓		✓	✓	✓
Child initiates interactions with others in work and play situations.		✓		✓	✓
Child shows empathy and care for others.	✓			✓	✓

Language and Communication	Day 1	2	3	4	5
Child demonstrates an understanding of oral language by responding appropriately.				✓	
Child begins and ends conversations appropriately.	✓				
Child exhibits an understanding of instructional terms used in the classroom.	✓				
Child understands or knows the meaning of many thousands of words, many more than he or she uses.	✓				
Child uses newly learned vocabulary daily in multiple contexts.	✓	✓	✓	✓	✓
Child uses individual words and short phrases to communicate. (ELL)			✓		✓

Emergent Literacy: Reading	Day 1	2	3	4	5
Child explores books and other texts to answer questions.	✓		✓		
Child names most upper- and lowercase letters of the alphabet.	✓	✓	✓	✓	✓
Child identifies the letter that stands for a given sound.	✓	✓	✓	✓	✓
Child produces the most common sound for a given letter.		✓	✓	✓	
Child asks and answers questions about books read aloud (such as "Who?" "What?" "Where?").	✓	✓	✓	✓	✓

Emergent Literacy: Writing	Day 1	2	3	4	5
Child participates in free drawing and writing activities to deliver information.		✓			
Child uses scribbles, shapes, pictures, symbols, and letters to represent language.		✓		✓	
Child writes own name or a reasonable approximation of it.				✓	
Child writes some letters or reasonable approximations of letters upon request.	✓	✓	✓	✓	
Child experiments with and uses some writing conventions when writing or dictating.		✓	✓		✓

Mathematics	Day 1	2	3	4	5
Child understands that objects, or parts thereof, can be counted.	✓				
Child recites number words in sequence from one to thirty.		✓			
Child counts 1–10 concrete objects correctly.			✓	✓	✓
Child demonstrates that, when counting, the last number indicates how many objects were counted.				✓	✓
Child understands that objects can be counted in any order.				✓	✓
Child tells how many are in a group of up to 5 objects without counting.		✓			
Child measures the length and height of people or objects using standard or non-standard tools.				✓	
Child measures passage of time using standard or non-standard tools.		✓			
Child sorts objects and explains how the sorting was done.			✓	✓	✓
Child identifies, duplicates, and creates simple patterns.				✓	

Science	Day 1	2	3	4	5
Child identifies organisms and describes their characteristics.				✓	
Child practices personal hygiene skills independently (for example, washes hands, blows nose, covers mouth, brushes teeth).	✓				

Social Studies	Day 1	2	3	4	5
Child identifies common events and routines.			✓		
Child identifies the U.S. Flag and state flag.			✓		
Child recites the Pledge of Allegiance.			✓		

Fine Arts	Day 1	2	3	4	5
Child uses and experiments with a variety of art materials and tools in various art activities.					✓
Child expresses emotions or ideas through art.	✓	✓	✓		✓
Child participates in a variety of music activities (such as listening, singing, finger plays, musical games, performances).			✓		✓
Child expresses thoughts, feelings, and energy through music and creative movement.				✓	✓
Child expresses ideas, emotions, and moods through individual and collaborative dramatic play.				✓	

Physical Development	Day 1	2	3	4	5
Child develops small-muscle strength and control.			✓		

Materials and Resources

DAY 1	DAY 2	DAY 3	DAY 4	DAY 5

Program Materials

DAY 1	DAY 2	DAY 3	DAY 4	DAY 5
• Teacher's Treasure Book • Oral Language Development Card 3 • Rhymes and Chants Flip Chart • Photo Library CD-ROM • ABC Picture Cards • *Yellowbelly and Plum Go to School* Big Book • ABC Big Book • Alphabet Wall Cards • Online Building Blocks Math Activities • Making Good Choices Flip Chart • Math and Science Flip Chart • Home Connections Resource Guide	• Teacher's Treasure Book • *Yellowbelly and Plum Go to School* Big Book • Rhymes and Chants Flip Chart • ABC Big Book • ABC Picture Cards • Online Building Blocks Math Activities • Making Good Choices Flip Chart • Dog Puppets 1 and 2 • Two-Color Counters • Math and Science Flip Chart • Home Connections Resource Guide	• Teacher's Treasure Book • Oral Language Development Card 4 • Rhymes and Chants Flip Chart • Concept Big Book 1 • ABC Big Book • Making Good Choices Flip Chart • Dog Puppets 1 and 2 • Home Connections Resource Guide	• Teacher's Treasure Book • Flannel Board Patterns for "Why Goldfinches Are Yellow Like the Sun" • Alphabet Wall Cards • ABC Big Book • Dog Puppets 1 and 2 • Alphabet Wall Cards • Home Connections Resource Guide	• Teacher's Treasure Book • Rhymes and Chants Flip Chart • *Yellowbelly and Plum Go to School* Big Book • Alphabet Wall Cards • Letter Tiles • Making Good Choices Flip Chart • Home Connections Resource Guide

Other Materials

DAY 1	DAY 2	DAY 3	DAY 4	DAY 5
• smocks, paint trays • construction paper • small sponges, paint brushes • picture cards of song words • chalk, pencil, newspaper • moist towel • drawing paper, crayons	• large trays or plastic table covers • shaving cream • paper, pencils, crayons, markers • items that begin with s, like soap, stick, stone • items that do not begin with s, like ball, apple • paper plate, cloth	• multi-colored construction paper masks, dress-up clothes • blocks • paper plates • tape • US and state flags, photographs of the US and state flags • construction paper (blue squares, red and white stripes, white stars) • glue; smocks; red, white, and blue paint; paintbrushes	• images of foxes, birds, animals, sun, moon, trees on tagboard pieces with sandpaper on back • crayons, construction paper • tissue paper scraps, yarn scraps • paste • paint, sponges, smocks • building blocks	• paper • small plastic containers • liquid starch • paintbrushes • colored chalk • variety of music selections and audio player • masking tape

Home Connection

DAY 1	DAY 2	DAY 3	DAY 4	DAY 5
Encourage children to show their families how they learned to sneeze and cough into their elbow. Send home the Weekly Family Letter, Home Connections Resource Guide, pp. 15–16; ABC Take-Home Book for *Aa,* (English) p. 7 or (Spanish) p. 35.	Invite children to sing the song "When I Was One" to their families. Send home the ABC Take-Home Book for *Ss,* (English) p. 25 or (Spanish) p. 56.	Have children bring their flags home and show them to their families. Send home the ABC Take-Home Book for *Mm,* (English) p. 19 or (Spanish) p. 49.	Remind children to tell their families about the story "Why Goldfinches are Yellow and Like the Sun." Send home ABC Take-Home Book for *Dd,* (English) p. 10 or (Spanish) p. 39; Storybook 1, Home Connections Resource Guide, pp. 81–84	Have children show their families different ways they can move to music.

Assessment

As you observe children throughout the week, you may fill out an Anecdotal Observational Record Form to document an individual's progress toward a goal or signs indicating the need for developmental or medical evaluation. You may also choose to select work for each child's portfolio. The Anecdotal Observational Record Form and Weekly Assessment rubrics are available In the assessment section of DLMExpressOnline.com.

More Literature Suggestions

• **D.W.'s Guide to Preschool** by Marc Brown
• **Cleo's Alphabet Book** by Caroline Mockford
• **Llama Llama Misses Mama** by Anna Dewdney
• **La clase de dibujo** por Tomi dePaola
• **El mejor libro para contar** por Richard Scarry

Week 2

Daily Planner

		DAY 1	**DAY 2**
Let's Start the Day **Language Time**	large group	**Opening Routines** p. 64 **Morning Read Aloud** p. 64 **Oral Language and Vocabulary** p. 64 Words about Pictures **Phonological Awareness** p. 64 Listen for Fun 	**Opening Routines** p. 70 **Morning Read Aloud** p. 70 **Oral Language and Vocabulary** p. 70 Busy at School **Phonological Awareness** p. 70 Listening for Names 
Center Time	small group	**Focus On:** **Creativity Center** p. 65 **Library and Listening Center** p. 65	**Focus On:** **ABC Center** p. 71 **Writer's Center** p. 71
Circle Time **Literacy Time**	large group	**Read Aloud** *Yellowbelly and Plum Go to School/Barrigota y Pipón van a la escuela* p. 66 **Learn About Letters and Sounds: Learn About the Alphabet** p. 66 	**Read Aloud** *Yellowbelly and Plum Go to School/Barrigota y Pipón van a la escuela* p. 72 **Learn About Letters and Sounds: Learn About the Alphabet** p. 72 
Math Time	large group	**Number Me** p. 67	**Count and Move** p. 73 **Sing "When I Was One "** p. 73
Social and Emotional Development	large group	**Clean-Up Time** p. 67 	**On the Job Help** p. 73 
Content Connection	large group	**Science:** **Oral Language and Academic Vocabulary** p. 68 Sneeze into Your Elbow **Observe and Investigate** p. 68 Personal Health and Hygiene 	**Math:** **Snapshots** p. 74 
Center Time	small group	**Focus On:** **Math and Science Center** p. 69 **Purposeful Play** p. 69	**Focus On:** **Math and Science Center** p. 75 **Purposeful Play** p. 75
Let's Say Good-Bye	large group	**Read Aloud** p. 69 **Writing** p. 69 **Home Connection** p. 69	**Read Aloud** p. 75 **Writing** p. 75 **Home Connection** p. 75

Building Blocks

Focus Question

What happens in our classroom?
¿Qué sucede en nuestro salón de clases?

DAY 3	DAY 4	DAY 5
Opening Routines p. 76 **Morning Read Aloud** p. 76 **Oral Language and Vocabulary** p. 76 Mask Making **Phonological Awareness** p. 76 Can You Hear It? 	**Opening Routines** p. 82 **Morning Read Aloud** p. 82 **Oral Language and Vocabulary** p. 82 Pretend Stories **Phonological Awareness** p. 82 Simon Says 	**Opening Routines** p. 88 **Morning Read Aloud** p. 88 **Oral Language and Vocabulary** p. 88 Words in Our Class **Phonological Awareness** p. 88 Sing and Listen 
Focus On: **Pretend and Learn Center** p. 77 **Construction Center** p. 77	**Focus On:** **Pretend and Learn Center** p. 83 **Creativity Center** p. 83	**Focus On:** **Library and Listening Center** p. 89 **Creativity Center** p. 89
Read Aloud *Welcome to School/Bienvenidos a la escuela* p. 78 **Learn About Letters and Sounds: Learn About the Alphabet** p. 78 	**Read Aloud** "Why Goldfinches Are Yellow Like the Sun"/"Por qué los jilgueros son amarillos como el sol" p. 84 **Learn About Letters and Sounds: Learn About the Alphabet** p. 84  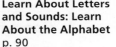	**Read Aloud** *Yellowbelly and Plum Go to School/Barrigota y Pipón van a la escuela* p. 90 **Learn About Letters and Sounds: Learn About the Alphabet** p. 90  
Find and Make Groups p. 79	**Count and Move in Patterns** p. 85 **Make Groups** p. 85	**Find and Make Groups** p. 91
It's Clean-Up Time! p. 79 	**Everyone Helps** p. 85	**The Importance of Clean-Up** p. 91
Social Studies: **Oral Language and Academic Vocabulary** p. 80 Looking at Our Flags **Understand and Participate** p. 80 My Own Flag	**Math:** **Find Groups** p. 86	**Music and Movement:** **Oral Language and Academic Vocabulary** p. 92 All Kinds of Moves **Explore and Express** p. 92 Move to the Music
Focus On: **Creativity Center** p. 81 **Purposeful Play** p. 81	**Focus On:** **Construction Center** p. 87 **Purposeful Play** p. 87	**Focus On:** **Pretend and Learn Center** p. 93 **Purposeful Play** p. 93
Read Aloud p. 81 **Writing** p. 81 **Home Connection** p. 81	**Read Aloud** p. 87 **Writing** p. 87 **Home Connection** p. 87	**Read Aloud** p. 93 **Writing** p. 93 **Home Connection** p. 93

Learning Centers

Math and Science Center

Good Health Habits
Children draw pictures of themselves practicing good health habits, p. 69.

More Camera Counting
Children count objects they see for just a moment, p. 75.

Good Habits
Provide pictures of children showing good and bad personal health habits. Children group good and bad health habit photos.

Groups of 2 and 3
Children choose groups of like items from a pile of various small items. They create as many groups of two and groups of three as they can.

Classroom 1 to 10
Children hold a Numeral Card from 1 to 10. In counting order, children name things in their classroom that correspond to the numbers they are holding.

ABC Center

Writing the Letter A
Children practice writing upper case and lower case A, p. 71.

ABC Train
Prepare an alphabet train with letters written on index cards. String the cards together with yarn. Children sing "The ABC Song" as they point to letters on the train.

Alphabet Match
Children match magnetic letters with letter cards.

Aa Flags
Children place sticky notes with the letter *Aa* on signs, books, and labels in the classroom. Help children count the *Aa*s.

Begins with /a/ or /s/
Prepare cards with images that begin with /a/ and /s/. Children turn over the cards and identify the image and the beginning letter sound on each, by saying, for example, "Sad. *Sad* begins with /s/."

Creativity Center

Sponge Painting
Children use paint to make sponge prints, p. 65.

Red, White, and Blue
Children use the colors of the flag in their paintings, p. 81.

Color Collages
Children choose one color to use in a collage, p. 83.

School Is Fun
Children use starch and chalk to make a picture, p. 89.

Healthy Habits Book
Children make a classroom book for healthy habits practiced in the classroom. Children create a "page" that illustrates a healthy habit.

Healthy Sneezer
Create cut-out figures of a child. Attach one arm with yarn so it is moveable. Children decorate a figure and place the arm so it is sneezing into its elbow or a tissue.

Library and Listening Center

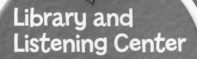

Listening for Words
Children will listen for certain words in a song, p. 65.

Listen for Fun
Children listen for specific words as they hear a song, p. 89.

Browse Pre-K Books
Pairs browse through books about going to school. Have them point out things that they like their school.

Books About Flags
Children browse through nonfiction and fiction stories that show flags. Have children ask and answer one another's questions about the different flags.

Yesterday, Today, Tomorrow
Children browse Pre-K books and identify pictures of things they did today and yesterday and hope to do tomorrow.

Listen to Big Book
Children listen in pairs to *Yellowbelly and Plum Go to School*/*Barrigota y Pipón van a la escuela.*

Construction Center

Building Inside and Outside
Children use blocks to make buildings, p. 77.

Make Buildings
Children count blocks after they use them to make buildings, p. 87.

Plan and Build
Children work in groups to plan and build a structure. Each child takes on a role and follows the group plan.

Build It Together
Children work together to build a structure that Yellowbelly and Plum could play on.

Building Names
Children take turns saying their names. Partners use two blocks to clap out the syllables in each name. Then they add those blocks to the Name Tower. Continue with other names in the class.

Writer's Center

Writing About Plum
Children write about a character in a story, p. 71.

Write the Answer
Children work in pairs. One child asks a question about Yellowbelly and Plum and the other child answers. Both draw and write the answer.

Write a Rule
Children draw a picture showing them carrying out a classroom rule. Then they label their drawing. Encourage all levels of writing.

Describing My Flag
Children describe their flags to a partner. They dictate or write words that tell about their flag and what it symbolizes.

Caring for a Friend
Children draw a picture of something they did to help a friend. Then they dictate or write about their pictures.

Pretend and Learn Center

Multi-Colored Dress Up
Children talk about masks before they play dress up, p. 77.

Make-Believe Fox and Bird Tales
Children make up stories about animals, p. 83.

Moving in Place
Children move to music, p. 93.

Play About Rules
Children use stuffed animals or puppets to act out how they play outside. Children discuss outdoor rules before they begin their play-acting.

Act Out Tomorrow
Children plan and act out an activity they would like to do at school tomorrow.

Act Out Answers
Children work in groups. One child asks a question about the story *Yellowbelly and Plum Go to School*/*Barrigota y Pipón van a la escuela* and the other children discuss and act out their responses.

DAY 1

Let's Start the Day

Focus Question

What happens in our classroom?

¿Qué sucede en nuestro salón de clases?

✓ Learning Goals

Language and Communication
• Child begins and ends conversations appropriately.
• Child uses newly learned vocabulary daily in multiple contexts.

Vocabulary

apron	delantal	brush	pincel
make	hacer	paint	cuadro
picture	pintura	smock	delantal

Differentiated Instruction

 Extra Support
Phonological Awareness
If…children have difficulty listening for the word *fun*, **then…**pause for just a second before you sing the word to signal that it's time to pay attention.

 Enrichment
Oral Language and Vocabulary
Challenge children to describe the tools they have used in the classroom to make pictures.

Accommodations for 3's
Phonological Awareness
If…children have difficulty standing up and turning around, **then…**have them stand up and sit down slowly.

 Opening Routines and Transition Tips
For **Opening Routines** and **Transition Tips** turn to pages 178–181 and visit **DLMExpressOnline.com** for more ideas.

Read **"With a Crayon in My Hand"**/**"Cuando en la mano tengo un crayón"** from the *Teacher's Treasure Book,* page 108, for your morning Read Aloud.

Language Time

 large group 15 minutes

👥👥👥 **Social and Emotional Development** Encourage children to listen to and comment on one another's ideas.

Oral Language and Vocabulary

✓ **Can children answer questions about the girl pictured, what she is doing, and the tools she is using?**

Words about Pictures Display *Oral Language Development Card 3*. Ask children to look at the girl and guess where she is and what she is going to do. Ask: **What will the girl use to make her picture?** *¿Qué usará la niña para hacer su pintura?* Explain that people make pictures in many different ways and that every activity has its own supplies and tools. Ask: **What supplies do you use to make pictures?** *¿Qué elementos usará la niña? ¿Qué elementos usan ustedes para hacer pinturas?* Discuss the tools the girl in the picture uses and the other tools children use. Then follow the suggestions on the back of the card.

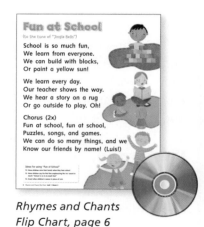

Oral Language Development Card 3

Phonological Awareness

✓ **Can children listen for and hear an individual word in a sentence?**

Listen for Fun Display the *Rhymes and Chants Flip Chart,* page 6. Introduce and sing the song "Fun at School." Remind children that a song is made up of individual words. Ask them to listen to the song, focusing especially on the word *fun*. Have children stand up each time they hear the word *fun*, turn around once, and then sit back down.

ELL Provide classroom examples of puzzles and games to help non-English-speaking children understand what the words *puzzle* and *game* mean.

Rhymes and Chants Flip Chart, page 6

Center Time

Center Rotation Center Time includes teacher-guided activities and independent activities. Refer to the **Learning Centers** on pages 62–63 for independent activity ideas.

 small group 60–90 minutes

Creativity Center

 Observe children using new vocabulary during center time.

Materials paintbrush, smocks, paint trays, construction paper, small sponges

Sponge Painting Hold up a paintbrush and ask children if they remember the name of the artist's tool. Ask: *What can you do with this kind of brush? ¿Qué pueden hacer con este tipo de pincel?* Ask children what other tools or supplies they need when they paint.

● Display sponges and model how to dip them in paint to make paint prints on paper.

● Have children put on paint smocks and choose a sponge and one color of paint to use for printing.

Center Tip
If...children have difficulty making textured prints, **then...**guide them to tap the painted sponges lightly on paper in order to make a texture appear.

Library and Listening Center

 Track children listening for a word while singing along with a music CD.

Materials *Rhymes and Chants CD, Photo Library CD-ROM*

Listening for Words Create and display picture cards of words from "Fun at School." Name each item and have children repeat after you. Then, turn all the cards upside down. Explain that children will listen for words while singing along with a music CD. Have children take turns picking a picture card that shows a focus word.

● Model choosing one card and turning it over.

● Place the picture card faceup and say: *This is the word we will listen for. Ésta es la palabra que estábamos buscando.* Then say the word. Tell children to raise both their hands when they hear the word.

Center Tip
If...children have difficulty hearing the words in recorded songs, **then...**sing the song, pausing before the focus word for emphasis.

Focus Question
What happens in our classroom?
¿Qué sucede en nuestro salón de clases?

 Learning Goals

Emergent Literacy: Reading
• Child explores books and other texts to answer questions.
• Child names most upper- and lowercase letters of the alphabet.
• Child identifies the letter that stands for a given sound.

Vocabulary

bear	oso	busy	ocupado
drums	tambores	excellent	excelente
games	juegos	music	música
shy	tímido		

Differentiated Instruction

✋ Extra Support
Learn About Letters and Sounds
If...children have difficulty tracing letters as you write, **then...**draw a mirror image of letters in the air, one line at a time, for children to copy.

⭐ Enrichment
Read Aloud
Challenge children to describe the games in the story that they liked best.

Accommodations for 3's
Learn About Letters and Sounds
If...children have difficulty making the /a/ sound, **then...**point out how their mouths are open like an alligator when they begin to say the word *apple* or *alligator*.

Literacy Time

📖 Read Aloud

✔ **Can children ask and answer questions about the story?**

Build Background Tell children you will read a story about two friends starting school. Say that one of the friends is a little shy about going to school.

● Explain that *shy* means being unsure about trying new things or meeting new people. Ask: **How did you feel when you came here the first day?** *¿Cómo se sintieron el primer día de clase?*

Listen for Enjoyment Display *Yellowbelly and Plum Go to School,* and read the title. Preview some of the pages in the book.

● Read the story, providing child-friendly explanations of vocabulary words. Have children point to pictures of activities they do at school.

● Ask: **Why do you think Yellowbelly brought Plum to school with him? How did Yellowbelly feel when Plum was lost? Why?** *¿Por qué crees que Barrigota lleva Pipón a la escuela? ¿Cómo se sintió Barrigota cuando Pipón se perdió? ¿Por qué?*

Respond to the Story Discuss the story and ask children to share their favorite parts. Ask: **What was your favorite part of the story?** *¿Cuál es tu parte favorita del cuento?* Then have children think of questions to ask the class about the story. Have other children answer the questions.

💡 **TIP** Pause as you read to explain the meaning of words children ask about, such as *submarine, meteor shower, orthodontist, glockenspiel,* and so on.

ELL Explain that *plum* can mean "the color purple," or "a purple fruit." Ask children to explain why they think Yellowbelly named his bear *Plum.*

Learn About Letters and Sounds

✔ **Can children identify the letter *Aa* and the /a/ sound?**

Learn About The Alphabet Invite children to sing "The ABC Song" with you, then ask: **What is the first letter in the alphabet?** *¿Cuál es la primera letra del alfabeto?* Display the *ABC Big Book*. Point out the letter *Aa* at the beginning of the book.

● Explain that each letter has a name, and also at least one sound. Point to the letter *Aa* and ask: **What is this letter's name?** *¿Cómo se llama esta letra?*

● Introduce the /a/ sound using the pictures in the *ABC Big Book*. Say: **The first sound you hear in the word** apple **is /a/, the sound the letter A makes.** *El primer sonido de la palabra apple es /a/; ése es el sonido que hace la letra A.* Have children say the sound. Repeat with the other pictures on the *Aa* page.

● Say: **Now let's learn to write it.** *Ahora, vamos a aprender a escribirla.* Display the *ABC Picture Card* for *Aa*. Trace upper and lowercase *Aa* with your finger as children trace along with you in the air. Review the letter name and sound.

Yellowbelly and Plum Go to School
Barrigota y Pipón van a la escuela

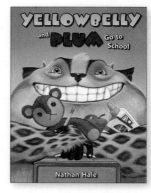
ABC Big Book

apple   acorn
ABC Picture Cards

Math Time

Observe and Investigate

Can children count objects?

Number Me Invite children to use their bodies to count and number objects. Ask them to tell you their age using their fingers, and count their body parts.

- Say: *How old are you? Show me with your fingers.* *¿Cuántos años tienen? Muéstrenlo con los dedos.*

- Next have children focus on their hands, fingers, legs, feet, toes, head, nose, eyes, and ears. Encourage children to add motion. Say: *How many legs do you have? Wiggle your two legs.* *¿Cuántas piernas tienen? ¡Jugueteen con las dos piernas y diviértanse!*

- Make silly, incorrect statements, such as: *I have four ears…three feet…five eyes.* *Tengo cuatro orejas…tres pies…cinco ojos.* Mix them with correct statements. Have children say whether or not you are correct. Ask: *How many do I have? How do you know? ¿Cuántos tengo? ¿Cómo lo saben?*

☩☩☩ Social and Emotional Development

Making Good Choices

Do children understand classroom routines and rules and show a desire to follow them?

Clean-Up Time Explain that in the classroom everyone has rules to follow. Ask: *Remember when we made the rule about cleaning up? Why did you make that rule? What would happen if nobody followed the clean-up rule? Who's going to follow the clean-up rule today? Las reglas los ayudan a saber cómo comportarse durante el día de escuela. Una regla que tenemos es ordenar después de una actividad. Todos debemos seguir las reglas de la clase. Así nos preocupamos por los demás.* Talk about the kinds of things children must clean up. Display the *Making Good Choices Flip Chart,* page 6, and explain that it's showing clean-up time. Ask children to name different clean-up jobs that children do each day in the classroom. Review transition routines for clean-up. Refer to Transition Tips on pages 180–181.

- Point to the boys in the picture, and ask what the boys are doing and why. Point to the girl and ask how other children might feel when they see what she has done.

- Ask: *Why is it better to help each other clean up instead of cleaning up by yourself? ¿Por qué es mejor trabajar juntos que ordenar todo uno solo?*

    ELL Explain that the word *accident* and *accidente* in Spanish sound very similar and mean the same thing. Ask: *What letter and sound are at the beginning of both words?*

Online Math Activity

Introduce Kitchen Counter (online activity). In Kitchen Counter, children need to click on each item to count it; explain that they should click each item only once. Each child should complete the activity this week.

Making Good Choices Flip Chart, page 6

 Learning Goals

Social and Emotional Development
- Child follows simple classroom rules and routines.
- Child uses classroom materials carefully.
- Child accepts responsibility for and regulates own behavior.

Language and Communication
- Child experiments with and produces a growing number of sounds in English words. (ELL)

Mathematics
- Child understands that objects, or parts thereof, can be counted.

Vocabulary

accident	accidente	rule	regla
wiggle	juguetear		

Differentiated Instruction

 Extra Support

Making Good Choices

If…children have difficulty explaining why it is important to clean up, **then…**ask them to describe what would happen in the classroom if no one ever put any supplies or materials away.

⭐ Enrichment

Making Good Choices

With a partner, children agree on and respond with one way they can help together.

Accommodations for 3's

Observe and Investigate

If…children have trouble holding up their fingers to show their age is three, **then…** provide individual support.

Learning Goals

Social and Emotional Development
• Child accepts responsibility for and regulates own behavior.

Language and Communication
• Child exhibits an understanding of instructional terms used in the classroom.

Science
• Child practices personal hygiene skills independently (for example, washes hands, blows nose, covers mouth, brushes teeth).

Vocabulary

cough	tos	elbow	codo
germs	gérmenes	habit	hábito
health	salud	sneeze	estornudar
spread	esparcir		

Differentiated Instruction

Extra Support

Observe and Investigate

If...children do not see any chalk on their partner's hands, **then...**help the child repeat the activity with more chalk.

Enrichment

Observe and Investigate

Invite children to draw a picture showing healthy personal care routines, such as brushing teeth and combing hair. The picture can be used as a reminder at home.

Accommodation for 3's

Oral Language and Academic Vocabulary

If...children are afraid of germs, **then...**explain that talking about germs is just another way to talk about being sick. When you feel better, the germs are going away.

Science Time

large group   20 minutes

Health Skills Model good habits of personal health in the classroom by washing your hands before and after eating.

Oral Language and Academic Vocabulary

✓ **Can children explain why they should sneeze into their elbow?**

Sneeze into Your Elbow Explain that germs are what make people feel sick. They live inside our bodies and can come outside and spread to other people when we cough or sneeze. Demonstrate by spraying water from a spray bottle into the air. Then spray water into your elbow.

● Point to the sneezing child in the *Math and Science Flip Chart,* page 7. Say: *This child is sneezing into an elbow and trying not to spread germs. Este niño está estornudando sobre el codo para no esparcir gérmenes.*

● Ask why the child is sneezing into an elbow. Say: *If you sneeze into your hand, the germs will be on your hand and can get on anything that you touch. You should cough into your elbow as well as sneeze into your elbow. Si estornudan sobre la mano, los gérmenes quedarán en la mano y pasarán a otras cosas que toquen.*

● Discuss why children should wash their hands after blowing their noses.

Observe and Investigate

✓ **Can children identify good habits of personal health and hygiene?**

Personal Health and Hygiene Pair children, and invite one child in each pair to rub colored chalk between his or her hands. Have that child touch a piece of white paper and then pass the paper to a partner. Have the partner wipe his or her hands with a moist towel.

● Ask: *What happened to the paper and to the partner's hand? ¿Qué le sucedió al papel y a la mano del compañero?* Explain that germs can move from person to person through touch just as the chalk did. Ask: *If you sneeze or cough into your elbow and wash your hands often, what will happen to the germs?* (The germs will not spread as easily.) *Si estornudan o tosen sobre el codo y se lavan las manos con frecuencia, los gérmenes no se transmitirán tan fácilmente.*

● Discuss other habits of good health and hygiene practiced in both the classroom and at home, such as washing hands before and/or after eating, using the toilet, brushing teeth, bathing, and washing clothing.

TIP Set up the chalk activity in a small, uncluttered area to facilitate clean-up. You may also want to lay down newspaper and limit the number of objects children touch with chalk on their hands. Have children wash their hands after the activity.

ELL Review body parts with the children. Play a game similar to "Simon Says" and include simulating sneezing into an elbow.

Good Health Habits
Hábitos de buena salud

Math and Science Flip Chart, page 7

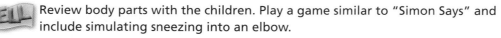

Center Time

▶ **Center Rotation:** Center Time includes teacher-guided activities and independent activities. Refer to the **Learning Centers** on pages 62–63 for independent activity ideas.

small group · 30 minutes

Refer to the **Learning Centers** on pages 62–63 for independent activity ideas.

Math and Science Center

	Center Tip

☑ **Encourage children to describe good health habits.**

Materials drawing paper, crayons, Sequence Cards set "Brushing Your Teeth"

Good Health Habits Tell children that they will be drawing pictures of themselves practicing a good health habit.

- Encourage children to name several good health habits, such as coughing and sneezing into elbows, washing hands after using the bathroom, washing hands before eating, and brushing teeth.

- Use the Sequence Cards set "Brushing Your Teeth" to illustrate a good health habit. Have children draw a picture of themselves practicing a good health habit.

Center Tip

If…children have difficulty drawing the good habit, **then…**place the *Math and Science Flip Chart* in the center as a reference.

Learning Goals

Emergent Literacy: Writing
• Child writes some letters or reasonable approximations of letters upon request.

Science
• Child practices personal hygiene skills independently (for example, washes hands, blows nose, covers mouth, brushes teeth).

Fine Arts
• Child expresses emotions or ideas through art.

Writing

Have children draw a picture of themselves and something that starts with the letter *A*. Explain that children can look at the *Alphabet Wall Cards* or *ABC Big Book* for ideas of words that begin with *Aa*. Ask them to label the picture with the letter *A*.

Purposeful Play

☑ **Observe children as they demonstrate the motions involved in different good health habits.**

Children choose an open center for free playtime. Encourage children to practice the motor skills involved in some good health habits by acting them out dramatically.

Let's Say Good-Bye

large group · 15 minutes

 Read Aloud Revisit "With a Crayon in My Hand"/"Cuando en la mano tengo un crayón" for your afternoon Read Aloud. Have children talk about art supplies they use at school.

 Home Connection Refer to the Home Connections activities listed in the Resources and Materials chart on page 59. Remind children to tell their families about the sound the letter *Aa* makes. Sing the "Good-Bye Song" as children prepare to leave.

Let's Start the Day

Focus Question

What happens in our classroom?

¿Qué sucede en nuestro salón de clases?

Learning Goals

Language and Communication
• Child uses newly learned vocabulary daily in multiple contexts.

Vocabulary

busy	ocupado	excellent	excelente
games	juegos	outside	afuera

Differentiated Instruction

 Extra Support

Oral Language and Vocabulary
If...children have difficulty naming an activity that kept them busy, **then...**ask: *What did you work very hard at yesterday? ¿En qué trabajaron mucho ayer?*

Enrichment

Oral Language and Vocabulary
Have children browse through *Yellowbelly and Plum Go to School* and find a page that shows Yellowbelly busy with an activity.

Accommodations for 3's

Phonological Awareness
If...three-year-olds have difficulty listening for a word in a song, **then...**sing slowly with clear enunciation. Give a visual cue to listen carefully, such as a head nod, when you are getting near to singing the chosen word, or sing the lyrics together accompanied by hand claps.

 Opening Routines and Transition Tips

For **Opening Routines** and **Transition Tips** turn to pages 178–181 and visit **DLMExpressOnline.com** for more ideas.

Read **"Smart Cookie's Clever Idea"/"La inteligente idea de Smart Cookie"** from the *Teacher's Treasure Book*, page 264, for your morning Read Aloud.

large group   15 minutes

Language Time

Social and Emotional Development Observe how children interact with others during work and play time during the day.

Oral Language and Vocabulary

Can children use new words to describe activities?

Busy at School Discuss the variety of activities children do everyday at school. Explain that with so much to do, they have been very busy each day. Explain that often, when someone is very busy because they are working hard, they do very good work, even excellent work. Say: *Yellowbelly and Plum were very busy in the story we read yesterday. Can you remember what they were doing? Barrigota y Pipón estaban muy ocupados en el cuento que leímos ayer. ¿Se acuerdan qué estaban haciendo?*

Ask children if they can name anything excellent that either Yellowbelly or Plum did at school. Have them give examples of excellent jobs they have done.

ELL Model how to use the word *busy* in a sentence. For example, say: *I was busy painting; I was busy building blocks; I was busy playing outside.* Encourage children to use a complete sentence to name times they were busy.

Phonological Awareness

Can children listen for a word spoken in a chant?

Listening for Names Display *Rhymes and Chants Flip Chart*, page 6, "Fun at School." Ask children if they remember the song, then have them sing it for you. Explain that you are going to play a listening game. This time, you are going to ask children to listen for new words that they have not practiced listening for before. Choose a word not used in previous listening games, such as *we, up, down,* or *outside.* Have children decide on an action to perform when they hear the word. For example, have children wave their hands, put their hands on their heads, or stand up when they hear the word. Then sing the song together.

Rhymes and Chants Flip Chart, page 6

Center Time

Center Rotation Center Time includes teacher-guided activities and independent activities. Refer to the **Learning Centers** on pages 62–63 for independent activity ideas.

 small group 60–90 minutes

ABC Center

| | **Center Tip** |

 Can children listen for an individual word in a sentence?

 Do children initiate interactions and discussions with others as they work?

Materials large trays or plastic table covers, shaving cream

Writing the Letter A Review with children how to write an upper case and lower case *Aa* and remind children of the /a/ sound they hear at the beginning of the word *alligator*.

- Model how to write the letter *Aa* with your finger in shaving cream. Have the children practice writing the letter *Aa*. Encourage them to draw alligators in shaving cream.

- Have children listen for anyone saying the word *alligator* as they work. Tell them if they hear the word *alligator*, they should reply by saying *alligator*. Alternatively, use rhyming words such as *and* and *sand*. Ask children for new focus words if time permits.

Center Tip

If...children have difficulty writing letters because they've filled up their trays with marks, **then...**remind them they can smooth over the shaving cream and start again on a clean surface.

Writer's Center

Center Tip

 Observe children as they write about games they like to play.

Materials paper, pencils, crayons, markers

Writing About Plum Remind children that Plum likes to play games. Ask children to think about what games they like to play at school. Have children draw and/or write about a game they like to play.

- Write children's sentences on their papers, including any additional thoughts they dictate.

- Have children draw pictures to illustrate their dictations.

- Make a class book of completed work for the classroom library.

Center Tip

If...children have difficulty thinking of a game they like to play, **then...**name some of the games you have observed children playing.

Learning Goals

Emergent Literacy: Writing
- Child writes some letters or reasonable approximations of letters upon request.
- Child experiments with and uses some writing conventions when writing or dictating.

Fine Arts
- Child expresses emotions or ideas through art.

Differentiated Instruction

Extra Support
Writer's Center
If...children have difficulty remembering things that Yellowbelly and Plum did together, **then...** invite them to browse through the book and review the illustrations.

Enrichment
ABC Center
Challenge children to also write any of the letters in their names that they know.

Accommodations for 3's
ABC Center
If...children have difficulty remembering how to write the letter *Aa*, **then...**demonstrate once more, tracing in the shaving cream, this time allowing the child to make the letter right beside yours. Some children may be more successful using the whole hand for this activity. Be sure to encourage the use of either hand.

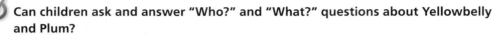

Circle Time

Focus Question
What happens in our classroom?
¿Qué sucede en nuestro salón de clases?

Literacy Time

large group · 15 minutes

📖 Read Aloud

✅ **Can children ask and answer "Who?" and "What?" questions about Yellowbelly and Plum?**

Build Background Discuss the reasons children might feel shy or lonely when they first start school.

● Ask: *What did Yellowbelly do to make new friends? ¿Qué hicieron Barrigota y Pipón para hacer nuevos amigos?*

● Ask: *What are some ideas for having fun with other children? ¿Qué pueden hacer los niños para divertirse juntos en la escuela?*

Listen for Understanding Display *Yellowbelly and Plum Go to School* and read the title.

● Pause after you read each page to give the children time to take in the illustrations.

● Ask: *What just happened? What do you think will happen next? ¿Qué sucedió recién? ¿Qué creén que pasará después?*

Respond to the Story Discuss the story and invite children to share thoughts about whether Plum could be shy or not. Ask them to explain their answers. If children are unsure about whether Plum could have real feelings, encourage them to ask questions to help them come to a conclusion.

ELL Break challenging words from the book, such as *submarine commander, orthodontist,* and *glockenspiel,* into syllables. Show children pictures in the book to help them understand their simpler meanings of a boat captain, a kind of a dentist, and a musical instrument.

Learn About Letters and Sounds

✅ **Can children identify the letter *S* and the /s/ sound?**

Learn About The Alphabet Share the *ABC Big Book* and introduce the sound the letter *S* makes by saying: *The first sound you hear in the word sun is /s/; /s/ /s/ sun. El primer sonido de la palabra Sun es /s/.* Have children repeat.

● Display several items, such as a bar of soap, a stick, a stone, a ball, and an apple. Name each item and have children repeat the names. Then ask children to identify items that begin with /s/.

● Display the *ABC Picture Cards* for *Ss* and *Aa*. Point out how the uppercase *A* is made up of straight lines and the uppercase *S* is a rounded line with two curves.

● Demonstrate how to write the letter *Ss*. Have children trace the *Ss* and repeat the /s/ sound.

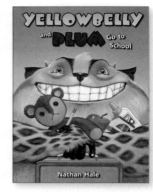

Yellowbelly and Plum Go to School
Barrigota y Pipón van a la escuela

ABC Big Book

ABC Picture Cards

large group • 15 minutes

Building Blocks

Online Math Activity

Introduce Kitchen Counter (online activity). In Kitchen Counter, children need to click on each item to count it; explain that they should click each item only once. Each child should complete the activity this week.

large group • 15 minutes

Making Good Choices Flip Chart, page 6

Math Time

Observe and Investigate

☑ **Can children use words to count?**

Count and Move Have children count from 1 to 10, clapping with each number. Say: **Count with me from 1 to 10. Let's clap with each number!** *Cuenten conmigo del 1 al 10. ¡Aplaudamos en cada número!*

● Repeat during the day and on different days using other motions, such as hopping or marching.

Sing "When I Was One" Invite children to sing the song "When I Was One" with you. The Spanish version of this song is located on page 128 of the *Teacher's Treasure Book.*

> **When I was one, I was so small.** *(Show one finger.)*
> **I could not speak a word at all.** *(Shake head left to right, "no.")*
> **When I was two, I learned to talk.** *(Show two fingers.)*
> **I learned to sing, I learned to walk.** *(Point to mouth and feet.)*
> **When I was three, I grew and grew.** *(Show three fingers.)*
> **Now I am four and so are you!** *(Show four fingers.)*

ELL Provide visual support by making sure children can see the motions. Check to see that they are correlating the motions with the appropriate words.

👤👤👤 Social and Emotional Development

Making Good Choices

☑ **Do children show an understanding of classroom routines, including cleaning up?**

☑ **Do children show a willingness to interact with others and help when completing classroom jobs?**

Help on the Job Discuss classroom jobs and responsibilities that children sometimes need help with. Display the *Making Good Choices Flip Chart,* page 6, and invite children to explain to a Dog Puppet what the children are doing.

● Say: **Can you tell the dogs why children clean up after they work?** *¿Pueden explicar a los perritos por qué los niños limpian después de una tarea?*

● Have the first dog ask: **When would you ask for help? When would you help a friend or classmate?** *¿Cuándo pedirían ayuda? ¿Cuándo ayudarían a un amigo?*

Learning Goals

Social and Emotional Development
● Child follows simple classroom rules and routines.

● Child initiates interactions with others in work and play situations.

Mathematics
● Child recites number words in sequence from one to thirty.

Vocabulary

fingers	dedos
small	pequeño
walk	caminar

Differentiated Instruction

✋ Extra Support
Observe and Investigate
If...children have difficulty counting from 1 to 10 as they clap, **then...**have them count first, and then add motions.

⭐ Enrichment
Observe and Investigate
Challenge children to count to a number higher than 10 as they clap.

Accommodations for 3's
Observe and Investigate
If...children are three years old, **then...**revise the song so that the last line tells that they are three.

Focus Question
What happens in our classroom?
¿Qué sucede en nuestro salón de clases?

Learning Goals

Mathematics

• Child tells how many are in a group of up to 5 objects without counting.

• Child measures passage of time using standard or non-standard tools.

Vocabulary

camera	cámara	photos	fotografías
pose	pose	smile	sonrisa
snapshots	instantáneas		

Differentiated Instruction

👏 Extra Support
Math Time
If...children are having difficulty naming the number of counters, **then...**use fewer counters.

⭐ Enrichment
Math Time
Use up to five classroom objects to challenge children.

Accommodations for 3's
Math Time
If...children are struggling to remember the number of objects, **then...**ask children to count aloud.

💜 Special Needs
Hearing Impairment
Instead of using counters on a plate, let the child hold a coffee can while you drop in the counters. She or he can count by feeling the counters hit the bottom of the can. If she or he still has difficulty, try using items heavier than a counter.

Math Time

 large group · 20 minutes

✓ **Can children identify the number of objects without counting?**

Snapshots Invite children to use their eyes and minds like a camera and take a "picture" of what they see. Display the *Math and Science Flip Chart*, page 8. Discuss what a camera is. Tell children that a camera copies an image of something. Say: *Has anyone taken your picture? Have you used a camera? ¿Alguna vez alguien les tomó una foto? ¿Alguna vez han usado una cámara?*

● Talk about the photos on the flip chart page and ask children to talk about the activities in the pictures.

● Point to any examples of photos around the classroom. If there are class photos of each child, for example, point to them and explain that they are photographs.

● For this activity, secretly place two counters on a paper plate, covering the plate with an opaque cloth.

● Show your covered plate, and explain that counters are hidden under the cloth. Say: *Watch the counters as I show them to you for a short time. How many counters are there? Take a picture of them in your mind. Observen las fichas mientras se las muestro. ¿Cuántas fichas hay? Saquen una fotografía de las fichas en su mente.* Uncover the plate for two seconds and cover it again.

● Have children show with their fingers how many counters they saw. Say: *Show me with your fingers how many counters there are. How many counters did you see? Muéstrenme con sus dedos cuántas fichas hay. ¿Cuántas fichas ven?* Repeat the uncovering if needed.

● Uncover the plate indefinitely. Say: *Now you can see the counters for a long time. How many do you see? Ahora pueden ver todas las fichas durante un rato largo. ¿Cuántas fichas ven?*

● Repeat with more counters. Discuss whether it was easier to tell how many counters when students saw them for a short time or a long time.

Math and Science Flip Chart, page 8

Center Time

► **Center Rotation** Center Time includes teacher-guided activities and independent activities. Refer to the **Learning Centers** on pages 62–63 for independent activity ideas.

small group · 30 minutes

Math and Science Center

Center Tip

☑ Observe children as they group items, using classroom manipulatives.

Materials plates, Two-Color Counters

More Camera Counting Children explore the camera activity in small groups.

- For this activity, secretly place two counters on a paper plate, covering the plate with an opaque cloth.

- Have one child uncover the counters and show them quickly to a small group of children.

- Have the other children show with their fingers how many counters they saw.

- Children can take turns and repeat with more counters.

If...children need help setting up the paper and counters, **then...**model the activity again.

Purposeful Play

☑ Observe children making groups.

Children choose an open center for free playtime. Encourage children to treat each other as they want to be treated. Remind them that anyone can ask for help at any time.

Let's Say Good-Bye

large group · 15 minutes

 Read Aloud Revisit the story, "Smart Cookie's Clever Idea"/"La inteligente idea de Smart Cookie" for your afternoon Read Aloud. Encourage children to ask "Who?" and "What?" questions about the story.

 Home Connection Refer to the Home Connections activities listed in the Resources and Materials chart on page 59. Invite children to sing the song "When I Was One" to their families. Sing the "Good-Bye Song" as children prepare to leave.

✔ Learning Goals

Emergent Literacy: Writing
- Child participates in free drawing and writing activities to deliver information.
- Child uses scribbles, shapes, pictures, symbols, and letters to represent language.

Mathematics
- Child tells how many are in a group of up to 5 objects without counting.
- Child measures passage of time using standard or non-standard tools.

Writing

Recap the day. Invite children to share what they felt was the best or most excellent part of the day. Invite them to write and draw about the best part of their day, encouraging them to write using letters, partial letters or words, or scribble. Invite several children to share the pictures and writing with the group. Have children take their pictures home to share with their families.

DAY 3

Let's Start the Day

Focus Question
What happens in our classroom?
¿Qué sucede en nuestro salón de clases?

Learning Goals

Social and Emotional Development
• Child accepts responsibility for and regulates own behavior.

Language and Communication
• Child uses newly learned vocabulary daily in multiple contexts.

Fine Arts
• Child participates in a variety of music activities (such as listening, singing, finger plays, musical games, performances).

Vocabulary

art	arte	colors	colores
mask	máscara	projects	proyectos
red	rojo	supplies	materiales

Differentiated Instruction

Extra Support
Phonological Awareness
If...children have difficulty hearing words in a song, **then...**use voice and facial expression to emphasize the chosen word as you sing it.

Enrichment
Phonological Awareness
Invite children to pick another song. Choose a familiar word in the song. Challenge them to sing the song, listening for the word and raising their hands when they hear it.

Accommodations for 3's
Oral Language and Vocabulary
If...three-year-olds have difficulty asking questions about the masks, **then...**ask: **What would you like to know about this mask? What do you see?** *¿Que les gustaría saber sobre esta máscara? ¿Qué ven aquí?*

 Opening Routines and Transition Tips
For **Opening Routines** and **Transition Tips** turn to pages 178–181 and visit **DLMExpressOnline.com** for more ideas.

Read **"Little Annie Oakley"/"La pequeña Annie Oakley"** from the *Teacher's Treasure Book,* page 253, for your morning Read Aloud.

Language Time

large group 15 minutes

Social and Emotional Development Encourage children to put away their backpacks and coats so they will be ready to begin the daily routines.

Oral Language and Vocabulary

✓ **Can children use new words when speaking about the mask picture?**

Mask Making Ask children what they can make or color in the classroom. Ask: **Have you ever made a mask?** *¿Alguna vez han hecho una máscara?*

● Display *Oral Language Development Card 4.* Invite children to ask questions about the child and the mask pictured to learn more about who might make masks at school and how they might do it. Then follow the suggestions on the back of the card.

Oral Language Development Card 4

Phonological Awareness

✓ **Can children distinguish an individual word while singing the song "Fun at School?"**

Can You Hear It? Display the *Rhymes and Chants Flip Chart,* page 6, and sing the song with the children. Review the vocabulary words contained in "Fun at School." Invite children to sing along with you. Name a word in the song and ask them to raise their hands when they hear the word. Have children sing the song again. This time, have children sing each of the words in the song in a whisper except for the focus word. Have children sing that word loudly.

ELL Children may not understand the phrase *line up one by one.* Have children demonstrate lining up one by one, and invite English learners to join in the line.

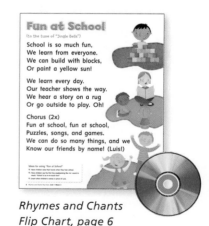

Rhymes and Chants Flip Chart, page 6

Center Time

▶ **Center Rotation** Center Time includes teacher-guided activities and independent activities. Refer to the **Learning Centers** on pages 62–63 for independent activity ideas.

 small group 60–90 minutes

Learning Goals

Social and Emotional Development
• Child accepts responsibility for and regulates own behavior.

Physical Development
• Child develops small-muscle strength and control.

Pretend and Learn Center

| **Center Tip** |

✓ **Observe children as they make predictions about a photograph.**

Materials multi-colored construction paper masks, dress-up clothes

Multi-Colored Dress Up Display *Oral Language Development Card 4*. Have children describe the mask and all the colors the child used. Explain how the child might use the mask.

● Ask: *What do you think the child will pretend to be?* *¿Qué personaje creen que representará cuando use la máscara?*

● Ask: *What would you like to pretend to be?* *¿Qué personaje les gustaría representar?*

● Display simple unpainted masks that children can use along with dress-up clothes to participate in pretend play.

● Encourage children to describe their pretend outfits using color words.

Center Tip

If...children have difficulty choosing something to pretend to be, **then**...offer two or three options to make the selection process easier.

Differentiated Instruction

 Extra Support
Construction Center
If...children have difficulty deciding how to build a structure, **then**...ask them to think of one thing about the building, such as tall or short, wide or narrow.

 Enrichment
Construction Center
Encourage children to use pencil, paper, and tape to label some of the buildings they make.

 Special Needs
Behavioral Social/Emotional
Real vs. make-believe is a critical concept for a child with severe emotional delays, as sometimes these children have considerable difficulty distinguishing what is real from what is make-believe. Throughout the week, look for opportunities to point out the difference. Encourage the child to point out pictures or objects and tell you whether or not they are real.

Construction Center

| **Center Tip** |

✓ **Look for examples of children listening for an individual word as they work together on a building project.**

✓ **Observe children accepting responsibility for and regulating their own behavior as they work together to build with blocks.**

Materials blocks, pencils, paper, tape

Building Inside and Outside Review the kinds of activities children do inside when they are at school, and the kinds of activities they do outside.

● Invite children to divide the block area into an inside classroom area and an outside classroom area.

● Ask: *What do you want to build inside your classroom? What do you want to build outside?* *¿Qué deben construir dentro del salón de clases? ¿Qué deben construir afuera?* Direct children to build the structures they describe.

● Challenge children to listen for the words *inside* and *outside*. Say: *Each time you hear someone say* inside, *answer by saying* outside. *Cada vez que oigan a alguien decir* inside, *respondan diciendo* outside.

Center Tip

If...children are unsure about what structures to build inside and outside, **then**...have them browse through the book *Yellowbelly and Plum Go to School* for ideas.

Circle Time

Focus Question
What happens in our classroom?
¿Qué sucede en nuestro salón de clases?

✓ Learning Goals

Social and Emotional Development
• Child follows simple classroom rules and routines.

Emergent Literacy: Reading
• Child explores books and other texts to answer questions.

Vocabulary

circle	círculo	classroom	salón de clases
exercise	ejercicio	habits	hábitos
healthy	saludable	learn	aprender
teacher	maestro		

Differentiated Instruction

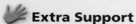

🖐 Extra Support

Learn About Letters and Sounds
If...children have difficulty saying the /m/ sound, **then...**show them how you begin with your lips closed. Say the following words slowly and have children repeat after you: *mouse, moon, monkey, man.*

⭐ Enrichment

Read Aloud
Challenge children to name two things that were described in the book and compare those things to what they have learned or done in their classroom this week.

Accommodations for 3's

Read Aloud
If...children have difficulty naming something they have learned or done, **then...**point to an illustration in the book and ask if they have done that activity at school.

Literacy Time

large group — 15 minutes

📖 Read Aloud

✓ Can children ask and answer questions about the book?

✓ Can children understand and follow classroom routines during circle time?

Build Background Tell children they have been going to school for almost two weeks and now know many things about preschool and classroom activities.

● Ask: **What are some things we do in our classroom every day? What things have you done for the first time since coming to preschool?** *¿Qué hacemos todos los días en el salón de clases? ¿Qué cosas hicieron por primera vez en Prekínder?*

Listen for Understanding Display *Concept Big Book 1: Welcome to School,* and read the title. Remind children that last week when you read the book, they were just beginning school. Now they know much more about school. Ask them to notice things in the book they have also done in the classroom.

● Ask: **What have you done that we also read about in the book?** *¿Qué cosas hicimos en clase que hayan aparecido en el cuento?*

● Read the book. Pause as you read to allow children the opportunity to answer questions and to ask any new questions they have about the written text.

Respond to the Story Invite children to share their ideas about activities in the book they have also done in the classroom. Ask: **What are some new things you have learned in our classroom? Who has helped you learn at school?** *¿Qué cosas nuevas han aprendido en el salón de clases? ¿Quién los ayudó a aprender en la escuela?*

ELL Point out some of the ways English and Spanish words can sound alike, such as *numbers/números*, and *circle/círculo*. Remind children that words they know can sometimes help them understand new words.

Learn About Letters and Sounds

✓ Can children identify the /m/ sound?

Learn About the Alphabet Display the *ABC Big Book* and introduce the letter *Mm* and the /m/ sound.

● Say: **The first sound you hear in the word mouse is /m/.** Say: /m/, /m/. *El primer sonido de la palabra* mouse *es /m/.* Have children repeat the sound.

● Play a game of "I Spy." Look directly at an object that begins with /m/ and say: **I spy something that starts with /m/. What do I see?** *Veo una cosa que empieza con /m/. ¿Qué es?* Guide children to name the object.

● Model how to write an uppercase *M*. Point out that it is made of four straight lines. Have children practice writing *M* in sand trays.

Welcome to School
Bienvenidos a la escuela

ABC Big Book

Building Blocks

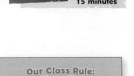

Online Math Activity

Children can complete Kitchen Counter during computer time or Center Time.

Math Time

Observe and Investigate

✔ **Can children make groups?**

Find and Make Groups Gather items from around the classroom for children to make and count groups.

- Place six different groups of classroom items on paper plates, beginning with groups of one to three items.

- Say: **What is a group of two?** *¿Cuál es el grupo de dos?* Have children work in pairs to find a group of two. Partners help and check each other while you observe and assist as needed. Vary the amount pairs are to find based on their ability.

- Now model making a group of two. Say: **Watch me make a group of two. Can you make a group of two.** *Observen cómo formo un grupo de dos. ¿Pueden formar un grupo de dos?* Have children make a group of two. Make sure they use two of the same object.

- Expand the activity to include other numbers if children are able.

☿☿☿ Social and Emotional Development

Making Good Choices

✔ **Do children show an understanding of classroom routines and rules?**

It's Clean-Up Time! Display the *Making Good Choices Chart*, page 6, and review some of the tasks involved in clean-up. Ask the children to help the dogs understand the importance of clean-up by role-playing with the puppets.

Have the children take turns pretending to be working at a center with the Dog Puppets when you announce clean-up time. Role-play several different situations for children to act out:

- The Dog Puppets don't want to stop working and clean up.

- The Dog Puppets would like help cleaning up.

- The Dog Puppets accidentally spill something and don't know what to do.

 Pair English learners with native English speakers. Track children's use of simple phrases to communicate meaning.

Making Good Choices Flip Chart, page 6

Learning Goals

Social and Emotional Development
- Child follows simple classroom rules and routines.

Language and Communication
- Child uses individual words and short phrases to communicate. (ELL)

Mathematics
- Child counts 1–10 concrete objects correctly.
- Child understands that objects can be counted in any order.

Vocabulary

classroom	salón de clases
group	grupo
objects	objetos

Differentiated Instruction

✋ **Extra Support**

Making Good Choices

If...children have difficulty talking to the Dog Puppets, **then...**ask them what they would tell a friend.

⭐ **Enrichment**

Observe and Investigate

Challenge children to find groups of more than two items.

Accommodations for 3's

Observe and Investigate

If...three-year-olds are having trouble making groups, **then...**place a sheet of paper with a drawing of two circles on the table. Have them put an object in each circle.

Focus Question
What happens in our classroom?
¿Qué sucede en nuestro salón de clases?

 Learning Goals

Social Studies
• Child identifies the U.S. Flag and state flag.
• Child recites the Pledge of Allegiance.

Fine Arts
• Child expresses emotions or ideas through art.

Vocabulary

blue	azul	flag	bandera
pledge	compromiso	red	rojo
stars	estrellas	stripes	rayas
symbol	símbolo	white	blanco

Differentiated Instruction

 Extra Support
Understand and Participate
If...children have difficulty comparing the flags in the classroom, **then...**provide pictures of the two flags for children to observe and compare.

Enrichment
Oral Language and Academic Vocabulary
Invite children to name both the state and the country in which they live.

Social Studies Time

  large group · 20 minutes

Oral Language and Academic Vocabulary

 Can children identify the United States flag?

Looking at Our Flags Show children where the United States flag and the flag of their state are displayed in the classroom. Share pictures of the United States flag and flag of their state. Tell children that the United States flag is a symbol of the country we live in. Explain that a pledge is a promise, and when children say the Pledge of Allegiance in the morning, they are making a promise to try to be a good American. Recite the Pledge of Allegiance to the United States flag. Observe a moment of silence.

● Have children compare the state flag to the United States flag.

● Ask: **What is the same about the two flags?** *¿En qué se parecen las dos banderas?*

● Ask: **What is different?** *¿En qué se diferencian?*

Understand and Participate

Can children learn the Pledge of Allegiance?

My Own Flag Have children design their own flags. When children have finished their flags, display them on the wall near the United States and state flags. Invite children to comment about the flags.

● Ask: **Which flags have stripes?** *¿Qué banderas tienen rayas?*

● Ask: **What colors are the flag of the United States, the flag of your state, and the flags of our classroom?** *¿De qué colores son la bandera de Estados Unidos, la de nuestro estado y la del salón de clases?*

● Invite children to stand and face the United States flag and echo you in the Pledge of Allegiance.

ELL Provide pictures to help children understand the words *stars*, *stripes*, and *flags*. Have children point out stripe patterns children might have on their clothing.

  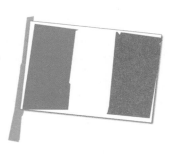 

Center Time

▶ **Center Rotation** Center Time includes teacher-guided activities and independent activities. Refer to the **Learning Centers** on pages 62–63 for independent activity ideas.

small group   30 minutes

Learning Goals

Social Studies
• Child identifies the U.S. Flag and state flag.

Fine Arts
• Child expresses emotions or ideas through art.

Creativity Center

	Center Tip

☑ **Observe as children identify the United States flag.**

Materials paper; smocks; paintbrushes; red, white, and blue paint

Red, White, and Blue Review the colors and design of the United States flag and your state flag. Remind children the United States flag has stars and stripes. Invite children to make decorative paintings in red, white, and blue. Have children include stars and stripes if they wish.

Center Tip

If... children have difficulty making stars, **then...** provide star-shaped sponges for star printing.

Writing

Tell children they can write a letter to their family about the book *Yellowbelly and Plum Go to School*. Use the following form:

Dear _____ ,

We have been reading the book *Yellowbelly and Plum Go to School.* It is about _____ .

My favorite part is when _____ .

Love _____ ,

Allow random drawing and scribbling along with experimental letter formation.

Purposeful Play

☑ **Observe children following classroom rules and routines.**

Children choose an open center for free playtime. Encourage children to follow classroom routines by putting away their supplies at clean-up time and getting ready to finish the school day.

Let's Say Good-Bye

large group   15 minutes

 Read Aloud Revisit "Little Annie Oakley"/"La pequeña Annie Oakley" for your afternoon Read Aloud. Encourage children to listen for the /m/ sound.

Home Connection Refer to the Home Connections activities listed in the Resources and Materials chart on page 59. Remind children to tell parents about the flags they made today. Sing the "Good-Bye Song" as children prepare to leave.

Let's Start the Day

Focus Question
What happens in our classroom?
¿Qué sucede en nuestro salón de clases?

 Learning Goals

Social and Emotional Development
• Child is aware of self in terms of abilities, characteristics and preferences, and respects personal boundaries.

Science
• Child identifies organisms and describes their characteristics.

Vocabulary

bird	pájaro	fox	zorro
helped	ayudó	sun	sol
tree	árbol	tummies	barriguitas

Differentiated Instruction

 Extra Support
Oral Language and Vocabulary
If...children have difficulty understanding the concept of a pretend story, **then...**explain it is a kind of make-believe story.

Enrichment
Phonological Awareness
Repeat the game using a different body part as the focus word.

Accommodations for 3's
Phonological Awareness
If...three-year-olds have difficulty listening for the focus word during the game, **then...**use the same word pattern for each instruction, changing only the command. For example, say: *Touch your toes. Touch your nose. Touch your tummies. Tóquense los pies. Tóquense la nariz. Tóquense la barriguita.*

 Opening Routines and Transition Tips

For **Opening Routines** and **Transition Tips** turn to pages 178–181 and visit **DLMExpressOnline.com** for more ideas.

Read **"Let's Pretend to Make Tortillas"/"Hagamos que estamos haciendo tortillas"** from the *Teacher's Treasure Book*, page 245, for your morning Read Aloud.

Language Time

 large group / 15 minutes

Social and Emotional Development Encourage children to gather in the group area and get ready to begin the day's routine.

Oral Language and Vocabulary

 Can children engage in conversation about pretend stories?

Pretend Stories Explain that sometimes books show things that really happened. Say: *Other times, books tell a made-up story. It's pretend; it never really happened. Otras veces, los libros cuentan historias inventadas: fantasías o cosas que nunca pasaron.*

● Ask children to talk about a pretend story they've told or heard.

● Tell children that later on you will read a pretend story about a kind of bird called a goldfinch. They will learn what happened when those birds helped a fox.

Phonological Awareness

Can children listen for and hear a specific word during a game?

Simon Says Invite children to play a modified game of Simon Says. Say: *I'm going to tell you what to do; I'm going to give you an instruction. Yo les diré que tienen que hacer. Voy a darles una instrucción.* Tell children to listen carefully to your words. Explain that they will do everything that you say to do, and everything that you do, with one exception. Say: *There is one time you should not do what I say or do what I do. Whenever I say the word* toes, *stand completely still. Sólo en un caso no tendrán que hacer lo que yo diga o haga. Cuando yo diga la palabra pies, ustedes se quedarán quietos.* Have the children stand up. Give instructions, such as: *Touch your head. Now touch your tummy. Now touch your toes. Wiggle your hands. Wiggle your toes. Tóquense la cabeza. Ahora tóquense la barriguita. Ahora tóquense los pies. Muevan sus manos. Muevan sus pies.*

ELL Review body parts before the game. Explain that *tummy* is another word for *stomach*, which is like the word *estómago* in Spanish. Have children touch their heads, arms, and tummies, and say: *This is my head; these are my arms; this is my tummy.*

Center Time

▶ **Center Rotation** Center Time includes teacher-guided activities and independent activities. Refer to the **Learning Centers** on pages 62–63 for independent activity ideas.

Pretend and Learn Center

Center Tip

☑ Observe children creating pretend stories.

☑ Look for examples of children initiating interactions with others as they work.

Materials flannel boards; pictures of foxes, birds, and other animals; the sun, moon, and trees glued to tagboard pieces with sandpaper glued to the back

Make-Believe Fox and Bird Tales Have children work in pairs to create make-believe stories using the tagboard animals and props.

● Have children dramatize their stories with the tagboard pieces, displaying them on the felt board.

Center Tip

If...children need more characters or props for their stories, **then...**provide blank tagboard pieces (with sandpaper attached to the back), along with crayons. Have children draw and create the extra pieces they need.

Creativity Center

Center Tip

☑ Observe children listening for and identifying individual color words as they work.

Materials construction paper, tissue-paper scraps, yarn scraps, paste, crayons, paint, sponges, smocks

Color Collages Have children choose one color with which to make a color collage. Explain that they can use any material for their collage, but each material they choose must be in the target color.

● Encourage children to listen for color words as they work, and to repeat any color word they hear another child say.

● Say: *If you hear someone say* yellow, *then say* yellow. *If you hear someone say* red, *say* red. *Si oyen a alguien decir* yellow, *entonces digan* yellow. *Si alguien dice* red, *ustedes dirán* red.

Center Tip

If...children have difficulty listening for words as they work, **then...**ask them to listen for a specific color word as you comment on their collages.

✓ Learning Goals

Social and Emotional Development
• Child initiates interactions with others in work and play situations.

Language and Communication
• Child uses newly learned vocabulary daily in multiple contexts.

Fine Arts
• Child participates in a variety of music activities (such as listening, singing, finger plays, musical games, performances).

• Child expresses ideas, emotions, and moods through individual and collaborative dramatic play.

Differentiated Instruction

👋 **Extra Support**
Creativity Center
If...children have difficulty listening for color words, **then...**ask everyone to listen for one color word as you discuss all the pictures with them.

⭐ **Enrichment**
Creativity Center
Invite children to take turns choosing a color word for the other children to listen for during discussion of all the collages.

Accommodations for 3's
Pretend and Learn Center
If...three-year-olds have difficulty making up a story, **then...**ask questions to help them make story choices, such as: *Will your story be about foxes or birds? Are the foxes mean or friendly?* *¿Tu cuento será sobre zorros o pájaros? ¿Los zorros son malos o amigables?*

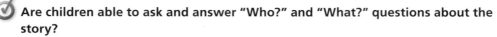

Focus Question
What happens in our classroom?
¿Qué sucede en nuestro salón de clases?

Learning Goals

Emergent Literacy: Reading
• Child names most upper- and lowercase letters of the alphabet.
• Child identifies the letter that stands for a given sound.
• Child produces the most common sound for a given letter.
• Child asks and answers questions about books read aloud (such as "Who?" "What?" "Where?").

Vocabulary

beak	pico	bird	pájaro
fox	zorro	helped	ayudó
sun	sol	tree	árbol

Differentiated Instruction

 Extra Support

Read Aloud
If...children have difficulty naming who helped whom, **then...**ask two questions: *Did the birds help the fox? Did the fox help the birds? ¿Ayudan los pájaros al zorro? ¿Y el zorro ayuda a los pájaros?*

 Enrichment

Read Aloud
Challenge children to tell where they think the story took place.

Accommodations for 3's

Learn About Letters and Sounds
If...three-year-olds have difficulty making the /d/ sound, **then...**guide them to place their tongue on the roof of the mouth before they make the sound.

Literacy Time

large group   15 minutes

📖 Read Aloud

 Are children able to ask and answer "Who?" and "What?" questions about the story?

Build Background Explain that you will be reading a story about a friendship between a fox and some goldfinches. Hold up a picture of a goldfinch and ask what it is. After children respond *a bird,* ask what color it is. Say: **This yellow bird is called a goldfinch.** *Este pájaro amarillo se llama jilguero.* Ask children what they know about foxes and birds.

● Ask: **Are birds and foxes usually friends?** *¿Los zorros y los pájaros siempre se llevan bien?*

Listen for Enjoyment Read the title of "Why Goldfinches Are Yellow Like the Sun" from the *Teacher's Treasure Book*, page 310. Tell children this is a make-believe story that tells what happened when animals helped each other.

● Ask: **What could a fox do to help a bird or a bird do to help a fox?** *¿El zorro ayuda al pájaro o el pájaro ayuda al zorro?*

● Read the story, using the flannel board characters to act out events.

Respond to the Story Discuss what happened in the story. Encourage children to recall who did what. Ask: **Did anyone ask for help?** *¿Alguien pide ayuda en el cuento?*

TIP Reinforce children's willingness to talk about what they know by discussing unusual animal friendships they've heard about or seen.

ELL Use pictures to help point out the different animal body words used in the story, such as *bellies, tummies, wings, beaks, feathers,* and *tail.*

After reading the story, use the same words to describe animals pictured on *Alphabet Wall Cards,* the *ABC Big Book,* or other storybooks.

Learn About Letters and Sounds

 Can children identify the /d/ sound?

 Can children accept responsibility for their own behavior and regulate it?

Learn About The Alphabet Display the *ABC Big Book* and introduce the letter *Dd* and the /d/ sound. Have one of the Dog Puppets point to the picture of the dog and say: **The first sound you hear in the word** dog **is /d/.** Say **/d/, /d/.** *El primer sonido de la palabra* dog *es /d/.* Ask children to repeat the sound.

● Display pictures of a duck, a donkey, a mouse, and a moose, and ask children which of the dog's friends starts with /d/.

● Display the *Alphabet Wall Card* and demonstrate how to write uppercase *D.* Provide children with sandpaper with uppercase *D* written on it. Have them trace the letter with their fingers.

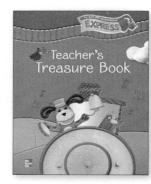

Teacher's Treasure Book, page 310

ABC Big Book

Math Time

Observe and Investigate

 Can children recognize and count patterns?

Count and Move in Patterns Invite children to count in patterns of 2. Have children count from 1 to 10 or another even number.

- Emphasize the even numbers by saying 1 quietly, 2 loudly, 3 quietly, 4 loudly, and so on.

- Add to the fun by having children march along as you say the numbers. Say: *1 step, 2 stomp!, 3 step, 4 stomp! 1 paso, 2 pisotón, 3 paso, 4 pisotón* and so on.

Make Groups Place classroom items in easy reach of all children, and have children use them to make groups of 3.

- As children work, say: *How do you know you made a group of 3? ¿Cómo saben que formaron un grupo de 3?*

- Repeat with larger numbers as long as children are successful.

  ELL Provide visual and auditory support by demonstrating with your fingers and slowly saying the number of objects to go in each group.

👥 Social and Emotional Development

Making Good Choices

 Do children show an understanding of classroom routines and rules?

Can children accept responsibility for their behavior and regulate it during a group discussion?

Everyone Helps Have the two Dog Puppets act out continuing to work on a project at clean-up time, including taking out more supplies instead of putting them away. After the teacher asks them to clean up and join the group several times, have the Dog Puppets leave all their supplies where they are and sneak into group time without putting anything away.

- Invite the children to comment on the dog's behavior.

- Ask: *What happens if someone doesn't clean up the place where they were working? ¿Qué sucede si alguien no limpia el lugar donde estaba trabajando?*

- Ask: *Why is it important for everyone to help at clean-up time? ¿Por qué es importante que todos ayudemos a limpiar?*

Differentiated Instruction

 Extra Support

Making Good Choices
If…children have difficulty commenting on the dog's failure to clean up, **then…**have the dogs prompt the discussion by asking questions, such as: *What difference does it make if we don't help? ¿Que sucede si no ayudamos?*

 Enrichment

Making Good Choices
Invite children to explain some of their ideas directly to the Dog Puppets to show they understand the value of cleaning up.

Special Needs

Behavioral Social/Emotional
Often, children with emotional issues think that they do not have to obey all the rules. Make a comparison, and ask the child to tell you about the school rules that apply to everyone. This is also a good opportunity to start helping the child understand that, when s/he does not follow the rules, there are consequences.

Focus Question
What happens in our classroom?
¿Qué sucede en nuestro salón de clases?

  Learning Goals

Mathematics
• Child identifies, duplicates, and creates simple patterns.

• Child understands that objects can be counted in any order.

• Child sorts objects and explains how the sorting was done.

Vocabulary

chairs	sillas	clocks	relojes
desks	escritorios	doors	puertas
toys	juguetes		

Differentiated Instruction

✋ Extra Support
Math Time
If...children struggle to find groups of two, **then...**ask them to find one item and see if they can find another like it in the classroom.

⭐ Enrichment
Math Time
Challenge children to find groups of three or four classroom objects.

Accommodations for 3's
Math Time
If...children are having difficulty finding groups of objects, **then...**pair them with children who are grouping items easily.

Math Time

large group · 20 minutes

 Can children find and group objects?

Find Groups Invite children to look around the classroom to find and count groups of objects and things.

● Ask children to find groups of 2 in the classroom, such as two doors, two clocks, and so on. Say: *Look around the classroom. Can you find groups of two?* *Busquen en todo el salón. ¿Pueden encontrar grupos de dos?*

● Help children understand that as long as each item is counted once and only once, objects can be counted in any order. Say: *If we count this one first, how many are there? If we count the other one first, how many are there?* *Si cuento primero éste y después el otro, ¿cuántos hay? Si cuento el otro primero y después éste, ¿cuántos hay?*

● Encourage children to walk around the classroom together. Say: *Take a friend with you to count groups of two!* *Busquen un amigo y cuenten grupos de dos.*

● Ask children to tell and show with fingers how many of a certain item are in the classroom.

Center Time

Center Rotation Center Time includes teacher-guided activities and independent activities. Refer to the **Learning Centers** on pages 62–63 for independent activity ideas.

Construction Center

☑ **Observe children grouping objects to make structures.**

Materials building blocks

Make Buildings Invite children to make buildings with groups of building blocks.

- Ask children how many blocks they used to make their building. Say: **Look at your building. How many blocks did you use to make your building?** *Miren su construcción. ¿Cuántos bloques usaron?*

- Have children tell the dimensions of their building by counting the number of blocks. Ask: **How many blocks high is your building? How many blocks wide is your building?** *¿Cuántos bloques mide de alto? ¿Cuántos bloques mide de ancho?*

Center Tip

If... children have trouble determining the dimensions of their building, **then...** count the height and length with them.

Purposeful Play

☑ **Observe the ways in which children demonstrate caring and empathy for one another.**

Children choose an open center for free playtime. Remind children to look around and think about all the activities they can work on in the classroom before choosing one activity for free playtime.

Let's Say Good-Bye

 Read Aloud Revisit the story, "Let's Pretend to Make Tortillas"/ "Hagamos que estamos haciendo tortillas" for your afternoon Read Aloud. Name a word for children to listen for as you talk about the story. Have them put their hands on their heads when they hear the word.

 Home Connection Refer to the Home Connections activities listed in the Resources and Materials chart on page 59. Remind children to tell their families about the story "Why Goldfinches Are Yellow Like the Sun." Sing the "Good-Bye Song" as children prepare to leave.

✔ Learning Goals

Social and Emotional Development
- Child shows empathy and care for others.

Emergent Literacy: Writing
- Child uses scribbles, shapes, pictures, symbols, and letters to represent language.
- Child writes own name or a reasonable approximation of it.

Mathematics
- Child measures the length and height of people or objects using standard or non-standard tools.

Writing

Recap the day, and review two stories children heard this week, *Yellowbelly and Plum Go to School*, and "Why Goldfinches Are Yellow Like the Sun." Ask: **Which story did you like best?** *¿Qué cuento les gustó más?* Provide a two-column graph and have children make a symbol or mark, write a letter, or write their name in the column under the book they liked best. If time permits, ask children why they selected that story. Display the completed graph.

Focus Question

What happens in our classroom?

¿Qué sucede en nuestro salón de clases?

✓ **Learning Goals**

Social and Emotional Development
• Child follows simple classroom rules and routines.
• Child accepts responsibility for and regulates own behavior.

Language and Communication
• Child uses newly learned vocabulary daily in multiple contexts.

Vocabulary

count	contar	day	día
paint	pintar	puzzles	rompecabezas
rug	alfombra	sing	cantar

Differentiated Instruction

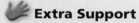 **Extra Support**

Oral Language and Vocabulary
If...children have difficulty identifying activities in the picture, **then...**point to an activity and guide them to describe what the pictured children are doing. Ask: *Do we also do that activity in our classroom? ¿Nosotros hacemos eso?*

 Enrichment

Phonological Awareness
Substitute a word that is not in the song for one that is, and have children listen for the new word without knowing where it will appear.

Let's Start the Day

▶ **Opening Routines and Transition Tips**
For **Opening Routines** and **Transition Tips** turn to pages 178–181 and visit **DLMExpressOnline.com** for more ideas.

 Read **"I Like School"/**"Me gusta la escuela" from the *Teacher's Treasure Book*, page 274, for your morning Read Aloud.

Language Time

👧👦👧 **Social and Emotional Development** Encourage children to accept responsibility for their own behavior and regulate it during a discussion.

Oral Language and Vocabulary

✓ **Can children use newly acquired vocabulary to name objects and activities?**

Words in Our Class Display the *Rhymes and Chants Flip Chart*, page 6. Invite children to point out pictures of objects and activities that they can identify. Ask children to point out similar objects in the classroom and tell how they use them. Have children describe times in the classroom that they do some of the same activities that are pictured. Encourage children to comment on one another's ideas. Then, sing the song "Fun at School" together.

Phonological Awareness

✓ **Can children listen for and hear a separate word in a whispered chant?**

Sing and Listen Display the *Rhymes and Chants Flip Chart*, page 6, and review the song words. Compliment children on what excellent listeners they are becoming, and how well they can listen for and hear words in a song. Ask children whether they think they could listen for a word if everyone whispered the song words instead of singing them. Choose a word to listen for. Ask children to whisper the words of the song along with you, but to shout the target word when they hear it.

ELL Use the *Rhymes and Chants Flip Chart* as a starting point to discuss some of the topics it touches on, such as the days of the week, number words, and names of children in the class.

 large group — 15 minutes

Rhymes and Chants Flip Chart, page 6

Center Time

▶ **Center Rotation** Center Time includes teacher-guided activities and independent activities. Refer to the **Learning Centers** on pages 62–63 for independent activity ideas.

 small group 60–90 minutes

Library and Listening Center | Center Tip

✓ Observe as children listen for and hear individual words in a song.

Materials *Rhymes and Chants Flip Chart*, page 6, "Fun at School;" *Rhymes and Chants CD*

Listen for Fun Have children listen to "Fun at School" and sing along as they listen for the word *fun*. Have them stand up and sit down each time they hear the word *fun*. Explain that after they listen to the song once, they can take turns choosing a new word to listen for.

- Say: **When it is your turn to pick the word, point to a picture of the word, say the word, and tell the children what they should do when they hear the word.** *Cuando sea su turno para elegir una palabra, digan la palabra y expliquen a sus compañeros lo que deben hacer cuando la escuchen.*

Center Tip

If...children have difficulty identifying words from the picture, **then...** review the words illustrated on the flip chart and point out each word pictured.

Creativity Center | Center Tip

✓ Encourage children to use newly learned vocabulary to describe their activities.

Materials paper, small plastic containers filled with liquid starch, paintbrushes, colored chalk

School Is Fun Have children use chalk and liquid starch to draw pictures of themselves doing something fun at school.

- Model painting the paper with starch and then drawing on the wet starch with colored chalk. Encourage discussion as they work.

Center Tip

If...children are unsure about what to draw, **then...**have them review the activities they did last week and ask what they enjoyed most.

 Learning Goals

Language and Communication
- Child uses newly learned vocabulary daily in multiple contexts.

Fine Arts
- Child expresses emotions or ideas through art.
- Child participates in a variety of music activities (such as listening, singing, finger plays, musical games, performances).

Differentiated Instruction

Extra Support
Creativity Center
If...children have difficulty covering their entire paper with starch, **then...**model how to start at the top and paint in stripes from top to bottom to cover the whole sheet.

Enrichment
Creativity Center
Challenge children to describe their completed pictures and explain why they enjoy the activity they have illustrated.

Accommodations for 3's
Creativity Center
If... children have difficulty drawing with large pieces of colored chalk, **then...** break the chalk into smaller pieces to make it more manageable.

Focus Question
What happens in our classroom?
¿Qué sucede en nuestro salón de clases?

Learning Goals

Emergent Literacy: Reading
• Child names most upper- and lowercase letters of the alphabet.
• Child identifies the letter that stands for a given sound.
• Child asks and answers questions about books read aloud (such as, "Who?" "What?" "Where?").

Vocabulary

bear	oso	busy	ocupado
drums	tambores	excellent	excelente
game	juego	music	música

Differentiated Instruction

Extra Support

Learn About Letters and Sounds
If...children are having difficulty identifying and matching the letters, **then...**focus on only one or two letters at a time instead of reviewing four at once.

Enrichment

Learn About Letters and Sounds
Challenge children to find the page in the *ABC Big Book* that displays each letter reviewed.

Special Needs

Vision Loss
Continue to introduce each new letter. Remember to give the child time to explore the letter and to touch either a magnetic letter or a cutout of the letter.

Literacy Time

 large group 15 minutes

Read Aloud

✓ **Can children ask and answer questions about the book?**

Build Background Invite children to talk about all the things they have learned since starting school, as well as new friends they have made.

Listen for Understanding Display *Yellowbelly and Plum Go to School*. Read the title, reminding children you will be reading a story about starting school. Ask if they remember who is going to school for the first time in the story.

● Ask: ***Do you remember who was an excellent student?*** *¿Recuerdan quién era un excelente estudiante?* ***Do you remember what happened in the story?*** *¿Recuerdan qué sucedía en el cuento?*

● Ask: ***Do you remember how Yellowbelly changed from the beginning to the end of the story?*** *¿Recuerdan cómo cambió Barrigota entre el principio y el final del cuento?*

Respond to the Story Discuss the story. Ask children what they think Yellowbelly said to his mother before he went to school in the morning. Ask what he might have told his family when he came home from his first day of school.

ELL Point out the similarity between the English and Spanish words *excellent/excelente* and explain that some words have the same meaning in different languages. Remind children that *excellent* means "very, very good." Ask them to remember who was excellent in the story and have them explain why or how they think he was excellent. Encourage them to name a time they have been excellent in school and explain why.

Learn About Letters and Sounds

✓ **Can children identify the letters *Aa, Ss, Mm*, and *Dd*?**

Learn About The Alphabet Write the upper case and lower case letters *Aa, Ss, Mm*, and *Dd* on chart paper or interactive whiteboard. Ask children to name the letters they know. Review each letter name and have children repeat it after you. Ask children to point out and name any of the focus letters they have in their own names.

● Have children point out each of the focus letters on the *Alphabet Wall Cards*. Review the sounds for each letter. Then display the Alphabet/Letter Tiles for uppercase and lowercase *Aa, Ss, Mm*, and *Dd*.

● Say: ***The first sound you hear in the word*** mouse ***is /m/. The letter*** M ***makes the /m/ sound. Can you find the upper case*** M ***and match it to the wall card?*** *El primer sonido de la palabra* mouse *es /m/. La letra* M *tiene el sonido /m/. Busquen la letra* M *mayúscula en el mural de la clase.* Repeat for each letter.

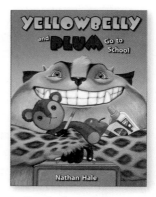

Yellowbelly and Plum Go to School
Barrigota y Pipón van a la escuela

Alphabet Wall Cards

Online Math Activity

Children can complete Kitchen Counter during computer time or Center Time.

Math Time

Observe and Investigate

 Can children make groups?

Find and Make Groups This lesson repeats the activity introduced on Day 3. Gather items from around the classroom for children to use while making and counting groups.

- Place six different groups of classroom items on paper plates, beginning with groups of one to three items.

- Say: *What is a group of two?* *¿Cuál es el grupo de dos?* Have children work in pairs to find the group of two. Partners help and check each other while you observe and assist as needed. Vary the amount pairs are to find based on their ability.

- Now model making a group of two. Say: *Watch me make a group of two. Can you make a group of two?* *Observen cómo formo un grupo de dos. ¿Pueden formar un grupo de dos?* Have children make a group of two. Make sure they use two of the same object.

- Expand the activity to include other numbers if children are able.

ELL Provide visual and auditory support by demonstrating with your fingers and saying slowly what number of objects should go in each group.

✺ Social and Emotional Development

Making Good Choices

 Do children demonstrate caring and empathy for others by listening to one another's comments and ideas?

 Do children initiate interactions with each other during group discussions?

The Importance of Clean-Up Display the *Making Good Choices Flip Chart*, page 6, and invite children to help review what they've learned during the week about cleaning up.

- Ask: *Who is helping to clean up in the picture?* *¿Quién está ayudando a limpiar en la ilustración?*

- Ask: *Who helps clean up in our room?* *¿Quiénes ayudan a limpiar en nuestro salón de clases?*

- Invite children to share examples of ways they have helped to keep the room clean during the week.

Making Good Choices Flip Chart, page 6

 Learning Goals

Social and Emotional Development
- Child shows empathy and care for others.

Mathematics
- Child counts 1–10 concrete objects correctly.
- Child understands that objects can be counted in any order.

Vocabulary

groups   grupos

Differentiated Instruction

✋ **Extra Support**

Observe and Investigate

If...children have trouble making groups of two or more, **then...** reduce the number of objects to choose from.

⭐ **Enrichment**

Making Good Choices

Challenge children to name other children in the room who did a good job cleaning up.

Accommodations for 3's

Observe and Investigate

If...three-year-olds are having trouble making groups, **then...**give them a sheet of paper with two circles on it. Ask them to put an object in each circle.

Focus Question
What happens in our classroom?
¿Qué sucede en nuestro salón de clases?

Learning Goals

Social and Emotional Development
• Child accepts responsibility for and regulates own behavior.

Language and Communication
• Child uses newly learned vocabulary daily in multiple contexts.

Fine Arts
• Child expresses thoughts, feelings, and energy through music and creative movement.

Vocabulary

gallop	galopar	hop	brincar
jump	saltar	march	marchar
slide	deslizarse	tiptoe	puntillas

Differentiated Instruction

Extra Support

Explore and Express
If...children have difficulty understanding different ways they can move, **then...** demonstrate several kinds of movement, asking them to repeat after you.

Enrichment

Explore and Express
Encourage children to experiment with different ways to move their arms and hands.

Accommodations for 3's

Explore and Express
If...three-year-olds have difficulty exploring different movement styles, **then...**make suggestions for children to try as the music is playing.

Music and Movement Time

large group   20 minutes

Personal Safety Skills Before beginning to explore movement styles, remind children to pick a space that is not too close to anyone else so they have enough room to move without bumping into anyone.

Oral Language and Academic Vocabulary

✓ **Can children use a variety or words to describe different ways of moving?**

All Kinds of Moves Have children move their feet and legs in different ways, such as galloping, hopping, running, tiptoeing, sliding, marching, and jumping. Label each movement.

● Encourage children to try out some of the different movement ideas discussed.

● Ask: *Can you think of any ways to move just your hands? ¿Se les ocurre alguna manera de mover sólo los pies?*

● Ask: *Can you show us how? ¿Pueden mostrarnos cómo lo hacen?*

Explore and Express

✓ **Do children enjoy participating in music and movement activities?**

✓ **Can children accept responsibility for their behavior during a group movement activity and regulate it?**

✓ **Are children able to use newly learned vocabulary to describe music movement?**

Move to the Music Play two to three minutes of a variety of music selections. Include different styles and tempos, such as waltz, polka, rap, Latin American, Asian, country and western, and so on. Identify each type of music. Encourage children to move to the music during each selection. Alternate between selections with fast and slow tempos.

● Have children comment on each of the selections by describing the movements they made to accompany the music and the way the music made them feel.

● Pause after several selections to rest and review. Ask: *Which music did you like best? Why? ¿Qué música les gustó más? ¿Por qué?*

ELL Help children understand the names for each kind of movement by demonstrating each one as you say the name.

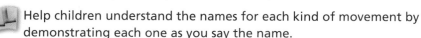

Center Time

▶ **Center Rotation** Center Time includes teacher-guided activities and independent activities. Refer to the **Learning Centers** on pages 62–63 for independent activity ideas.

 small group · 30 minutes

Learning Goals

Emergent Literacy: Writing
• Child experiments with and uses some writing conventions when writing or dictating.

Fine Arts
• Child participates in a variety of music activities (such as listening, singing, finger plays, musical games, performances).
• Child expresses thoughts, feelings, and energy through music and creative movement.

Pretend and Learn Center

✓ **Encourage children to explore moving in place to music.**

Materials CD or tape of quiet instrumental music, masking tape

Moving in Place Tell children that earlier they explored moving around to music. Now, they will explore moving in place. Invite children to try moving their bodies while sitting, standing, and crouching.

• Provide each child with masking tape and guide them to find a spot on the floor where they can move without touching another child. Help children tape an *X* on their spot.

• Have children stand on their taped spots. Say: *Can you find a way to move to the music while you stay on your spot? ¿Pueden moverse al ritmo de la música mientras en su lugar?*

Center Tip

If...children have difficulty thinking of ways to move in place, **then...**ask: *What parts of your body can you move when your feet stay in one place? ¿Qué partes del cuerpo pueden mover cuando sus pies están quietos en su lugar?*

 Writing

Review the day and ask children to report on the most important or newsworthy events that took place. Make a class newspaper by recording the date, weather, and two or three of the events that children mention. Read the date, weather, and children's dictated sentences back to them, tracking the words from left to right as you read. Point out any vocabulary words or children's names that are part of the news report. Post the newspaper in the classroom.

Purposeful Play

✓ **Observe children as they put away materials in one area before moving on to another.**

Children choose an open center for free playtime. Encourage children to think of all the things they did in the classroom this week and make a list or draw a picture of some of them.

Let's Say Good-Bye

 large group · 15 minutes

 Read Aloud Revisit **"I Like School"**/*"Me gusta la escuela"* for your afternoon Read Aloud. Have students demonstrate different ways they moved in school today.

 Home Connection Refer to the Home Connections activities listed in the Resources and Materials chart on page 59. Have children show their families different ways they can move to music. Sing the "Good-Bye Song" as children prepare to leave.

Week 3

Focus Question

What makes a good friend?
¿Cómo es un buen amigo?

This week children will make a friendship collage, sing a song about a baker, and count pizza toppings. They will also learn more about making friends and how friends talk to each other.

Social and Emotional Development

Social and Emotional Development	1	2	3	4	5
Child shows eagerness, curiosity, and confidence while learning new concepts and trying new things.	✓				✓
Child demonstrates positive social behaviors, as modeled by the teacher.			✓		✓
Child shows empathy and care for others.	✓	✓	✓	✓	✓
Child learns how to make and keep friends.	✓	✓			✓
Child understands and respects the different ideas, feelings, perspectives, and behaviors of others.			✓	✓	

Language and Communication

Language and Communication	1	2	3	4	5
Child demonstrates an understanding of oral language by responding appropriately.	✓			✓	✓
Child begins and ends conversations appropriately		✓	✓	✓	
Child follows basic rules for conversations (taking turns, staying on topic, listening actively).				✓	✓
Child uses appropriate nonverbal skills during conversations (making eye contact; using facial expressions).		✓			
Child names and describes actual or pictured people, places, things, actions, attributes, and events.	✓		✓		✓
Child uses newly learned vocabulary daily in multiple contexts.	✓	✓		✓	✓
Child builds English listening and speaking vocabulary for common objects and phrases. (ELL)	✓			✓	
Child speaks in complete sentences of four or more words including a subject, verb, and object.			✓	✓	

Emergent Literacy: Reading

Emergent Literacy: Reading	1	2	3	4	5
Child independently engages in pre-reading behaviors and activities (such as, pretending to read, turning one page at a time)					✓
Child listens for words (for example, hears and separates individual words within a four-word sentence).	✓	✓	✓	✓	✓
Child names most upper- and lowercase letters of the alphabet.	✓	✓	✓	✓	✓
Child identifies the letter that stands for a given sound.		✓	✓	✓	✓
Child produces the most common sound for a given letter.		✓		✓	
Child retells or reenacts poems and stories in sequence.	✓	✓	✓		✓
Child asks and answers questions about books read aloud (such as, "Who?" "What?" "Where?").				✓	✓

Emergent Literacy: Writing

Emergent Literacy: Writing	1	2	3	4	5
Child participates in free drawing and writing activities to deliver information.		✓		✓	
Child uses scribbles, shapes, pictures, symbols, and letters to represent language.	✓				✓
Child writes some letters or reasonable approximations of letters upon request.					✓
Child experiments with and uses some writing conventions when writing or dictating.	✓	✓	✓	✓	

Mathematics

Mathematics	1	2	3	4	5
Child counts 1–10 concrete objects correctly.	✓	✓		✓	
Child demonstrates that, when counting, the last number indicates how many objects were counted.			✓	✓	✓
Child understands that objects can be counted in any order.		✓			
Child tells how many are in a group of up to 5 objects without counting.		✓			
Child sorts objects and explains how the sorting was done.	✓		✓		
Child identifies, duplicates, and creates simple patterns.					✓

Science

Science	1	2	3	4	5
Child uses senses to observe, classify, investigate, and collect data.	✓	✓			
Child identifies organisms and describes their characteristics.	✓				

Social Studies

Social Studies	1	2	3	4	5
Child identifies similarities and differences among people.			✓	✓	
Child identifies the U.S. Flag and state flag.			✓		
Child recites the Pledge of Allegiance.			✓		
Child respects/appreciates the differing interests, skills, abilities, cultures, languages, and family structures of people.			✓	✓	

Physical Development

Physical Development	1	2	3	4	5
Child develops small-muscle strength and control.	✓	✓			

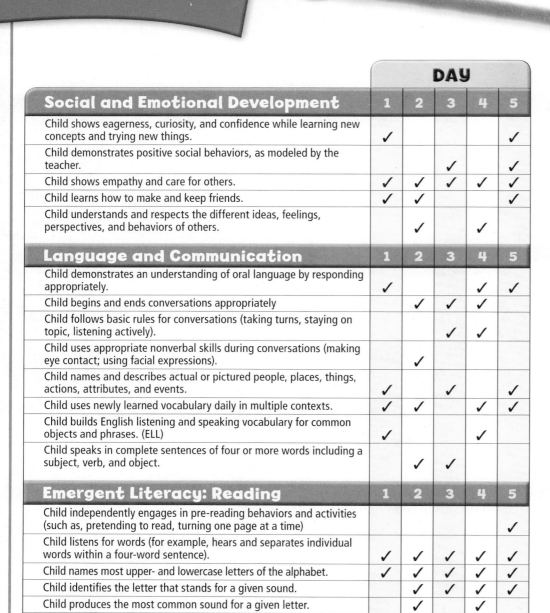

Materials and Resources

DAY 1	DAY 2	DAY 3	DAY 4	DAY 5

Program Materials

• Teacher's Treasure Book • Oral Language Development Cards 5, 9, 10 • Rhymes and Chants Flip Chart • Sequence Cards: "Building Blocks" • Connecting Cubes • *Max and Mo's First Day at School* Big Book • ABC Picture Cards • Online Building Blocks Math Activities • Making Good Choices Flip Chart • Math and Science Flip Chart • Home Connections Resource Guide	• Teacher's Treasure Book • *Max and Mo's First Day at School* Big Book • Dog Puppets • ABC Picture Cards • Making Good Choices Flip Chart • Math and Science Flip Chart • Two-Color Counters • Online Building Blocks Math Activities • Home Connections Resource Guide	• Rhymes and Chants Flip Chart • Teacher's Treasure Book • Oral Language Development Card 6 • ABC Picture Cards • Concept Big Book 1 • Alphabet/Letter Tiles • Two-Color Counters • Making Good Choices Flip Chart • Oral Language Development Card 2 • Pattern Blocks • Jumbo Hand Lenses • Home Connections Resource Guide	• Teacher's Treasure Book • Two-Color Counters • Alphabet Wall Cards • ABC Picture Cards • Dog Puppets • Making Good Choices Flip Chart • Magnetic Wands • Online Building Blocks Math Activities • Vehicle Counters • Home Connections Resource Guide	• Teacher's Treasure Book • Rhymes and Chants Flip Chart • ABC Picture Cards • *Max and Mo's First Day at School* Big Book • ABC Big Book • Two-Color Counters • Making Good Choices Flip Chart • Dog Puppets • Home Connections Resource Guide

Other Materials

• drawing paper, crayons • building blocks • pictures of a baker, muffins, bread, other baked goods • markers • yellow and orange strips of paper	• index cards • 9"× 12" construction paper • collage materials (such as paper scraps, ribbon, feathers, toothpicks, and so on) • glue, paste • writing paper, markers, crayons • paper plates • clear containers	• picture cards for friend, laugh, school • books about friends • magazines, scissors, glue or paste • plastic containers • U.S. and state flags • books of holidays and celebrations • pad of washable ink; wet wipes • 4-inch squares of drawing paper	• hand mirror • 6" paper circles (flesh tones) • crayons • yarn (brown, yellow, red, black) • scissors, glue or paste • boxes (many sizes) • blocks • pillows • dress-up clothes • clear containers	• books about friends • sticky notes • sand tray • paper folded in 4 sections • crayons • toy telephones

Home Connection

Invite children to discuss with their families the differences between plants in their house or yard. Send home the Weekly Family Letter, Home Connections Resource Guide, pp. 17–18; ABC Take-Home Books for *Oo* and *Uu*, (English) pp. 21, 27, or (Spanish) pp. 52, 58.	Tell children to practice counting at home with their families.	Encourage children to discuss with their families what is the same and different about them.	Encourage children to tell their families what they learned about making new friends. Send home Storybook 4, Home Connections Resource Guide, pp. 85–88.	Remind children to show their families how they introduce themselves to new friends.

Assessment

As you observe children throughout the week, you may fill out an Anecdotal Observational Record Form to document an individual's progress toward a goal or signs indicating the need for developmental or medical evaluation. You may also choose to select work for each child's portfolio. The Anecdotal Observational Record Form and Weekly Assessment rubrics are available In the assessment section of DLMExpressOnline.com.

More Literature Suggestions

• **Being Friends** by Karen Beaumont
• **My Friend and I** by Lisa Jahn-Clough
• **Bear Snores On** by Karma Wilson
• **Friends Forever: The Adventures of Melrose and Croc** by Emma Chichester Clark
• **¿Qué te gusta?** por Michael Grejniec
• **Maisy y sus amigos** por Lucy Cousins
• **Y el oso ronca sin parar** por Karma Wilson

Week 3

Daily Planner

		DAY 1	**DAY 2**
Let's Start the Day Language Time	large group	**Opening Routines** p. 102 **Morning Read Aloud** p. 102 **Oral Language and Vocabulary** p. 102 Helping a Friend **Phonological Awareness** p. 102 Concept of Word	**Opening Routines** p. 108 **Morning Read Aloud** p. 108 **Oral Language and Vocabulary** p. 108 Retelling Story Events **Phonological Awareness** p. 108 Concept of Word
Center Time	small group	**Focus On:** **Writer's Center** p. 103 **Construction Center** p. 103	**Focus On:** **Creativity Center** p. 109 **Writer's Center** p. 109
Circle Time Literacy Time	large group	**Read Aloud** *Max and Mo's First Day at School/Max y Mo van a la escuela* p. 104 **Learn About Letters and Sounds: Learn About the Letters** *Aa* and *Ss* p. 104	**Read Aloud** *Max and Mo's First Day at School/Max y Mo van a la escuela* p. 110 **Learn About Letters and Sounds: Learn About the Letters** *Aa* and *Ss* p. 110
Math Time	large group	Our Friend the Baker p. 105	Making Matches p. 111
Social and Emotional Development	large group	Making Friends p. 105	Making New Friends p. 111
Content Connection	large group	**Science:** **Oral Language and Academic Vocabulary** p. 106 **Observe and Investigate** p. 106	**Math:** Compare Number Pizzas p. 112
Center Time	small group	**Focus On:** **Math and Science Center** p. 107 **Purposeful Play** p. 107	**Focus On:** **Math and Science Center** p. 113 **Purposeful Play** p. 113
Let's Say Good-Bye	large group	Read Aloud p. 107 Writing p. 107 Home Connection p. 107	Read Aloud p. 113 Writing p. 113 Home Connection p. 113

DAY 3

Opening Routines p. 114
Morning Read Aloud p. 114
Oral Language and Vocabulary
p. 114 What Is a Friend?
Phonological Awareness
p. 114 Find a Word

Focus On:
Library and Listening Center p. 115
ABC Center p. 115

Read Aloud *Welcome to School/Bienvenidos a la escuela* p. 116
Learn About Letters and Sounds: Matching Letters and Sounds p. 116

Fill and Spill p. 117

A Good Friend p. 117

Social Studies:
Oral Language and Academic Vocabulary
p. 118
Understand and Participate
p. 118 Holidays and Celebrations

Focus On:
Pretend and Learn Center p. 119
Purposeful Play p. 119

Read Aloud p. 119
Writing p. 119
Home Connection p. 119

DAY 4

Opening Routines p. 120
Morning Read Aloud p. 120
Oral Language and Vocabulary
p. 120 Real or Make-Believe
Phonological Awareness
p. 120 Listen and Count

Focus On:
Creativity Center p. 121
Pretend and Learn Center p. 121

Read Aloud "The Lion and the Mouse"/"El león y el ratón agradecido" p. 122
Learn About Letters and Sounds: Alphabet Match p. 122

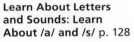

Count and Move in Patterns p. 123
Number Me p. 123

Making a Friend p. 123

Building **B**locks

Math:
Demonstrate Counting p. 124

Focus On:
Math and Science Center p. 125
Purposeful Play p. 125

Read Aloud p. 125
Writing p. 125
Home Connection p. 125

DAY 5

Opening Routines p. 126
Morning Read Aloud p. 126
Oral Language and Vocabulary
p. 126 Friends at School
Phonological Awareness
p. 126 Be the Word

Focus On:
Library and Listening Center p. 127
ABC Center p. 127

Read Aloud *Max and Mo's First Day at School/Max y Mo van a la escuela* p. 128
Learn About Letters and Sounds: Learn About /a/ and /s/ p. 128

Demonstrate Counting p. 129

Making Friends p. 129

Dramatic Play Time:
Oral Language and Vocabulary
p. 130 Making Friends
Explore and Express
p. 130 Making New Friends

Focus On:
Pretend and Play Center p. 131
Purposeful Play p. 131

Read Aloud p. 131
Writing p. 131
Home Connection p. 131

Learning Centers

Math and Science Center

Same and Different
Children work with a friend to find things that are the same or different, p. 107.

Find the Number
Children count pizza toppings, p. 113.

Say the Number
Children count vehicle counters and indicate the last number counted, p. 125.

What's the Same?
Children observe objects from nature. Partners choose objects that are the same in some way and tell how they are alike.

Match How Many
Children match Dot Cards with pasta shapes. Partners choose a Dot Card and work together to paste the given number of pasta pieces on another card.

Triangles and Squares
Children work in pairs. One child counts out and lines up square pattern blocks. A partner counts and matches the amount using triangles.

ABC Center

The Sound of *S*
Children find pictures of objects that begin with the /s/ sound, p. 115.

Make a Letter
Children practice writing *Aa* and *Ss*, p. 127.

Max and Mo's *Aa* and *Ss*
Partners find the letters *Aa* and *Ss* in the book *Max and Mo's First Day at School/Max y Mo van a la escuela*. One partner points to an *Aa* or *Ss* and stops to ask a question about the picture on the page.

I Spy *Aa* and *Ss*
Children use a hand lens to find the letters *Aa* or *Ss* in the classroom. One child gives a clue, such as, *I spy an Aa in the teacher's name card*. A partner uses the lens to "find" the letter.

Alphabet Match
Children match magnetic letters with ABC Picture cards. Focus on upper case and lower case *Aa* and *Ss*.

Creativity Center

Friendship Collage
Children make a collage about friendship, p. 109.

Alike and Different
Children create self-portraits, p. 121.

Circle of Friends
Children sit in a circle. One child rolls a beach ball to another and says, *My name is [name] and [classmate's name] is my friend.* Continue until all children have had a turn.

Same in Nature
Children gather items from nature, such as acorns, leaves, and so on, while on a class nature walk. Use these items and art supplies to create nature collages, grouping things that are the same.

Friendship Card
Children draw a picture of a friend on the front of an index card. Then they draw a picture of themselves doing something with the friend on the back. Hang friendship cards around the classroom.

Library and Listening Center

What Friends Do
Pairs talk about a picture of friends helping each other, p. 115.

Browsing Books
Children look through books for pictures of friends, p. 127.

Listen and Feel
Children browse through instrument books and explore the sound and feel of rhythm instruments.

Children Are the Same; Children Are Different
Children browse books that have images of children of various ethnicities. Partners discuss characteristics that are the same or different in the children.

Listen to Big Book
Children listen in pairs to *Max and Mo's First Day at School*/*Max y Mo van a la escuela* and point out things the friends do together.

Construction Center

Taking Turns Tower
Children build a tower together out of blocks, p. 103.

Build with a Friend
Show friendly behaviors when building a bridge with a partner.

Two Castles
Partners build side-by-side castles using blocks, boxes, and other items in the construction area. They talk about things that are the same or different in their finished castles.

Friend Hut
Small groups show positive behaviors as they work together to build a Friend Hut in the construction area. Have them build a structure that they would like to play in with their friends.

Writer's Center

Helping Others
Children draw a picture of themselves helping a friend, p. 103.

Animal Friends
Children write a note, p. 109.

My Friends
Children draw a picture of two or three friends playing together. They dictate or write two things that are the same about the friends. Encourage them to write any letters they know.

A Pile of Pictures
Children choose two pictures from a pile of image cards. They describe something similar about the two pictures. Help them write how they are the same.

Tell About It
Children listen to a Read Aloud story they have heard. Have them retell an event and draw a picture of it. Then have them retell it again as you help them label the drawing.

Pretend and Learn Center

Fingerprint Detectives
Children look at their fingerprints with a hand lens, p. 119.

Let's Pretend
Children role-play being a different person, p. 121.

Call a Friend
Children pretend to call a friend on the phone, p. 131.

A Good Friend
Children use stuffed animals to act out something they do that makes them a good friend.

Help a Friend
Children act out how to help a friend who is having difficulty waiting for a turn on the swings.

Retell It
Children choose a page or event from *Max and Mo's First Day at School*/*Max y Mo van a la escuela* and retell what happened. They act out the event with friends.

Focus Question
What makes a good friend?
¿Cómo es un buen amigo?

Opening Routines and Transition Tips
For **Opening Routines** and **Transition Tips** turn to pages 178–181 and visit DLMExpressOnline.com for more ideas.

Read **"Make New Friends"/"Amigos"** from the *Teacher's Treasure Book*, page 74, for your morning Read Aloud.

✓ Learning Goals

Social and Emotional Development
• Child shows eagerness, curiosity, and confidence while learning new concepts and trying new things.
• Child shows empathy and care for others.

Language and Communication
• Child names and describes actual or pictured people, places, things, actions, attributes, and events.
• Child builds English listening and speaking vocabulary for common objects and phrases. (ELL)

Emergent Literacy: Reading
• Child listens for words (for example, hears and separates individual words within a four-word sentence).

Vocabulary

friend	amigo	help	ayuda
learn	aprender	shoe	zapato
tie	amarrar	together	juntos

Differentiated Instruction

 Extra Support
Oral Language and Vocabulary
If...children have difficulty naming the setting of the picture, **then...**provide clues by pointing to a detail about the setting and asking: *What is this? Where would you see it? ¿Qué es esto? ¿Dónde podrían verlo?*

Enrichment
Phonological Awareness
Challenge children to separate words in a full line of the song.

Let's Start the Day

Language Time

large group   15 minutes

👥 **Social and Emotional Development** Acknowledge and encourage children when you observe them helping and taking care of each other.

Oral Language and Vocabulary

✓ **Can children describe people, places, and actions in a picture?**

Helping a Friend Explain that a friend is someone whom you like and who likes you. Friends care about each other and help each other. Ask: *How do friends act? What are some ways friends help each other? ¿Cómo actúan los amigos? ¿Cómo se ayudan unos a otros?*

● Display *Oral Language Development Card 5*. Discuss the setting of the picture. Ask: *Where are these children? What are they doing? ¿Dónde están estos niños? ¿Qué están haciendo?* Then follow the suggestions on the back of the card.

Oral Language Development Card 5

Phonological Awareness

✓ **Can children isolate words within a four-word phrase?**

Concept of Word Display *Rhymes and Chants Flip Chart*, page 7. Remind children to listen to the words as you sing "Make a Friend!" Demonstrate separating phrases into words. Say: *Some fun at school,* clapping once for each word. Have children repeat, using other four-word phrases from the song.

ELL Use *Oral Language Development Cards 9* and *10* to review and extend children's vocabulary. For example, point to the children on card 10 and ask: *How are these children learning together? How might two friends or classmates help each other at school?*

Rhymes and Chants Flip Chart, page 7

Center Time

▶ **Center Rotation** Center Time includes teacher-guided activities and independent activities. Refer to the **Learning Centers** on pages 100–101 for independent activity ideas.

small group   60–90 minutes

Writer's Center | Center Tip

 Look for ways that children are helping each other and being a good friend.

Materials drawing paper, crayons

Helping Others Have children draw a picture to show something they have done recently to help a friend or classmate.

- Have children draw themselves helping a friend or classmate.

- Ask: *How did you help your friend? ¿Cómo ayudaron a su amigo?*

- Ask children to label the drawing by writing or dictating their name and their friend's name.

Center Tip

If...children have difficulty thinking of a situation to draw, **then**...encourage them to look around the room to recall classroom activities in which they may have helped a friend.

Construction Center | Center Tip

 Listen for positive interactions between children as they construct their towers.

Materials building blocks, Sequence Cards set "Building Blocks"

Taking Turns Tower Model working with one child to build a block tower. Explain that partners will work together to build their own block towers.

- Use the Sequence Cards set "Building Blocks" to illustrate a building sequence.

- Explain that children should take turns adding one block at a time to make a tower. Model the concept of "taking turns."

- Have children dismantle the tower in the same way.

Center Tip

If...children find it difficult to build a tower together without knocking the blocks over, **then**... have them work side-by-side to build individual towers.

✓ Learning Goal

Social and Emotional Development
- Child learns how to make and keep friends.

Emergent Literacy: Writing
- Child writes own name or a reasonable approximation of it.

Fine Arts
- Child expresses emotions or ideas through art.

Physical Development
- Child completes tasks that require eye-hand coordination and control.

Differentiated Instruction

👋 **Extra Support**
Writer's Center
If...children have difficulty writing their names, **then**...help them write just the first letter and allow them to use any other kind of marks to finish the name.

⭐ **Enrichment**
Writer's Center
Challenge children to dictate or scribble write to add a sentence that tells what they are doing with their friend.

Accommodations for 3's
Construction Center
If...children have difficulty manipulating blocks to make a tower, **then**...have them make towers from Connecting Cubes.

Focus Question
What makes a good friend?
¿Cómo es un buen amigo?

Learning Goals

Social and Emotional Development
• Child shows eagerness, curiosity, and confidence while learning new concepts and trying new things.

Language and Communication
• Child demonstrates an understanding of oral language by responding appropriately.

Emergent Literacy: Reading
• Child names most upper- and lowercase letters of the alphabet.
• Child retells or reenacts poems and stories in sequence.

Vocabulary

cage	jaula	friend	amigo
hamster	hámster	name tag	cartel
rolling	rodar	tilt	inclinarse

Differentiated Instruction

 Extra Support
Read Aloud
If...children have difficulty remembering what character they are acting out, **then...**have them hold up an image of the character from the book. The image should be photocopied on both sides of the paper and labeled with the character's name.

 Enrichment
Read Aloud
Challenge children to use the illustrations to retell the story to a friend.

Literacy Time

large group · 15 minutes

📖 Read Aloud

✓ **Can children name story events as they help you retell the story?**

Build Background Tell children that you will be reading a book about two animals that go to school for the first time. Ask: ***Do you have pets? Tell me about them.*** *¿Qué saben sobre los hámsters?*

● Ask: ***Can real hamsters talk, read, and write?*** *¿Pueden los hámsters hablar, leer y escribir?*

● Explain that they will act out the story as you retell it.

Listen for Enjoyment Display *Max and Mo's First Day at School,* and read the title. Explain that Max and Mo are the names of the two hamsters.

● Take a picture walk through the book, pointing out the things the animals are doing.

● Track the print as you read the book aloud.

Respond to the Story Discuss the story. Review the illustrations. Ask: ***What do the children call Max and Mo? How do Max and Mo solve their problem?*** *¿Cómo llamaron los niños a Max y a Mo? ¿Cómo solucionaron su problema?* Ask two children to help you retell the story. Have pairs act out the animals as you retell the story.

 ELL As you read aloud, encourage children to point to and name familiar objects such as a *scissors* and *tape.* To support comprehension, use gestures and role-play for more abstract vocabulary such as *climb up* and *slide down.*

TIP Ask children who "the big ones" are. Point out that the hamsters do not talk to "the big ones." Ask children what the hamsters might say to "the big ones" if they could talk to them.

Learn About Letters and Sounds

✓ **Can children identify and compare and contrast letters *Aa* and *Ss*?**

Learn About the Letters *Aa* and *Ss* Display the *ABC Picture Card* for *Aa*. Say the letter name, make the letter sound, and review the formation strokes. Then have children name the letter. Repeat with the *ABC Picture Card* for *Ss*.

● Ask: ***How are uppercase and lowercase A the same? How are they different?*** *¿En qué se parecen la a minúscula y la A mayúscula? ¿En qué se diferencian?*

● Guide children to compare and contrast not only the letter shapes, but also the sounds they represent and the way children make the sounds.

● Ask: ***How are uppercase and lowercase S the same? How are they different?*** *¿En qué se parecen la s minúscula y la S mayúscula? ¿En qué se diferencian?*

Max and Mo's First Day at School
Max y Mo van a la escuela

ABC Picture Cards

Online Math Activity

Demonstrate Pizza Pizzazz 1: Match Collections (online activity). In this activity, children help twins choose a pizza to match another pizza with a certain number of toppings. Each child should complete the activity this week.

Math Time

Observe and Investigate

✓ **Can children count 1–10 items?**

Our Friend the Baker Invite children to sing a song with you about a baker who drives a truck. Explain that a baker is someone who bakes bread, muffins, and other delicious food. Ask children to share what kinds of foods they like to bake and eat.

- Demonstrate the actions as you sing the song.
  Our friend the baker drives a truck down the street,
  Filled with everything good to eat.
  Two doors the baker opens wide. (Outstretch arms.)
  Let's look at the shelves inside, (Cup hands over eyes to look.)
  What do you see? What do you see?
  Three big muffins for you and me! (Show three fingers.)
- Say: *Now you sing the song with me and show the number of muffins with your fingers. Ahora ustedes cantarán la canción conmigo y mostrarán el número de galletas con los dedos.*
- Adapt the final number of muffins in the finger play to reinforce numbers up to 10.

 Provide visual support for the content of the song with pictures of a baker, muffins, bread, and other baked goods. Ask children to count the items before you sing the song. Model a sentence pattern for them, such as: *Three big muffins for me!*

✖✖✖ Social and Emotional Development

Making Good Choices

✓ **Do children understand how to make new friends?**

Making Friends Ask children to tell about a time when they made a new friend. Display the *Making Good Choices Flip Chart*, page 7. Point to the boy standing alone by the fence.

- Ask: *What do you think the boy in the picture is feeling? How can you tell? Do you agree, or do you think something else? Does he look like he knows the other children? What might happen next? ¿Cómo creen que se siente el niño? ¿Cómo saben que se siente así? ¿Están todos de acuerdo? ¿Creen que el niño conoce a los otros niños? ¿Qué creen que pasará después?*
- Then discuss what activities the other children could invite the boy to join.

Making Good Choices Flip Chart, page 7

 Learning Goals

Social and Emotional Development
- Child shows empathy and care for others.
- Child learns how to make and keep friends.

Mathematics
- Child counts 1–10 concrete objects correctly.

Vocabulary

baker	panadero	lonely	solo
muffin	galleta		

Differentiated Instruction

 Extra Support

Observe and Investigate

If...children have trouble with any of the movements, **then...**practice the song several times and exaggerate the actions.

 Enrichment

Making Good Choices

Challenge children to make up a story about the boy. Have them tell the story to a friend or classmate.

♥ **Special Needs**

Vision Loss

Since most people use visual cues to tell how someone is feeling, this concept may be difficult for children with vision loss. Let the child feel your face when you are sad. Then say: *I'm sad when no one plays with me. What makes you sad? Me pongo triste cuando nadie quiere jugar conmigo. ¿Qué los pone triste a ustedes?*

Focus Question
What makes a good friend?
¿Cómo es un buen amigo?

Learning Goals

Language and Communication
• Child names and describes actual or pictured people, places, things, actions, attributes, and events.

Mathematics
• Child sorts objects and explains how the sorting was done.

Vocabulary

alike	parecido
different	diferente
materials	materiales
tree	árbol

Differentiated Instruction

✋ Extra Support
Oral Language and Academic Vocabulary
If...children cannot name how the trees are different, **then...**narrow the choices by asking specific questions, such as if all the colors are the same.

⭐ Enrichment
Oral Language and Academic Vocabulary
Challenge children to name other items from nature in the illustration, such as *clouds, grass*, and so on.

Accommodations for 3's
Observe and Investigate
If...children have trouble drawing a tree, **then...** supply a blackline outline of a tree for them to color in.

Science Time

large group 20 minutes

Language and Communication Skills Model effective communication by using complete sentences of four or more words.

Oral Language and Academic Vocabulary

✓ **Can children understand when something is the same or different about objects?**

Point to the trees shown in the *Math and Science Flip Chart*, page 9. Say: ***The trees are the same in some ways. The trees are different in other ways.*** *Los tres árboles se parecen en algunos aspectos. Los tres árboles son diferentes en otros aspectos.*

● Explain that things can be the same in some ways and different in others. Ask: ***How are these trees the same?*** *¿En qué se parecen estos árboles?*

● Encourage children to observe and discuss how things, such as leaves, can be the same and different, such as being the same shape but a different color.

Observe and Investigate

✓ **Can children name characteristics that are the same and different about objects?**

Provide a variety of drawing materials that children can use to draw a picture of a tree. Provide materials in colors that are similar to nature. Have children draw a picture of a tree. Allow children to work in pairs and observe trees outside the window or in books before drawing.

● Hang pictures on a wall and have children discuss what is the same about them and what is different.

● Allow children to take turns going to the pictures and pointing to things that are the same and different. Help them find the words to describe the characteristics.

Tell children they will have another chance to use the books and materials in the Math and Science Center.

ELL Display a red crayon and a red marker. Ask: ***What is the same about these two things?*** Help children identify the color red by making strokes on a sheet of paper. Have children compare the results and tell how they are different.

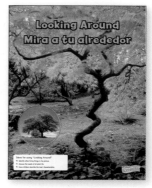
Math and Science Flip Chart, page 9

Center Time

▶ **Center Rotation** Center Time includes teacher-guided activities and independent activities. Refer to the **Learning Centers** on pages 100–101 for independent activity ideas.

 small group · 30 minutes

Math and Science Center

✓ **Encourage children to identify materials that are the same and different.**

Materials drawing paper; 2 of each: red crayons; yellow crayons; yellow strips of paper; orange strips of paper; orange markers. Display the variety of materials. Tell children they will work with a friend to find things that are the same or things that are different.

- Supply sheets of drawing paper that have a line down the middle.

- Have children draw two items that are the same in some way or different in some way.

- Allow time to have children tell you what is the same or different about their choices.

Center Tip

If... children cannot describe what is the same or different, **then...** ask a specific question, such as: *What color is this crayon? What color is this piece of paper?* *¿De qué color es el crayón? ¿De qué color es este pedazo de papel?*

Purposeful Play

✓ **Observe children's spontaneous social interaction as they play.**

Children choose an open center for free playtime. Encourage interaction by suggesting that children choose a classmate to work with.

Let's Say Good-Bye

 large group · 15 minutes

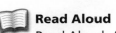 **Read Aloud** Revisit "Make New Friends"/"Amigos" for your afternoon Read Aloud. After reading, ask children to talk about a friend.

Home Connection Refer to the Home Connections activities listed in the Resources and Materials chart on page 97. Invite children to discuss with their families the differences among plants in their house and yard. Sing the "Good-Bye Song" as children prepare to leave.

✓ Learning Goals

Language and Communication
- Child names and describes actual or pictured people, places, things, actions, attributes, and events.

Emergent Literacy: Writing
- Child experiments with and uses some writing conventions when writing or dictating.

Mathematics
- Child sorts objects and explains how the sorting was done.

Science
- Child uses senses to observe, classify, investigate, and collect data.

Writing

Review the day. Have children recall things they have done to make new friends. Build children's concept of word by pointing to each word as you read back their ideas. Gather the children's work into a class book. Make a cover with the title *How We Are Friends* and place in the classroom library.

Let's Start the Day

Focus Question
What makes a good friend?
¿Cómo es un buen amigo?

Opening Routines and Transition Tips
For **Opening Routines** and **Transition Tips** turn to pages 178–181 and visit **DLMExpressOnline.com** for more ideas.

Read **"Pam and Sam"/"Pam y Sam"** from the *Teacher's Treasure Book*, page 195, for your morning Read Aloud.

Learning Goals

Language and Communication
• Child uses newly learned vocabulary daily in muitiple contexts.

• Child speaks in complete sentences of four or more words. including a subject, verb, and object.

Emergent Literacy: Reading
• Child listens for words (for example, hears and separates individual words within a four-word sentence).

• Child retells or reenacts poems and stories in sequence.

Vocabulary

cage	jaula	climb	trepar
cozy	cómodo	rolling	rodar

Differentiated Instruction

 Extra Support
Oral Language and Vocabulary
If...children cannot retell a full event in the story, **then...**offer specific clues to help them. Say: *Max and Mo needed to get out of the cage. How did they get out?* *Max y Mo querían salir de su jaula. ¿Cómo lo hicieron?*

 Enrichment
Oral Language and Vocabulary
Challenge children to re-enact the events in the story.

Language Time

large group 15 minutes

👫👫 **Social and Emotional Development** Encourage children to look for ways to help each other during the day.

Oral Language and Vocabulary

✓ **Can children retell events in a story?**

Retelling Story Events Display *Max and Mo's First Day at School*. Model retelling an event in the story. Ask: **What did Max and Mo do when the children left?** *¿Qué hicieron Max y Mo cuando se fueron los ¨grandotes¨?* Then say: **Max and Mo made a name tag.** *Max y Mo hicieron un cartel con sus nombres.*

● Take a picture walk through the book, pausing to ask questions and retell the story events that happened. Include new vocabulary in questions and answers.

● Ask: **Where did Max and Mo learn to make the name tag?** Say: **Max and Mo learned from a book.** *¿Dónde aprendieron a hacer el cartel? En un libro.*

● Ask: **How did they stop the name tag from rolling?** *¿Qué problema tuvieron con el cartel? ¿Cómo lo solucionaron?*

ELL Provide support for children by drawing simple stick-figure sketches of story events on index cards. Place the cards in sequence, and work with children to orally identify the sequence. Then shuffle the cards and help children sequence and describe the events.

Phonological Awareness

✓ **Can children isolate words in a sentence?**

Concept of Word Display a Dog Puppet. Say: **Say this sentence with me, and clap once for each word.** **[Dog's name] is my friend.** *Digan esta oración conmigo y den una palmada por cada palabra. [___] Es mi amigo.* If children have difficulty separating the words, model the exercise for them. Say: **The first word in this sentence is [dog's name].** **Clap as we say [dog's name].** **Repeat for each word in the sentence.** *La primera palabra de esta oración es [___]. Demos una palmada cuando decimos [___]*

Max and Mo's First Day at School
Max y Mo van a la escuela

Center Time

▶ **Center Rotation** Center Time includes teacher-guided activities and independent activities. Refer to the **Learning Centers** on pages 100–101 for independent activity ideas.

Creativity Center

Center Tip

✓ **Track how children help one another while working together to create a piece of art.**

Materials 9×12 construction paper, collage materials (paper scraps, ribbon, feathers, toothpicks, and so on), glue or paste

Friendship Collage Have children work in pairs to create collages.

● Have partners each choose 4 items to use in their collage. One item should show something they like about their classmate or friend.

● Ask children to work together to position and glue the items onto construction paper.

● Have them work together to decide where to write their names.

Center Tip

If...children have difficulty counting out 4 items, **then...**provide them with a visual cue, such as 4 counters, and have them pick one item for each counter.

Writer's Center

Center Tip

✓ **Note children's ability to write some letter forms on their own.**

Materials writing paper, crayons, markers

Animal Friends Children name an animal friend and mimic the sounds it makes as you say a sentence about it.

● Ask children to name an animal they know or like. Write the name at the bottom of the page. Have them draw a picture of the animal.

● Have children model the sound the animal makes. Partners mimic the sound after the first child says each word in the following sentence frame: [Kitty] [meow] is [meow] my [meow] friend. [meow]

Center Tip

If...children have difficulty mimicking the animal sound, **then...**ask the partner to say it along with them.

Learning Goals

Emergent Literacy: Writing
• Child participates in free drawing and writing activities to deliver information.
• Child experiments with and uses some writing conventions when writing or dictating.

Mathematics
• Child counts 1–10 concrete objects correctly.

Fine Arts
• Child uses and experiments with a variety of art materials and tools in various art activities.

Differentiated Instruction

🖐 **Extra Support**
Writer's Center
If...children have difficulty thinking of an animal, **then...**hold up pictures for them to choose from.

⭐ **Enrichment**
Writer's Center
Challenge children to draw their animal friend in its natural or domestic setting.

Accommodations for 3's
Creativity Center
If...three-year-olds have difficulty applying glue to specific areas of the paper, **then...**provide them with a visual clue by making Xs on the paper where they want to attach items.

Focus Question
What makes a good friend?
¿Cómo es un buen amigo?

Circle Time

Learning Goals

Social and Emotional Development
• Child understands and respects the different ideas, feelings, perspectives, and behaviors of others.

Language and Communication
• Child uses appropriate nonverbal skills during conversations (making eye contact; using facial expressions).

Emergent Literacy: Reading
• Child names most upper- and lowercase letters of the alphabet.
• Child produces the most common sound for a given letter.

Vocabulary

lift up	levantar	tilt up	inclinar
together	juntos		

Differentiated Instruction

 Extra Support

Learn About Letters and Sounds
If...children have difficulty saying the sound /s/, **then...**demonstrate the correct position of the tongue. Say these words slowly and have children repeat after you: *sad, some, said, sun/ sol, sopa, saco, seta.*

Enrichment
Read Aloud
Challenge children to choose one feeling the hamsters show in the story. Ask children if they've ever had the feeling the hamsters had. Ask them to draw a picture of themselves that shows a time they felt that way. Have them dictate a sentence that describes the feeling.

Literacy Time

 large group · 15 minutes

📖 Read Aloud

✓ **Can children re-enact a story with support?**

Build Background Say: *Yesterday we read about two hamsters that are best friends.* *Ayer leímos sobre dos hámsters que eran mejores amigos.*

• Ask: *What did the children call Max and Mo?* *¿Cómo llamaban a Max y a Mo los niños?*

• Ask: *How did Max and Mo feel about being called "Tummy" and "Fluffy?"* *¿Cómo se sintieron Max y Mo cuando los llamaron "Pancita" y "Peluchín"?*

Listen for Understanding Display *Max and Mo's First Day at School.* Help children re-enact the hamsters' activities as you review the events.

• Read the story and track the text.

• Review the events as you re-enact them.

Say: *When I turn a page, I will read the text and you will act out what Max and Mo are doing.* *Cuando dé vuelta una página, leeré el cuento y ustedes representarán lo que están haciendo Max y Mo.*

Respond to the Story Discuss the story. Help children recall the events in the story. Say: *Max and Mo work together very well. How do you feel when you work well with someone?* *Max y Mo trabajan muy bien juntos. ¿Cómo se sienten cuando trabajan con un amigo?*

ELL Help children understand the concept of working together. Ask a child to stand up. Say: *We are going to work together.* Hold up a paper towel tube. Have the child hold one end while you hold the other. Say: *Lift up!* Lift the tube and have the child do the same. Then say: *Tilt up!* Signal to the child to raise his or her end.

TIP As you discuss the story, point out body language that shows Max and Mo's feelings. For example, when the children greet them, Max waves his paws wildly.

Learn About Letters and Sounds

✓ **Can children identify the sounds /a/ and /s/?**

Learn About the Letters Aa and Ss Display the *ABC Picture Cards* for *Aa* and *Ss.* Review the letter sounds and names and how to form each letter.

• Point to the picture on the *Aa* card. Ask: *What letter is this? Do you hear the /a/ sound at the beginning of the word* alligator? *¿Qué letra es ésta? ¿Escuchan la /a/ al principio de la palabra* alligator?

• Slow down the focus word and stress the target sound. Have children point to the letter *Aa* as you say the target sound. Say: *Point to the letter as I say the letter sound.* *Señalen la letra mientras yo digo el sonido que tiene.*

• Repeat for the *Ss* card, using the focus word *sun.*

Max and Mo's First Day at School
Max y Mo van a la escuela

ABC Picture Cards

Math Time

Observe and Investigate

✓ **Can children count 1–10 items?**

Making Matches Invite children to make their plates match yours.

- Make sure each pair of children has a paper plate and several counters.

- Display a plate with three counters. Say: *Put the same number of counters on your plate as I have on mine. Pongan en su plato la misma cantidad de fichas que ven en mi plato.*

- When pairs have finished, ask: *How many counters are on your plate? How do you know? ¿Cuántas fichas hay en su plato? ¿Cómo lo saben?*

- Discuss the various arrangements children made with their counters, and whether the number can be the same if the plates look different.

- Repeat with numbers up to five or more.

✗✗✗ Social and Emotional Development

Making Good Choices

✓ **Do children understand how to initiate new friendships?**

Making New Friends Talk about making new friends. Ask: *What are some things you can do to make a new friend? ¿Qué cosas puedes hacer para encontrar un nuevo amigo?* Display the *Making Good Choices Flip Chart,* page 7. Model using a Dog Puppet to review the chart.

- Ask: *Who do you see in this picture? How do you think he might be feeling? Why might he be feeling this way? ¿A quién ven en esta ilustración? ¿Cómo creen que se siente? ¿Por qué se siente así?*

Making Good Choices Flip Chart, page 7

- Ask: *Who can use the puppet to say the words the boy might be thinking? ¿Quién puede usar el títere para contar lo que está pensando el niño?*

Have children take turns using the puppet. Encourage other children to react to the puppet as children in the picture might react.

ELL Help children understand the relationship between the words *alone* and *lonely.* Stress the root word *lone* as you say: *A boy who is alone may be lonely when he has no one to play with.*

Focus Question
What makes a good friend?
¿Cómo es un buen amigo?

 Learning Goals

Mathematics
• Child tells how many are in a group of up to 5 objects without counting.

Physical Development
• Child develops small-muscle strength and control.

Vocabulary

chef	cocinero	compare	comparar
counters	fichas	match	igualar
same	igual		

Differentiated Instruction

 Extra Support
Math Time
If...children cannot match the pizzas, **then...** cover all except three of the pizzas on the chart.

Enrichment
Math Time
Invite a child to help you choose the number of counters to put on the plate and present the pizza to the class.

Special Needs
Delayed Motor Development
Instead of counters, use large objects for the child to pick up. Attach hook and loop fasteners to the top of items, and provide a pointer with matching hook and loop fasteners attached to the end. This can enable children to pick up items more easily.

Math Time

Fine Motor Skills Model correct pincer movements with your fingers to help children pick up small manipulatives, such as counters.

Compare Number Pizzas

 Can children identify the number of slices of pepperoni on each pizza without counting?

Tell the children a story about a pizza chef. Explain that the chef makes pizza for his friends, but each pizza has a different number of pepperoni slices. Say: **We need to tell the pizza chef how many slices of pepperoni are on each pizza.** *Debemos decirle al cocinero cuántas rebanadas de pepperoni hay en cada pizza.*

- Use a paper plate for pizza crust and Two-Sided Counters for pepperoni. Display your pizza with two "pepperoni slices."

- Display the *Math and Science Flip Chart*, page 10. Ask children to describe the scene on the chart. Ask: **What kind of pizzas did the chef make?** *¿Qué clase de pizzas preparó el cocinero?*

- Ask children to point to the pizza that has the same number of pepperoni slices as the one on the paper plate. Ask: **How do you know the matching pizza had the same number of slices?** *¿Cómo saben que esa pizza tenía la misma cantidad de rebanadas de pepperoni?*

- Repeat the activity with the paper plate and more counters. Have children match amounts of three or more as their ability allows.

To provide English Language Learners with additional visual support, you can make the pizza and pepperoni slices out of felt or construction paper for this activity.

Math and Science Flip Chart, page 10

Building Blocks

Online Math Activity
Demonstrate Pizza Pizzazz 1: Match Collections. In this activity, children help twins choose a pizza to match another pizza with a certain number of toppings. Each child should complete the activity this week.

Center Time

▶ **Center Rotation** Center Time includes teacher-guided activities and independent activities. Refer to the **Learning Centers** on pages 100–101 for independent activity ideas.

 small group 30 minutes

Math and Science Center

☑ **Observe whether children can match pizzas with the same number of counters without counting.**

Materials paper plates, Two-Color Counters, clear containers, Counting Cards (*Teacher's Treasure Book,* pages 506–507)

Find the Number Before children get to the center, conceal several pizzas (paper plates), each with a different number (1–5) of pepperoni slices (counters), under its own clear container. Place Counting Cards that match the pizzas in the center.

- Have children choose a card to represent the target number. Then have them find the pizza that matches the card.

- Children can show their answer to a partner.

Center Tip

If...children need help during the activity,
then...reduce the number of hidden pizzas and leave them all uncovered.

Purposeful Play

☑ **Praise children's use of appropriate language as they interact socially.**

Children choose an open center for free playtime. Suggest that children work together to act out meeting each other at school and becoming friends.

Let's Say Good-Bye

 large group 15 minutes

 Read Aloud Revisit "Pam and Sam"/"Pam y Sam" for your afternoon Read Aloud. Remind children to listen for the /s/ sound.

 Home Connection Refer to the Home Connections activities listed in the Resources and Materials chart on page 97. Tell children to practice counting at home with their families. Sing the "Good-Bye Song" as children prepare to leave.

✓ Learning Goals

Emergent Literacy: Reading
• Child identifies the letter that stands for a given sound.

Emergent Literacy: Writing
• Child experiments with and uses some writing conventions when writing or dictating.

Mathematics
• Child tells how many are in a group of up to 5 objects without counting.

Physical Development
• Child develops small-muscle strength and control.

Writing

Ask children to recall a time when they were lonely. Ask: **How can a friend help you when you are lonely?** *¿Cómo puede ayudarlos un amigo cuando se sienten solos?* Record their ideas on chart paper or an interactive whiteboard. Read the sentences back as you track the print. Then name a word on one line and ask the child who contributed the idea to point out the word.

DAY 3

Let's Start the Day

Focus Question
What makes a good friend?
¿Cómo es un buen amigo?

Learning Goals

Social and Emotional Development
• Child demonstrates positive social behaviors, as modeled by the teacher.

Language and Communication
• Child names and describes actual or pictured people, places, things, actions, attributes, and events.

Emergent Literacy: Reading
• Child listens for words (for example, hears and separates individual words within a four-word sentence).

Vocabulary

blocks	bloques	building	construyen
friend	amigo	helpful	amable
work	trabajan		

Differentiated Instruction

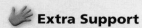

✋ Extra Support

Phonological Awareness
If...children stand at the wrong time, **then...** group children who have the same word together.

⭐ Enrichment

Phonological Awareness
Give children two words and actions and repeat the song. If children master two words and actions, give them three.

▶ **Opening Routines and Transition Tips**
For **Opening Routines** and **Transition Tips** turn to pages 178–181 and visit **DLMExpressOnline.com** for more ideas.

📖 Read **"Miguel and Maribel: Dance of Opposites"**/"Miguel y Maribel: Un baile de opuestos" from the *Teacher's Treasure Book*, page 258, for your morning Read Aloud.

Language Time

large group 15 minutes

👪 **Social and Emotional Development** Encourage children to follow your positive behavior by listening to each other as they work and play.

Oral Language and Vocabulary

✓ **Can children describe how they work together and help each other at school?**

What Is a Friend? Talk about how children work together and help each other. Ask: **What do friends and classmates do in the classroom to help each other?** ¿Cómo se ayudan los amigos unos a otros en el salón de clases?

● Display *Oral Language Development Card 6*. Discuss what the children are doing. Ask: **What do these children need to do with the blocks when they are done playing? How can they help each other?** ¿Qué deben hacer estos niños con los bloques cuando terminen de jugar? ¿Cómo pueden ayudarse unos a otros? Then review the suggestions on the back of the card.

Oral Language Development Card 6

Phonological Awareness

✓ **Can children hear individual words in a sentence?**

Find a Word Prepare and display individual picture cards for *friend, laugh,* and *school.* Display the *Rhymes and Chants Flip Chart,* page 7. Say: **Listen as I sing "Make a Friend!"** *Escuchen como canto la canción.* Then distribute the picture cards to children. Say: **This time, stand up when I sing the word pictured on your card. Because you have different words, everyone will not stand at the same time.** *Esta vez, pónganse de pie cuando yo diga la palabra de su tarjeta. Como tienen diferentes palabras, no todos se pararán al mismo tiempo.* Repeat the first verse.

ELL Use the *Rhymes and Chants Flip Chart* to review vocabulary. Say the word *share*, then pantomime sharing with a child. Have English Language Learners say *share* as you perform the pantomime.

Rhymes and Chants Flip Chart, page 7

Center Time

▶ **Center Rotation** Center Time includes teacher-guided activities and independent activities. Refer to the **Learning Centers** on pages 100–101 for independent activity ideas.

small group **60–90 minutes**

Library and Listening Center

 Listen for the use of a wide variety of words to describe people and actions.

Materials books about friends

What Friends Do Have children browse through books to find illustrations of friends working or playing together.

● Have each child pick one illustration and tell a partner what is happening. Then have the partner pick an illustration to talk about.

● Ask: *Can you find a picture that shows friends doing a job or activity that you do at school? ¿Pueden encontrar una ilustración que muestre amigos haciendo algo que ustedes hagan en la escuela?*

Center Tip

If...some children have difficulty taking turns talking and listening, **then...**provide toy microphones. Explain that the child holding the microphone is the child whose turn it is to talk.

ABC Center

 Note children's ability to identify objects that start with the sound /s/.

Materials *ABC Picture Card* for *Ss,* paper, magazines, scissors, glue or paste

The Sound of S Review the letter *Ss* and its sound.

● Have children cut out magazine pictures of five things that start with the /s/ sound, for example, *school*. Have them glue their pictures on their papers.

● Have children whisper the word *cool* when they hear *school* spoken aloud.

Center Tip

If...children have difficulty labeling their collages, **then...**have them use a finger to trace the letter *s* on the picture card before writing.

Learning Goals

Language and Communication
● Child uses oral language for a variety of purposes.
● Child follows basic rules for conversations (taking turns, staying on topic, listening actively).
● Child names and describes actual or pictured people, places, things, actions, attributes, and events.

Emergent Literacy: Reading
● Child identifies the letter that stands for a given sound.

Differentiated Instruction

✋ **Extra Support**
Library and Listening Center
If...children have difficulty describing a situation, **then...**give them a clue by asking a question, such as: *What are the boys doing at the park? ¿Qué están haciendo los niños en el parque?*

⭐ **Enrichment**
ABC Center
Challenge children to label their pictures by using what they know about sounds to write the name of each object.

♥ **Special Needs**
Behavioral Social/Emotional
If children have issues with texture and do not like to work with glue, allow them to tape their pictures on their papers.

Focus Question
What makes a good friend?
¿Cómo es un buen amigo?

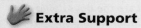

✓ Learning Goals

Language and Communication
• Child speaks in complete sentences of four or more words, including a subject, verb, and object.

Emergent Literacy: Reading
• Child names most upper- and lowercase letters of the alphabet.
• Child identifies the letter that stands for a given sound.
• Child retells or reenacts poems and stories in sequence.

Vocabulary

circle	círculo	classroom	salón de clases
exercise	ejercitar	habit	hábitos
healthy	saludable	learn	aprender
teacher	maestro		

Differentiated Instruction

👋 Extra Support

Read Aloud
If...children have difficulty remembering important details when retelling part of the book, **then...**use the illustrations to prompt them. For example, on page 7, ask: **What is this child doing?** *¿Qué está haciendo este niño?*

⭐ Enrichment

Learn About Letters and Sounds
Invite children to have fun with alliterative phrases that feature the /s/ sound. Say: **See the snakes slither,** or **Six silly sisters sang.** Have children repeat the phrases.

Literacy Time

large group / 15 minutes

📖 Read Aloud

✓ **Can children retell the story?**

Build Background Say: *You are all in school! Think of all the things you do in school. ¡Todos estamos en la escuela! Piensen en todas las cosas que hacen en la escuela.*

● Ask: **What do you do with friends or classmates?** *¿Qué cosas hacen con sus amigos?*

● Ask: **What new things have you learned?** *¿Qué cosas nuevas han aprendido?*

Listen for Understanding Display *Concept Big Book 1: Welcome to School/ Bienvenidos a la escuela.* Read the title. Say: **The school in the book is a lot like our school.** *La escuela del libro se parece mucho a nuestra escuela.*

● Browse through the pages. Name some of the activities shown. Occasionally ask a question showing a similarity to your school day, such as: **Do you learn healthy habits at school?** *¿Aprenden hábitos saludables en la escuela?*

● Open the book to the first page. Ask: **Where should I start reading on this page?** *¿Por dónde debería comenzar a leer esta página?* Read the book aloud.

Respond to the Book Discuss the book by having children retell what happens in preschool. Ask: **What do children do at the preschool?** *¿Qué hacen los niños en Prekinder?* Revisit several photographs and ask children to use complete sentences to retell the part of the book shown.

💡 **TIP** Ask children to identify similarities between the classroom activities shown in the book and their own.

ELL Enhance children's vocabulary by pantomiming some of the activities in the story, such as exercise, singing, and so on, as you read them.

Learn About Letters and Sounds

✓ **Can children name and identify the sound of Aa and Ss?**

Matching Letters and Sounds Display *Rhymes and Chants Flip Chart,* page 7.

● Display the Alphabet/Letter Tile for *Ss.* Ask: **What is this letter? What sound does it make?** *¿Qué letra es ésta? ¿Cuál es el sonido de esta letra?*

● Hand the letter to a child and ask him or her to match it to the same letter on the flip chart. Read the word the child indicates, stressing the /s/ sound.

● Repeat with the Alphabet/Letter Tile for *Aa.*

● Ask other children to take turns matching *Aa* or *Ss* on the flip chart.

Welcome to School
Bienvenidos a la escuela

Rhymes and Chants Flip Chart, page 7

Math Time

Observe and Investigate

✓ **Can children tell how many cubes are in the container?**

Fill and Spill Place a Counting Card (*Teacher's Treasure Book,* pages 506–507) on the table to indicate a target number, such as three. Ask: *How many circles are on this card? ¿Cuántos círculos hay en esta tarjeta?* Explain that children should put that many Connecting Cubes into the container.

● Have a child count three cubes and put them into a plastic container. Count as you drop them in. Ask: *How many cubes are in there? ¿Cuántos cubos hay?*

● Then spill all the cubes out of the container. Ask: *How many cubes spilled out? ¿Cuántos cubos se volcaron?* Count the cubes to check.

● Put different Counting Cards on the table and provide support as children repeat the activity in small groups.

 Group together children with varying levels of English proficiency. Encourage children to model the activity for each other and use vocabulary words to describe what they are doing.

✗✗✗ Social and Emotional Development

Making Good Choices

✓ **Do children understand that being friendly means helping one another?**

A Good Friend Display the *Making Good Choices Flip Chart,* page 7. Point to the boy in the sandbox.

● Ask: *How is he being friendly? How can the girl be friendly, too? ¿Por qué podemos decir que este niño está actuando de una manera amigable? ¿Cómo puede la niña ser también amigable?*

● Use the Dog Puppets to role-play having the girl give the boy a turn to use the sand toys. Model using the words *please* and *thank you.* Then invite children to use the puppets to role-play.

 Help children understand what it means to take turns. Display a crayon and say: *It is my turn to use this crayon.* Draw a circle. Then hand the crayon to a child. Say: *Now it is your turn to use the crayon.*

Making Good Choices Flip Chart, page 7

Focus Question
What makes a good friend?
¿Cómo es un buen amigo?

Learning Goals

Language and Communication
• Child begins and ends conversations appropriately.
• Child follows basic rules for conversations (taking turns, staying on topic, listening actively).

Social Studies
• Child identifies similarities and differences among people.
• Child respects/appreciates the differing interests, skills, abilities, cultures, languages, and family structures of people.

Vocabulary

celebrate	celebrar	culture	cultura
different	diferente	language	lengua
same	igual		

Differentiated Instruction

 Extra Support

Oral Language and Academic Vocabulary
If...children have difficulty identifying ways the children are the same and different, **then...**ask questions that focus on physical characteristics, such as: *Is she as tall as you? ¿Tienen la misma altura?*

Enrichment

Understand and Participate
Provide children with a variety of photographs of people from magazines. Challenge them to categorize the people by putting them into groups based on similarities such as height, hair color, emotion being expressed, and so on.

large group   20 minutes

Social Studies Time

👥 **Social and Emotional Development** Model positive behaviors such as saying *please* and *thank you* when appropriate.

Oral Language and Academic Vocabulary

☑ **Can children identify similarities and differences among himself or herself and his or her classmates?**

Have children identify the United States and state flags, and then practice reciting the Pledge of Allegiance to the United States flag. Observe a moment of silence. Explain that saying the Pledge of Allegiance is part of our culture. Hold up pictures of people as you talk about how we are alike and different. Include children of all ethnicities and cultural celebrations in your picture selection. Say: *Look around at your classmates. Observen a sus compañeros.* Ask: *How are we all alike? Can you name one way you are different from the child beside you? ¿Son todos iguales? ¿Pueden decir en qué se diferencian del niño que está al lado?*

• Talk about languages. Explain that many people speak English, but many others speak different languages. Say: *When I meet a friend I say, "Hello."* Ask: *Does anyone say* hello *in a different way? Cuando me encuentro con un amigo, digo "Hola". ¿Alguno de ustedes saluda de otra manera?* (buenos días, bonjour, pá prama) Have children say *hello* in their first language.

• Review how people are alike and different in size, color, and languages they speak. Introduce the idea that people are alike and different in many other ways, too, such as, family size, things they celebrate, homes they live in, and so on.

TIP Have children bring in photos, clothing, instruments, books, or other items to share and display in a My Culture corner of the room.

Understand and Participate

☑ **Can children identify similarities and differences among themselves and others from other cutures?**

Holidays and Celebrations Display books of holiday and family celebrations from different cultures. Have children identify their own celebrations.

• Hold up books, one at a time, and talk about the traditional celebrations in the pictures. Ask: *Who celebrates this holiday? Can you tell us something special about that day? ¿Quién ha participado alguna vez de una celebración como ésta? ¿Pueden comentar algo especial que se hace ese día?* Elicit information about food, clothing, decoration, parades, and so on.

ELL Enhance children's understanding of *same* and *different*. Give children several pattern blocks in different shapes and colors. Hold up a block and ask them to find one that is the same color. Then have them find a block that is a different color. Repeat with same and different shapes.

Center Time

▶ **Center Rotation** Center Time includes teacher-guided activities and independent activities. Refer to the **Learning Centers** on pages 100–101 for independent activity ideas.

 small group   30 minutes

Pretend and Learn Center

	Center Tip
✓ **Encourage children to identify similarities and differences in fingerprints.** **Materials** pad of washable ink, wet wipes, 4-inch squares of drawing paper, Jumbo Hand Lenses **Fingerprint Detectives** Invite children to pretend to be detectives as they study fingerprints. Explain that no two people have fingerprints that are exactly the same. ● Have children press a finger on the inkpad, then on paper to make a fingerprint. Have them clean the ink off their hands with a wet wipe. ● Ask children to use the hand lenses to study their own fingerprints. Then ask them to pair up with another child and observe how their fingerprints are the same and different.	**If...**children have difficulty making clear fingerprints, then...help them press a fingertip on the paper.

Learning Goals

Emergent Literacy: Writing
• Child experiments with and uses some writing conventions when writing or dictating.

Social Studies
• Child identifies similarities and differences among people.

Writing

Give each child a paper with *We all* _____. written at the bottom. Help children write or dictate the rest of the sentence. Encourage children to illustrate their sentence. Display the pages in the classroom.

Purposeful Play

✓ **Observe children taking turns using materials and saying *please* and *thank you* when appropriate.**

Children choose an open center for free playtime. Encourage social interaction by suggesting that they help a friend choose and complete an activity.

Let's Say Good-Bye

 large group   15 minutes

 Read Aloud Revisit "Miguel and Maribel: Dance of Opposites"/"Miguel y Maribel: Un baile de opuestos" for your afternoon Read Aloud. Remind children to listen for the /s/ sound.

Home Connection Refer to the Home Connections activities listed in the Resources and Materials chart on page 97. Remind children to find characteristics that are the same and different among family members. Sing the "Good-Bye Song" as children prepare to leave.

Let's Start the Day

Focus Question
What makes a good friend?
¿Cómo es un buen amigo?

Opening Routines and Transition Tips
For **Opening Routines** and **Transition Tips** turn to pages 178–181 and visit **DLMExpressOnline.com** for more ideas.

Read **"Eye Rhyme"**/**"Ojos que riman"** from the *Teacher's Treasure Book*, page 79, for your morning Read Aloud.

Learning Goals

Language and Communication
• Child begins and ends conversations appropriately.
• Child follows basic rules for conversations (taking turns, staying on topic, listening actively).

Emergent Literacy: Reading
• Child listens for words (for example, hears and separates individual words within a four-word sentence).

Vocabulary

make-believe fantasía real real

Differentiated Instruction

 Extra Support
Phonological Awareness
If...children have difficulty with two-syllable words when counting words in sentences, **then...**use one-syllable words exclusively.

 Enrichment
Phonological Awareness
Challenge children to count the words in sentences you say that include two- and three-syllable words, such as **Samantha is very friendly** *Samanta es bastante amigable* and **Let's play soccer together** *Nos encanta jugar juntos al fútbol.*

Language Time

large group   15 minutes

👪 **Social and Emotional Development** Model listening quietly when children contribute to the discussion and encourage others to do the same.

Oral Language and Vocabulary

✓ **Can children distinguish between real and make-believe?**

Real or Make-Believe Talk about real animals. Ask: **Is a dog a real animal? Can you name other real animals?** *¿Un perro es un animal real? ¿Puedes nombrar otros animales reales?*

● Display a Dog Puppet. Ask: **Is this a real animal?** *¿Es éste un animal real?* Discuss what makes the dog make-believe.

● Say: **A make-believe dog can talk. A real dog cannot.** *Un perro de fantasía puede hablar. Un perro real, no.* Ask children to tell what a make-believe rabbit could do that a real rabbit could not do. Then have children describe other things make-believe animals can do that real animals cannot.

ELL Extend children's understanding of the difference between real and make-believe by browsing through several books of each type. Point to appropriate illustrations and say: **This is real** or **This is not real. It is make-believe**.

Phonological Awareness

✓ **Can children identify the number of words they hear in a sentence?**

Listen and Count Explain that children are going to count the words in sentences. Provide each child with 4 Two-Color Counters. Say: **We are friends.** *Somos buenos amigos.* Model putting down a counter for each word you say. Then ask children to put down a counter each time they hear a word in sentences you say, such as **Friends work at school. Friends help each other. Reading books is fun.**
Los amigos hacen cosas juntos. Los amigos se ayudan. Leer libros es divertido.

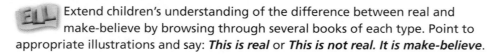

Center Time

Center Rotation Center Time includes teacher-guided activities and independent activities. Refer to the **Learning Centers** on pages 100–101 for independent activity ideas.

 small group 60–90 minutes

Creativity Center

 Track children's use of descriptive words to tell how they are similar to and different from their friends or classmates.

Materials hand mirror, 6-inch paper circles (in flesh tones), crayons, yarn (shades of brown, yellow, red, black), scissors, glue or paste

Alike and Different Explain that children will make a face that looks like their own.

- Have children study their faces in the hand mirror.

- Ask them to draw eyes, a nose, and a mouth on the circle. Have them color the circle and the features to make the face look like theirs. Then have them cut yarn and add hair.

- Have children share their faces and talk about how they are all alike and how they are different.

Center Tip

If...children have difficulty identifying similarities and differences, **then...**offer prompts such as: *What color is your hair? What color is (child's name)'s hair? ¿De qué color es tu pelo? ¿De qué color es el pelo de (child's name)?*

Pretend and Learn Center

 Look for and point out examples of children's understanding of real and make-believe.

Materials various-size boxes, blocks, pillows, dress-up clothing

Let's Pretend Explain that pretending to be someone or something else is making believe.

- Have clothes and props available for children to dress up. Explain that they can make themselves look any way they want: silly, pretty, brave, scary, and so on.

- Have children build a structure where their character lives, works, plays, and so on.

- Ask children to role-play being the make-believe person in their make-believe place.

Center Tip

If...children have difficulty thinking of a make-believe person to dress up as, **then...**offer suggestions based on the clothing choices, such as princess, robot, clown, and so on.

Learning Goals

Social Studies
- Child identifies similarities and differences among people.
- Child respects/appreciates the differing interests, skills, abilities, cultures, languages, and family structures of people.

Fine Arts
- Child expresses emotions or ideas through art.
- Child expresses ideas, emotions, and moods through individual and collarborative dramatic play.

Differentiated Instruction

Extra Support

Creativity Center
If...children have difficulty identifying similarities and differences, **then...**model an example such as: *We are the same because we both have a nose and two eyes. We are different because my eyes are brown and yours are blue. Somos parecidos porque los dos tenemos narices y ojos. Somos diferentes porque nuestro color de ojos es distinto.*

Enrichment

Pretend and Learn Center
Challenge children to work together to put on a performance starring their make-believe characters. Encourage them to talk as if they were the characters.

Accommodations for 3's
Creativity Center
If...three-year-olds have difficulty knowing how to space facial features on the circle, **then...**draw light pencil guidelines to show where they could draw eyes, nose, and a mouth.

Focus Question
What makes a good friend?
¿Cómo es un buen amigo?

Circle Time

Literacy Time

 large group 15 minutes

📖 Read Aloud

✓ **Can children answer questions about the story?**

Build Background Say: *Today we'll read about a mouse and a lion who become good friends.* Hoy vamos a leer un cuento que habla sobre un ratón y un león que se convierten en buenos amigos.

● Ask: *What is a real mouse like?* ¿Cómo es un ratón real?

● Ask: *What is a real lion like?* ¿Cómo es un león real?

● Ask: *Can a real mouse or lion talk?* ¿Un ratón y un león reales pueden hablar?

● Explain that this story is make-believe.

Listen for Enjoyment Display "The Lion and the Mouse"/"El león y el ratón agradecido" from *Teacher's Treasure Book*, page 171. Read the title of the story. Explain that a mouse talks a lion out of eating him. Later, the mouse helps the lion.

● Ask: *How might a tiny creature like a mouse help a huge lion?* ¿Cómo un animal tan pequeño como un ratón puede ayudar a un enorme león?

● Say: *Listen to find out what the mouse does.* Escuchen para descubrir lo que hace el ratón. Read the story, using the flannel board patterns to act out events.

Respond to the Story Have children recall details by re-enacting events from the story with flannel board patterns. Say: *Let's act out the story. What happens first?* Representemos el cuento. ¿Qué sucede en primer lugar? Have children take turns acting out events, such as the mouse running across the lion's nose, the lion catching the mouse, and so on.

 ELL Enhance children's vocabulary by acting out phrases from the story such as: *rising up angrily*, *roared with laughter*, or *gnawed the ropes*.

Learn About Letters and Sounds

✓ **Can children match letters by observing similarities and differences?**

Alphabet Match Prepare letter cards by printing individual letters *A*, *a*, *S*, and *s*. Display the *Alphabet Wall Card* for *Ss*. Say: *This is* **S**. *Ésta es la* S. Have children repeat the letter name. Say: **S** *makes the /s/ sound.* La S hace el sonido /s/. Then have them trace the letters in the air, pointing out the way both upper- and lowercase *s* curve.

● Repeat with the *Alphabet Wall Card* for *Aa*.

● Display one of the prepared cards. Say: *Look at the letter cards. Which letter does this match?* Observen las tarjetas. ¿A qué letra corresponden?

● Repeat with the other letter cards.

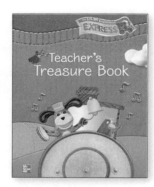

Teacher's Treasure Book, page 171

Alphabet Wall Cards

Learning Goals

Language and Communication
● Child demonstrates an understanding of oral language by responding appropriately.
● Child uses newly learned vocabulary daily in multiple contexts.
● Child builds English listening and speaking vocabulary for common objects and phrases. (ELL)

Emergent Literacy: Reading
● Child names most upper- and lowercase letters of the alphabet.
● Child asks and answers questions about books read aloud (such as "Who?" "What?" "Where?").

Vocabulary

creature	animal	friends	amigos
gnawed	roer	grateful	agradecido
roared	rugiente	surprised	sorpendido

Differentiated Instruction

 Extra Support

Learn About Letters and Sounds
If...children have difficulty matching a letter, **then...**have them note the similarities as they trace that letter on the *Alphabet Wall Card* and on each of the cards you prepared.

 Enrichment

Read Aloud
Encourage children to work with a friend to act out the story. Challenge them to use story vocabulary such as *surprised, grateful,* and *creature* as they role-play being the mouse or lion.

Math Time

Observe and Investigate

 Can children follow along with the patterns in your voice?

Count and Move in Patterns

- Spend some time counting in patterns of 3. Have children count from 1 to 15. For example, say 1 loudly, 2 loudly, 3 quietly, 4 loudly, 5 loudly, 6 quietly, and so on.

- Ask: *Can you hear the pattern in the way I am counting? You can try it too!*
  ¿Pueden oír la forma en que estoy contando? ¡Ustedes también pueden hacerlo!

- Add to the fun by marching along with the counting: 1 (stomp), 2 (stomp), 3 (step), and so on. Ask children to add their own ideas to the pattern.

 Can children show you five of something?

Number Me

- Tell children to show you five of something on their bodies. They will most likely show their fingers on one hand. Ask how they know there are five. Some children might answer by counting their fingers.

- Make silly statements, such as *I see six fingers on your hand, Yo vi seis dedos en tu mano,* encouraging them to prove there are only five by counting.

  ELL The silly statements may confuse children. Instead, ask them, *Does your friend have 5 fingers? How do you know?* Repeat the activity.

✖✖✖ Social and Emotional Development

Making Good Choices

 Can children demonstrate empathy and caring for others?

Making a Friend Use the Dog Puppets to role-play a scenario.

- Have one puppet say: *I am new here. I don't know anyone. Soy nuevo aquí. No conozco a nadie.* Have the other puppet turn to the children and ask: *What should I do? ¿Qué tengo que hacer?* Ask children what they think, and have them tell their answers to the puppet. Then have that puppet tell the other something like: *I remember when I was new here too. Don't be sad. Let's play together. Recuerdo cuando yo era nuevo. No te pongas triste. Vamos a jugar juntos.*

- Ask: *How is the second dog showing that he understands how the other dog feels? ¿Cómo demuestra el segundo perro que comprende cómo se siente el primero?* Explain that when two people like each other, understand and care about each other, and help each other, they can become friends.

Focus Question
What makes a good friend?
¿Cómo es un buen amigo?

Learning Goals

Mathematics
• Child demonstrates that, when counting, the last number indicates how many objects were counted.

Vocabulary

all	todo	counting	contar
many	muchos	together	juntos

Differentiated Instruction

 Extra Support
Math Time
If...children cannot demonstrate "how many," **then**...repeat the activity with more verbal modeling and questioning.

 Enrichment
Math Time
Try this activity with 10 or more counters.

Accommodations for 3's
Math Time
If...children struggle with the activity, **then**...use fewer counters.

 Special Needs
Behavioral Social/Emotional
If group activities involving counting are too overwhelming for the child, give her or him opportunities to practice in small groups or one-on-one with a peer.

Math Time

  large group 20 minutes

✓ **Can children say how many counters, based on the final count?**

Demonstrate Counting The goal of this activity is to teach object counting, emphasizing that counting tells how many. Hide four counters in your hand.

• Say: *I have some counters in my hand. Can you count aloud to tell how many?* *Tengo algunas fichas en mi mano. ¿Pueden contar en voz alta para decir cuántas hay?*

• Remove one of the counters and place it where the children can see and focus on it.

• Say: *This is ONE. One tells how many counters there are.* *Ésta es UNA. Entonces hay UNA.*

• Repeat until you have displayed all four counters. Then show your empty hand.

• Ask: How many counters are there in all? If children reply *four,* agree and reiterate that, together, you counted four counters.

ELL Work on a simple sentence pattern with the children to emphasize the math concept. Hold a counter and say: *This is ONE. One tells how many counters there are. How many are there?* Repeat the sentence pattern with other amounts.

Building Blocks

Online Math Activity
Children can complete Pizza Pizzazz during computer time or Center Time.

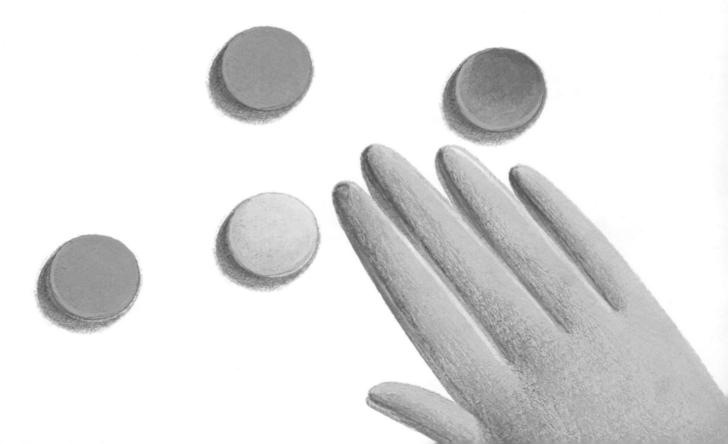

Center Time

▶ **Center Rotation** Center Time includes teacher-guided activities and independent activities. Refer to the **Learning Centers** on pages 100–101 for independent activity ideas.

 small group 30 minutes

Math and Science Center

✓ **Encourage children to count objects and tell how many, indicating the last number counted.**

Materials Vehicle Counters, clear containers

Say the Number Before children get to the center, put groups of one to ten Vehicle Counters in several containers.

- Children should work in small groups. One child can choose a container and count the vehicles.

- The child should tell his or her partner the final count. Then the other child should count the vehicles and say the final count as well.

- Children can take turns with other containers and talk about how many vehicles are in each.

Center Tip

If... children need help during the activity,
then... reduce the number of vehicle counters in each container.

 Writing

Ask children to draw a picture of how they are a good friend. Have them write or dictate a sentence that tells about their picture. Children can use invented spelling or scribble writing for sounds they do not know. Add children's creations to the class book *How We Are Friends* (page 107).

Purposeful Play

✓ **Observe children's use of vocabulary to describe what they did in school.**

Children choose an open center for free playtime. Suggest that children work together to draw and write about something they learned today.

Let's Say Good-Bye

 large group 15 minutes

Read Aloud Revisit "Eye Rhyme"/"Ojos que riman" for your afternoon Read Aloud. Remind children to listen for the sounds of /s/ and /a/.

Home Connection Refer to the Home Connections activities listed in the Resources and Materials chart on page 97. Encourage children to tell their families what they learned about making new friends. Sing the "Good-Bye Song" as children prepare to leave.

Unit 1 All About Pre-K

Week 3 Let's Be Friends

DAY 5

Let's Start the Day

Focus Question

What makes a good friend?

¿Cómo es un buen amigo?

 Learning Goals

Social and Emotional Development
• Child shows empathy and care for others.

Language and Communication
• Child names and describes actual or pictured people, places, things, actions, attributes, and events.

Emergent Literacy: Reading
• Child listens for words (for example, hears and separates individual words within a four-word sentence).

Vocabulary

friends	amigos	game	juego
play	jugar	school	escuela
share	compartir		

Differentiated Instruction

 Extra Support

Phonological Awareness

If...children have difficulty remembering their word when others have different words, **then...** work on one word at a time as a group.

⭐ **Enrichment**

Oral Language and Vocabulary

Challenge children to use the song on the flip chart as a guide for making up a story about friends. Have them tell their stories to a classmate

▶ **Opening Routines and Transition Tips**

For **Opening Routines** and **Transition Tips** turn to pages 178–181 and visit **DLMExpressOnline.com** for more ideas.

📖 Read **"Helpful Friends"/**"*Amigos útiles*" from the *Teacher's Treasure Book,* page 168, for your morning Read Aloud.

 large group   15 minutes

Language Time

👪 **Social and Emotional Development** Encourage children to share and help each other as they work and play.

Oral Language and Vocabulary

✓ **Do children use a variety of words to describe how friends or classmates play and work together?**

Friends at School Discuss what children do together at school. Ask: **How do we help each other?** *¿Cómo nos ayudamos unos a otros?*

● Display the *Rhymes and Chants Flip Chart,* page 7. Ask: **What might the children be doing?** *¿Qué están haciendo las niñas?* Explain that the children could be taking turns as they play a game. Say: **Tell about a time when you and a friend took turns doing something.** *Cuéntenos si alguna vez hicieron algo por turnos con un amigo.*

ELL Explain that when people share, they both get a chance to do something together. Discuss things that can be shared, such as a book or a toy, and how they can be shared.

Phonological Awareness

✓ **Can children identify discrete words in a spoken sentence?**

Be the Word Display the *Rhymes and Chants Flip Chart,* page 7. Say: **Today we will listen for words.** *Hoy escucharemos palabras.*

● Assign words from the song to pairs of children. Have them practice saying the word to help remember it.

● Explain that you will sing a verse from "Make a Friend!" When a pair hears their word, they will stand.

● Practice the song several times until the pairs are able to isolate their assigned word.

Rhymes and Chants Flip Chart, page 7

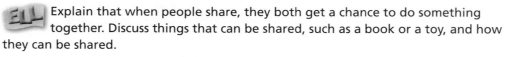

Center Time

▶ **Center Rotation** Center Time includes teacher-guided activities and independent activities. Refer to the **Learning Centers** on pages 100–101 for independent activity ideas.

 small group | 60–90 minutes

Library and Listening Center

☑ Note children's use of vocabulary words, such as *share* and *game*.

Materials books that feature friends (animal or human), sticky notes

Browsing Books Have children browse books to find pictures of friends who are sharing or taking turns.

- Have children mark the pages with the pictures of friends with sticky notes.

- Have them choose one picture to share. Ask: **How can you tell these are friends? How are they acting like friends?** *¿Qué están haciendo estos amigos? ¿De qué manera actúan como amigos?*

Center Tip

If...children have difficulty identifying situations in which children are sharing, **then...**give clues by pointing out situations where children are using the same materials or toys.

ABC Center

☑ Observe children as they form letters in sand and on paper.

Materials *ABC Picture Cards Aa* and *Ss*, sand tray, paper folded to make 4 sections, crayons

Make a Letter Have children make letters in sand, and then write the letters.

- Ask children to trace a letter on an *ABC Picture Card,* and then use a finger to form that letter in sand.

- Have children then write the letter in one section of their papers.

- Ask children to repeat until they have practiced and written the upper- and lowercase forms of both letters.

Center Tip

If...children confuse letters, **then...**point out unique details, such as the point at the top of *A* and the curves of *S* and *s*.

Learning Goals

Social and Emotional Development
- Child shows eagerness, curiosity, and confidence while learning new concepts and trying new things.

Emergent Literacy: Reading
- Child independently engages in pre-reading behaviors and activities (such as, pretending to read, turning one page at a time).

- Child names most upper- and lowercase letters of the alphabet.

Differentiated Instruction

👋 Extra Support
ABC Center

If...a child has difficulty writing a letter, **then...** place your hand over the child's, and guide him or her through the formation of the letter.

⭐ Enrichment
ABC Center

Challenge children to add a drawing of something that starts with the letter in each section of their paper.

Accommodations for 3's
ABC Center

If...three-year-olds have difficulty writing letters independently, **then...**write the letter on their paper and have them trace it.

💜 Special Needs
Vision Loss

Explain to the class that people with vision impairments often listen to books on tape as a way to learn about things. Allow students to record personal examples of sharing or taking turns instead of finding examples in books.

Circle Time

Focus Question

What makes a good friend?

¿Cómo es un buen amigo?

Literacy Time

large group · 15 minutes

Read Aloud

 Can children answer questions about the story?

Build Background Say: *We're going to revisit* **Max and Mo's First Day at School,** *the story about two hamsters that are best friends.* Vamos a releer Max y Mo van a la escuela, el cuento acerca de dos hámsters amigos.

● Ask: *Are the hamsters in this story real or make-believe?* ¿Son los hámsters en este cuento reales o de fantasía?

● Ask: *How do you know?* ¿Cómo lo saben?

Listen for Enjoyment Display *Max and Mo's First Day at School,* and read the title.

● Browse the book. Build print awareness by pointing to individual words. For example, point to a sentence and say: *This sentence says "We need name tags." Let's point to each word.* Esta oración dice "A la escuela". Señalemos cada palabra. Track the print as children count.

● Read the book aloud, using a pointer to track the print.

Respond to the Story Return to the first illustration. Model retelling the story. Say: **Max and Mo live in a cage.** Max y Mo vivían en su jaula. Turn to the next illustration. Ask: **What is happening?** ¿Qué sucede aquí? Continue using the illustrations as a guide to retelling the story.

TIP Help children understand that words are separated by spaces. Have them count the words on a page of the book.

Learn About Letters and Sounds

 Can children identify the /a/ and /s/ sounds?

Learn About /a/ and /s/ Review the sounds /a/ and /s/. Display the *Aa* page in the *ABC Big Book.* Ask: **What is this letter?** ¿Qué letra es ésta?

● Point to the apple. Ask: **What sound does** a **make in** apple? **Let's say the word:** /a/ **-pple.** ¿Qué sonido tiene la letra a en la palabra apple? Digamos la palabra: /a/ -pple. Point to the ape. Ask: **What sound does** a **make in** ape? **Say the word with me:** /ā/ **-pe.** ¿Qué sonido tiene la letra a en la palabra ape? Digan la palabra conmigo: /ā/ -pe.

● Turn to the *Ss* page and ask children to identify the letter. Point to the socks. Ask: **What sound does** s **make in** socks? **Say the word with me:** /s/ **-ocks.** ¿Qué tiene hace la letra s en socks? Digan la palabra conmigo: /s/ -ocks.

● Review with children how to form the letters *Aa* and *Ss*.

ELL Help children understand the relationship between the words *read* and *reading* and *write* and *writing.* Say: *I can write.* Then write a word and say: *Now I am writing.* Say: *I can read.* Pick up a book. Say: *Now I am reading.*

Learning Goals

Emergent Literacy: Reading

• Child names most upper- and lowercase letters of the alphabet.

• Child identifies the letter that stands for a given sound.

• Child retells or reenacts poems and stories in sequence.

• Child asks and answers questions about books read aloud (such as "Who?" "What?" "Where?").

Vocabulary

climb	trepar	cozy	cómodo
friend	amigo	hamster	hámster
make-believe	fantasía	revisit	releer

Differentiated Instruction

✋ Extra Support
Read Aloud

If...children have difficulty recalling details from the story, **then...**point out clues in the illustrations to prompt their recall.

★ Enrichment
Read Aloud

Encourage children to work with a classmate to act out the story. Challenge them to use story vocabulary such as *cozy, hamster,* and *friend.*

Accommodations for 3's
Learn About Letters and Sounds

If...three-year-olds have difficulty identifying long and short *Aa* sounds, **then...**say: *The letter A sometimes says its own name.* Esta letra A a veces tiene el sonido de su nombre. Have them repeat: /ā/ -corn, *acorn;* /ā/ /p/, ape. Then say: *Sometimes A makes the /a/ sound.* Y a veces tiene el sonido /a/. Digan estas palabras conmigo. **Say with me:** /a/ /m/, am, /a/ -nt, ant.

Max and Mo's First Day at School
Max y Mo van a la escuela

ABC Big Book

Math Time

large group · 15 minutes

Observe and Investigate

✓ **Can children count items one at a time?**

Demonstrate Counting

- Hide five counters in your hand. Ask children to count aloud with you to find out how many.

- Remove one counter and place it where children can see and focus on it.

- Repeat until you have counted and displayed all five counters. Then show your empty hand.

- Ask: *How many counters are there in all? ¿Cuántas fichas hay en total?* If they reply *five,* agree and say: *Together, you counted five counters. Juntos, contaron cinco fichas.*

- Repeat with different numbers of counters, making sure children count aloud with you.

large group · 15 minutes

👫 Social and Emotional Development

Making Good Choices

✓ **Can children describe how to make new friends?**

Making Friends Display the *Making Good Choices Flip Chart,* page 7. Ask: *Who wants to make friends? ¿Quién quiere hacer amigos?* Review the scenario on the chart page.

- Ask: *What can the boy do to get to play with the other children? ¿Qué puede hacer el niño para hacerse amigo de otros niños?*

- Ask: *What can the other children do to help make sure the boy gets to play with them? ¿Qué pueden hacer los demás niños para que el niño acepte jugar con ellos?*

- Have children draw a picture showing themselves with a new friend from school.

ELL Be sure children understand that in the phrase *make friends,* the word *make* does not mean "to build or create." Explain that the children make friends when they play with someone they didn't know before.

Making Good Choices Flip Chart, page 7

Focus Question
What makes a good friend?
¿Cómo es un buen amigo?

Learning Goals

Social and Emotional Development
• Child demonstrates positive social behaviors, as modeled by the teacher.

Language and Communication
• Child demonstrates an understanding of oral language by responding appropriately.

Fine Arts
• Child expresses ideas, emotions, and moods through individual and collaborative dramatic play.

Vocabulary

friend	amigo	introduce	presentarse
meet	encontrar	name	nombre
pretend	simular		

Differentiated Instruction

 Extra Support
Oral Language and Vocabulary
If...children have difficulty introducing themselves to a partner, **then...**have them echo you as you dramatize meeting the new friend.

 Enrichment
Oral Language and Vocabulary
Challenge children to introduce their "new friend" to you by saying "This is my new friend. Her (or his) name is _____."

Accommodations for 3's
Oral Language and Vocabulary
If...three-year-olds have difficulty working with a partner to dramatize making a friend, **then...** ask them to introduce themselves to you.

Dramatic Play Time

Social and Emotional Development Model using appropriate and polite language to introduce yourself to someone.

Oral Language and Vocabulary

Can children use language appropriately to make an introduction?

Making Friends Say: *When I meet someone new, I introduce myself. I tell her my name. How do you introduce yourself when you meet someone new? What do you say or do?* Cuando conozco a alguien, me presento. Le digo mi nombre. ¿Cómo se presentan cuando conocen a alguien? ¿Qué hacen o qué dicen?

• If possible, arrange for someone the children don't know to come into the classroom. Have the visitor say: *Hello, I am (visitor's name). What is your name?* Hola, soy (su nombre). ¿Cuál es tu nombre?

• After child responds, the visitor should say an appropriate response, such as: *I am happy to meet you!* ¡Encantado de conocerte!

• Ask another child to introduce him or herself to the visitor.

Explore and Express

Can children dramatize meeting a new friend?

Making New Friends Say: *Let's pretend to make new friends.* Simulemos que hacemos nuevos amigos.

• Say: *First, use dress-up clothes to make yourself look different. Pretend to be someone else, such as a doctor, your mother, or a bus driver.* Primero, usen un disfraz para verse diferentes. Simulen ser otra persona, como su mamá, un doctor o su papá.

• Encourage students to introduce themselves to each other in character.

• Praise children's use of appropriate language and actions as they interact.

ELL Encourage students to introduce themselves in their first language for English speakers to learn.

• For additional suggestions on how to meet the needs of children at the Beginning, Intermediate, Advanced, and Advanced-High levels of English proficiency, see pages 184–187.

Center Time

Center Rotation Center Time includes teacher-guided activities and independent activities. Refer to the **Learning Centers** on pages 100–101 for independent activity ideas.

small group **30 minutes**

Refer to the **Learning Centers** on pages 100–101 for independent activity ideas.

Pretend and Learn Center

	Center Tip

✔ Observe children's ability to use appropriate language as they interact.

Materials toy telephones

Call a Friend Tell children they will be pretending to call a friend on the telephone. Say: *Remember to introduce yourself when you call. Be polite and say* good-bye *when you are done talking. Recuerden presentarse cuando llamen por teléfono. Sean educados y despídanse cuando terminen de hablar.*

- Distribute toy phones to pairs of children.

- Observe them as they pretend to call each other.

Center Tip

If...there are not enough toy telephones for all the children, **then...**have some children who are waiting their turn use other objects, such as blocks, as phones.

Purposeful Play

✔ Observe children interacting appropriately as they work and play together.

- Children choose an open center for free playtime.

- Suggest that children work together to have the Dog Puppets make friends by introducing themselves to each other.

Let's Say Good-Bye

large group **15 minutes**

Read Aloud Revisit "Helpful Friends"/"Amigos útiles" for your afternoon Read Aloud. Ask children to listen to find out how friends act.

Home Connection Refer to the Home Connections activities listed in the Resources and Materials chart on page 97. Remind children to practice introducing themselves to a family member. Sing the "Good-Bye Song" as children prepare to leave.

Refer to the Home Connections activities listed in the Resources and Materials chart on page 97.

✔ **Learning Goals**

Language and Communication
- Child demonstrates an understanding of oral language by responding appropriately.

Emergent Literacy: Writing
- Child uses scribbles, shapes, pictures, symbols, and letters to represent language.
- Child writes some letters or reasonable approximation of letters upon request.

Fine Arts
- Child expresses ideas, emotions, and moods through individual and collaborative dramatic play.

Writing

Have children draw pictures of themselves. Add the sentence frame: *Hello, my name is* _____. Ask children to finish the sentence by writing their name. Send the pages home for students to share with their families.

Week 4

Focus Question

How can we play and learn together?

¿Cómo jugamos y aprendemos juntos?

This week children talk about the ways people are different and the things we have in common. They will match shapes to make a picture, pretend to play in a marching band, and use a hand lens to look at things up close. Together, they will make a class book about things they like to learn in school.

Social and Emotional Development	DAY 1	2	3	4	5
Child is aware of self in terms of abilities, characteristics and preferences, and respects personal boundaries.	✓				✓
Child begins to show a greater ability to control intense feelings.		✓	✓	✓	
Child begins to be responsible for individual behavior and actions.	✓		✓	✓	
Child recognizes and manages feelings and impulses; increasingly maintains self-control in difficult situations (can increase or decrease intensity of emotions with guidance).			✓		
Child shows eagerness, curiosity, and confidence while learning new concepts and trying new things.		✓	✓	✓	✓
Child demonstrates positive social behaviors, as modeled by the teacher.	✓				✓
Child initiates play scenarios with peers that share a common plan and goal.	✓		✓		
Child learns how to make and keep friends.		✓	✓		
Child understands and respects the different ideas, feelings, perspectives, and behaviors of others.	✓	✓	✓	✓	✓

Language and Communication	DAY 1	2	3	4	5
Child demonstrates an understanding of oral language by responding appropriately.	✓			✓	
Child names and describes actual or pictured people, places, things, actions, attributes, and events.	✓		✓	✓	✓
Child uses newly learned vocabulary daily in multiple contexts.	✓	✓	✓	✓	
Child speaks in complete sentences of four or more words including a subject, verb, and object.		✓	✓		

Emergent Literacy: Reading	DAY 1	2	3	4	5
Child independently engages in pre-reading behaviors and activities (such as, pretending to read, turning one page at a time).			✓		
Child listens for words (for example, hears and separates individual words within a four-word sentence).	✓	✓	✓	✓	✓
Child names most upper- and lowercase letters of the alphabet.	✓	✓	✓	✓	✓
Child identifies the letter that stands for a given sound.	✓	✓	✓	✓	✓
Child produces the most common sound for a given letter.		✓			
Child describes, relates to, and uses details and information from books read aloud.		✓	✓	✓	✓
Child asks and answers questions about books read aloud (such as, "Who?" "What?" "Where?").		✓		✓	✓

Emergent Literacy: Writing	DAY 1	2	3	4	5
Child writes own name or a reasonable approximation of it.	✓				
Child writes some letters or reasonable approximations of letters upon request.		✓		✓	
Child experiments with and uses some writing conventions when writing or dictating.	✓	✓	✓	✓	✓

Mathematics	DAY 1	2	3	4	5
Child counts 1–10 concrete objects correctly.					✓
Child recognizes, names, describes, matches, compares, sorts common two-dimensional shapes (such as circle, square, rectangle, triangle, rhombus).	✓	✓	✓	✓	✓
Child creates two-dimensional shapes; recreates two-dimensional shapes from memory.		✓		✓	

Science	DAY 1	2	3	4	5
Child uses senses to observe, classify, investigate, and collect data.	✓				✓

Social Studies	DAY 1	2	3	4	5
Child identifies similarities and differences among people.			✓		
Child respects/appreciates the differing interests, skills, abilities, cultures, languages, and family structures of people.			✓		

Fine Arts	DAY 1	2	3	4	5
Child uses and experiments with a variety of art materials and tools in various art activities.					✓
Child expresses emotions or ideas through art.			✓	✓	✓
Child participates in a variety of music activities (such as listening, singing, finger plays, musical games, performances).	✓			✓	

Physical Development	DAY 1	2	3	4	5
Child engages in a sequence of movements to perform a task.					✓
Child develops small-muscle strength and control.		✓			✓
Child completes tasks that require eye-hand coordination and control.			✓		✓

Materials and Resources

DAY 1	DAY 2	DAY 3	DAY 4	DAY 5
Program Materials				
• Teacher's Treasure Book • Oral Language Development Card 7 • Rhymes and Chants Flip Chart • Online Building Blocks Math Activities • *Amelia's Show-and-Tell Fiesta* Big Book • ABC Big Book • Shape Sets • Making Good Choices Flip Chart • Jumbo Hand Lenses • Math and Science Flip Chart • Sequence Cards: "Seed to Flower" • Home Connections Resource Guide	• Teacher's Treasure Book • *Amelia's Show-and-Tell Fiesta* Big Book • Dog Puppets 1 and 2 • ABC Big Book • Online Building Blocks Math Activities • Making Good Choices Flip Chart • Shape Sets • Math and Science Flip Chart • Home Connections Resource Guide	• Teacher's Treasure Book • Oral Language Development Card 8 • Rhymes and Chants Flip Chart • Concept Big Book 1 • ABC Picture Cards • Shape Sets • Making Good Choices Flip Chart • Dog Puppets 1 and 2 • Home Connections Resource Guide	• Teacher's Treasure Book • Dog Puppets 1 and 2 • Flannel Board Characters for "The Gingerbread Man" • Alphabet Wall Cards • Shape Sets • Home Connections Resource Guide	• Teacher's Treasure Book • Rhymes and Chants Flip Chart • *Amelia's Show-and-Tell Fiesta* Big Book • ABC Picture Cards • Making Good Choices Flip Chart • Home Connections Resource Guide
Other Materials				
• musical instruments • construction paper (6" circles of skin-tone colors) • crayons • plastic mirror • photographs of things in nature • objects from nature (pine cones, acorns, and so on) • cloth texture squares	• blocks • hula hoop • sentence strips • word cards; blank cards	• books about children playing and learning outside the classroom • square sheets of drawing paper • crayons • construction paper • magazines • books about people of different cultures • dress-up clothes • yarn (brown, yellow, red, black) • photos of people and things from different cultures	• photo chart of actions from "Wheels on the Bus" • recording of "Wheels on the Bus" and audio player • magazines • scissors • glue or paste • large construction paper • cylindrical aluminum cans	• gingerbread man outlines • scissors • crayons • buttons • glue • building blocks, sample block tower • drawing paper
Home Connection				
Remind children to show their families how to use a hand lens to observe things more closely. Send home the following materials. Weekly Family Letter, Home Connections Resource Guide, pp. 19–20	Encourage children to show their families different things at home that are shaped like circles.	Invite children to talk with their families about things they learn when they explore outside.	Tell children to retell the story of the *Gingerbread Man* to their families. Storybook 3, Home Connections Resource Guide, pp. 89–92	Encourage children to teach their families how to play "Run, Run, As Fast As You Can!"

Assessment

As you observe children throughout the week, you may fill out an Anecdotal Observational Record Form to document an individual's progress toward a goal or signs indicating the need for developmental or medical evaluation. You may also choose to select work for each child's portfolio. The Anecdotal Observational Record Form and Weekly Assessment rubrics are available In the assessment section of DLMExpressOnline.com.

More Literature Suggestions

- **Mouse Shapes** by Ellen Stoll Walsh
- **Brown Rabbit's Shape Book** by Alan Baker
- **Splat the Cat** by Rob Scotton
- **Chicka Chicka Boom Boom** by Bill Martin Jr. and John Archambault
- **Perro y gato** por Ricardo Alcántara
- **Hasta el ratón y el gato pueden tener un buen trato** por Silvia Molina

Week 4

Daily Planner

		DAY 1	**DAY 2**
Let's Start the Day Language Time	large group	Opening Routines p. 140 Morning Read Aloud p. 140 Oral Language and Vocabulary p. 140 Playing with Friends Phonological Awareness p. 140 Concept of Word	Opening Routines p. 146 Morning Read Aloud p. 146 Oral Language and Vocabulary p. 146 Amelia's Classroom Phonological Awareness p. 146 Concept of Word
Center Time	small group	Focus on: Pretend and Play Center p. 141 Creativity Center p. 141	Focus on: Construction Center p. 147 Library and Listening Center p. 147
Circle Time Literacy Time	large group	Read Aloud *Amelia's Show-and-Tell Fiesta/Amelia y la fiesta de "muestra y cuenta"* p. 142 Learn About Letters and Sounds: Learn About the Letters *Dd* and *Mm* p. 142	Read Aloud *Amelia's Show-and-Tell Fiesta/Amelia y la fiesta de "muestra y cuenta"* p. 148 Learn About Letters and Sounds: Review the Letters *Mm, Dd, Ss, and Aa* p. 148
Math Time	large group	Match Blocks p. 143	Circle Time! p. 149
Social and Emotional Development	large group	Making Friends p. 143	Making New Friends p. 149
Content Connection	large group	Science: Oral Language and Academic Vocabulary p. 144 Observing Nature Observe and Investigate p. 144 Observing Nature	Math: Match and Name Shapes p. 150
Center Time	small group	Focus on: Math and Science Center p. 145 Purposeful Play p. 145	Focus on: Math and Science Center p. 151 Purposeful Play p. 151
Let's Say Good-Bye	large group	Read Aloud p. 145 Writing p. 145 Home Connection p. 145	Read Aloud p. 151 Writing p. 151 Home Connection p. 151

DAY 3

Opening Routines p. 152
Morning Read Aloud p. 152
Oral Language and Vocabulary
p. 152 Outside the Classroom
Phonological Awareness
p. 152 Concept of Word

Focus on:
Library and Listening Center p. 153
Writer's Center p. 153

Read Aloud
Welcome to School/
Bienvenidos a la
escuela p. 154
Learn About Letters
and Sounds:
Name and Write
Letters p. 154

Match and Name Shapes p. 155

A Helpful Classmate
p. 155

Social Studies:
Oral Language and Academic Vocabulary
p. 156 Different People
Understand and Participate p. 156
Different Interests

Focus on:
Pretend and Learn Center p. 157
Purposeful Play p. 157

Read Aloud p. 157
Writing p. 157
Home Connection p. 157

DAY 4

Opening Routines p. 158
Morning Read Aloud p. 158
Oral Language and Vocabulary
p. 158 Let's Make-Believe
Phonological Awareness
p. 158 Listen and Clap

Focus on:
Library and Listening Center p. 159
ABC Center p. 159

Read Aloud
"The Gingerbread Man"/
"El hombrecito de jengibre"
p. 160
Learn About Letters and
Sounds: Alphabet Match p. 160

Match Blocks p. 161

Classroom Rules p. 161

Math:
Circles and Cans p. 162

Focus on:
Math and Science Center p. 163
Purposeful Play p. 163

Read Aloud p. 163
Writing p. 163
Home Connection p. 163

DAY 5

Opening Routines p. 164
Morning Read Aloud p. 164
Oral Language and Vocabulary
p. 164 Work and Play
Phonological Awareness
p. 164 Concept of Word

Focus on:
Construction Center p. 165
Creativity Center p. 165

Read Aloud
Amelia's Show-and-Tell
Fiesta/Amelia y la fiesta de
"muestra y cuenta" p. 166
Learn About Letters
and Sounds:
Sounds of *Aa, Dd,*
Mm, and Ss p. 166

Circle or Not? p. 167

Making Friends p. 167

Outside Play Time:
Oral Language and Vocabulary
p. 168 Inside or Outside
Move and Learn p. 168 Run, Run!

Focus on:
Writer's Center p. 169
Purposeful Play p. 169

Read Aloud p. 169
Writing p. 169
Home Connection p. 169

Learning Centers

Math and Science Center

Looking Closely
Children look at objects up close, p. 145.

Explore Shape Sets
Children match shapes to make a picture, p. 151.

Tracing Shapes
Children trace shapes and identify them, p. 163.

Count the Shape
Place in separate paper bags 1–10 round buttons, Connecting Cubes, and triangular pattern blocks. Pairs choose a bag, empty out the shapes, name the shape, and count how many.

Look and Observe
Children use a hand lens to look at two flower petals or leaves. Then they draw a picture to record their observations.

Count and Connect
Children collect cubes of one color from a pile. They count their cubes as they connect them.

ABC Center

Letter Sounds
Children find pictures that begin with certain letter sounds, p. 159.

Letter People
Children build Letter People. Hold up a letter card and have children determine how many people they need to build the letter. Allow children to lie on chart paper to build letters.

Circle *Aa*, *Ss*, *Dd*, or *Mm*
Provide copies of pages from children's books. Children work in pairs. One circles capital letters, and a partner circles lowercase letters *Aa, Ss, Dd* or *Mm*.

Alphabet Books
Children create Alphabet Books pages *Mm* and *Dd*. Supply folded paper. Label one page *Mm* and another *Dd*. Children draw something that begins with each letter.

Creativity Center

Make a Happy Face
Children make face masks, p. 141.

Make a Gingerbread Man
Children make gingerbread man figures, p. 165.

Mixed-Up Socks
Partners make unmatched sock pairs using various art supplies. Pairs choose a pair of paper cut-out socks. One child decorates the right; the partner decorates the left. Hang the mismatched socks together.

Special Day
Children use art supplies to make a picture of a special day their family celebrates. Encourage children to show clothing, food, colors, and transportation associated with that day.

Matching Mittens
Partners make identical mitten pairs using various art supplies. Pairs choose a pair of paper cut-out mittens. One child decorates the right; the partner decorates the left. Hang the matching mittens together.

Library and Listening Center

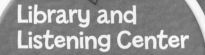

Word Puzzle
Children put together a word puzzle, p. 147.

Outside the Classroom
Pairs talk about pictures of things outside the classroom, p. 153.

Get on the Bus!
Children listen to a popular song about a bus, p. 159.

Observe Closely
Children browse nonfiction nature books and discuss what they know about the images. Then they use a hand lens to look at the images closely to gain more information about the objects in the photos.

Celebrations
Have children browse books that have images of celebrations. Encourage them to listen to other children tell about their special celebrations.

Construction Center

Build with Blocks
Pairs build towers from blocks, p. 147.

Building Directions
Children follow directions to make a building, p. 165.

Shape Structures
Pairs choose a block shape (or pattern blocks) and use only that shape to build a structure. Extend the activity by allowing each child to choose a different shape.

Height Towers
Children work in pairs to build side-by-side towers that equal their height.

Sentence Tower
Hang simple four-word sentences in the block area. Tape individual words on blocks. Children build the sentences by following the word sentences and placing blocks one by one. They place sentences on top of one another.

Writer's Center

Make a Book
Children make a class book about things they like to do, p. 153.

Class Book
Children make a book about outside activities, p. 169.

Special Things
Children draw a picture of something special in their family. Have them dictate and write to label the item. Allow children to talk about their special things.

What We Like
Children draw a picture of something a friend likes to do. Then they draw a picture of something they like to do. Help them fill in the sentence frame, *Anna likes to _____. I like to _____.*

Name Trace
Write children's full names on index cards. Tape a sheet of tracing paper on the card. Children trace the letters in their name.

Pretend and Learn Center

Marching Band
Children pretend to march in a band, p. 141.

Time to Explore!
Children pretend to be someone in a picture, p. 157.

Caring for Friends
Children act out scenarios that show them helping or caring for a friend. Groups work together to create the scenario.

Fiesta Time
Children dress up and pretend to be at a fiesta. Encourage children to look at pictures of fiestas before acting out their celebration.

Explore Together
Children pretend to be detectives. Have them use simple tools to go on an investigation around the classroom.

Let's Start the Day

Focus Question

How can we play and learn together?

¿Cómo jugamos y aprendemos juntos?

Learning Goals

Social and Emotional Development
• Child initiates play scenarios with peers that share a common plan and goal.

Language and Communication
• Child names and describes actual or pictured people, places, things, actions, attributes, and events.

Emergent Literacy: Reading
• Child listens for words (for example, hears and separates individual words within a four-word sentence).

Vocabulary

drum	tambor
instrument	instrumento
musical	musical
playing	tocar
sound	sonido

Differentiated Instruction

Extra Support

Oral Language and Vocabulary
If...children don't understand how a pictured instrument is played, **then...**say: *This is how you play a [instrument]. Play the [instrument] with me. Así se toca el/la _____. Toquen el/la _____ conmigo.* Have children pantomime as you pretend to play the instrument.

Enrichment

Phonological Awareness
Challenge children to listen to the CD and clap to isolate the individual words in a four-word phrase from the *Rhymes and Chants Flip Chart*.

▶ **Opening Routines and Transition Tips**
For **Opening Routines** and **Transition Tips** turn to pages 178–181 and visit **DLMExpressOnline.com** for more ideas.

📖 Read **"Five Little Monkeys"**/**"Cinco monitos"** from the *Teacher's Treasure Book*, page 80, for your morning Read Aloud.

large group | 15 minutes

Language Time

 Social and Emotional Development Encourage children to initiate play and learning activities with their friends.

Oral Language and Vocabulary

✓ **Can children use words that describe playing and learning together?**

Playing with Friends Talk about different kinds of play that you can do at school. Ask: *Do you like to play with friends or classmates? What do you like to play together? Do you ever play musical instruments with your friends? ¿Les gusta jugar con amigos? ¿A qué les gusta jugar juntos? ¿Alguna vez tocaron instrumentos musicales con sus amigos?*

● Display *Oral Language Development Card 7*. Ask: *Where are these children? What are they doing? ¿Dónde están estos niños? ¿Qué están haciendo?* Then follow the suggestions on the back of the card.

ELL Use the *Oral Language Development Card* to review and extend children's vocabulary. For example, point to the girl and ask: *Is this a girl or a boy? What instrument is she playing?*

Oral Language Development Card 7

Phonological Awareness

✓ **Can children isolate words within a sentence?**

Concept of Word Display the *Rhymes and Chants Flip Chart*, page 8. Say: *Let's sing a song about circle time. Listen for the word* circle. *Cantemos esta canción sobre sentarse en un círculo. Presten atención para escuchar la palabra círculo.* Sing "Circle Time" and raise your hand each time you sing the word *circle*. Have children join in as you sing it again. Then sing the first line of the song, clapping as you sing to isolate each word. Have children clap with you to isolate words in other sentences.

Rhymes and Chants Flip Chart, page 8

Center Time

Center Rotation Center Time includes teacher-guided activities and independent activities. Refer to the **Learning Centers** on pages 138–139 for independent activity ideas.

small group 60–90 minutes

Pretend and Learn Center | Center Tip

 Track children's willingness to participate in musical activities with others.

Materials musical instruments

Marching Band Tell children to pretend to be in a marching band. Say: *Pick an instrument to play in your pretend band.* *Elijan un instrumento para tocar en la banda imaginaria.*

- Have children form a circle, holding their instruments. Model how to march in place without hitting other people. Then say: *March!* *¡A marchar!* Have children march in a circle while playing the instruments.

- Have children exchange instruments and march again.

Center Tip

If...children have difficulty playing an instrument, **then**...demonstrate how to make sound with that instrument.

Creativity Center | Center Tip

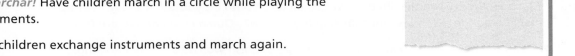

Can children work together and use words to label and describe their masks?

Can children write letters in their own name?

Materials 6-inch construction-paper circles in a variety of skin-tone colors, crayons, plastic mirror

Make a Happy Face Display the *Rhymes and Chants Flip Chart*, page 8. Sing the song "Circle Time." Say: *The classroom is full of happy faces while the children are learning.* *La ilustración muestra las caras felices de los niños que aprenden las letras.* Model a happy face and then have children make happy face masks. Allow children to look at their face in a mirror.

- Have children choose a circle and draw their smiling face on it.

- Ask them to write their names on the back of their circles. Encourage all levels of writing.

Center Tip

If...children have difficulty writing letters in their name, **then**...write their name on a piece of paper and help them trace a letter before writing it independently.

Learning Goals

Social and Emotional Development
- Child is aware of self in terms of abilities, characteristics and preferences, and respects personal boundaries.

Emergent Literacy: Writing
- Child writes own name or a reasonable approximation of it.

Fine Arts
- Child participates in a variety of music activities (such as listening, singing, finger plays, musical games, performances).

Differentiated Instruction

Extra Support
Pretend and Play Center
If...children have difficulty sharing instruments, **then**...set a timer and have them exchange instruments when it rings.

Enrichment
Pretend and Play Center
Challenge children to work with a partner to copy a rhythm. One child should beat a drum or toot on a horn, and then the other child should copy the rhythm. Have children switch roles as leader and follower.

 Focus Question

How can we play and learn together?
¿Cómo jugamos y aprendemos juntos?

 Learning Goals

Language and Communication
• Child demonstrates an understanding of oral language by responding appropriately.
• Child uses newly learned vocabulary daily in multiple contexts.

Vocabulary

fiesta	fiesta
red	rojo
show-and-tell	muestra y cuenta
skirt	vestido
white	blanco
yellow	amarillo

Differentiated Instruction

 Extra Support

Read Aloud

If...children seem confused about how Ameiia's skirt is described, **then...**help them understand that the pictures of the peppers, corn, and birds show the colors in Amelia's skirt.

Enrichment

Read Aloud

Challenge children to use the illustrations to retell the story to a friend.

Accommodations for 3's
Read Aloud

If...children have difficulty focusing for the entire book in one sitting, **then...**break the reading into shorter segments.

Literacy Time

  large group / 15 minutes

📖 Read Aloud

✓ Can children demonstrate understanding of the story by responding appropriately?

✓ Can children use prior knowledge to enhance their understanding of the read-aloud?

Build Background Tell children that you will be reading a book about a girl who wears a special skirt to show-and-tell Ask: *Do you have any special clothes you like to wear? ¿Tienen un objeto o una vestimenta que les resulte especial y que les gustaría compartir con sus amigos?* Describe what show-and-tell means to the children.

Listen for Enjoyment Display *Amelia's Show-and-Tell Fiesta*, and read the title. Point to Amelia and say: *This is Amelia. Ella es Amelia.* Say: **Fiesta** *is the Spanish word for* **party.** *Fiesta y party significan lo mismo.*

● Turn to the first page. Draw on children's prior knowledge by asking questions such as: **Where are the children in this picture? Who do you think the grown-up is?** *¿En dónde están los niños de esta ilustración? ¿Quién creen que es adulto?*

● Read the book aloud. Pause when you read Spanish words to clarify meaning. Use pictures to help children understand. Say: *This book has many words in a language called Spanish. Amelia speaks Spanish at home. Este libro tiene muchas palabras en español. Amelia habla español en su casa.*

Respond to the Story Discuss the story. Review the illustrations and talk about what Amelia is doing.

 ELL Invite Spanish-speaking children to help define and explain familiar words in Spanish.

 TIP Check children's understanding by having them point to Ameila's skirt in different illustrations in the book.

Learn About Letters and Sounds

✓ Can children compare the letters *Dd* and *Mm*?

Learn About the Letters Dd and Mm Display the *Dd* page in the *ABC Big Book*. Say the letter name.

● Point to the dog. Say: *This is a dog. What sound do you hear at the beginning of the word* dog? *What letter makes the /d/ sound? Éste es un dog ¿Con qué sonido empieza dog? ¿A qué letra corresponde?* Then review the formation strokes and have children trace the letter in the air.

● Repeat with the *Mm* page, pointing to the moon to review the sound of the letter.

● Ask: *How are upper case and lower case* Dd (Mm) *the same or different? ¿En qué se parecen las letras M (D) mayúscula y m (d) minúscula? ¿En qué se diferencian?*

Amelia's Show-and-Tell Fiesta
Amelia y la fiesta de "muestra y cuenta"

ABC Big Book

Building Blocks

Online Math Activity

Introduce Mystery Pictures 1: Match Shapes (online activity). In this activity, children match shapes to outlines in order to construct a mystery picture.

large group 15 minutes

Making Good Choices Flip Chart, page 8

Math Time

Observe and Investigate

✓ **Can children recognize common shapes?**

Match Blocks Have children match various block shapes to objects in the classroom. Tell children that you can see many shapes in the objects around you.

- Place different block shapes in front of you; children sit in a circle around you.

- Show one face of a block. Say: *Look at this block. Now look around the classroom. Can you find another object that is the same shape?* *Observen este bloque. Ahora, miren en el salón de clases. ¿Pueden encontrar otro objeto con la misma forma?*

- Repeat with each block shape. Accept all reasonable answers, including items that are not in the room but are the correct shape.

ELL Provide support by naming the shape for children. Describe the shape for children, asking how many sides it has and what other characteristics can be used to identify it.

✟✟✟ Social and Emotional Development

Making Good Choices

✓ **Do children understand that people might react differently to a situation?**

✓ **Do children show positive behavior toward the situation?**

Making Friends Ask children to tell about things they do at preschool. Display the *Making Good Choices Flip Chart*, page 8.

- Say: *What are these children doing at preschool?* *¿Qué están haciendo estos niños en la escuela?* Ask: *What happened to the girl's puzzle? How do you think this happened? How might she feel? Has anything like this ever happened to you? What happened?* *¿Qué pasó con el rompecabezas de la niña? ¿Cómo piensan que ocurrió esto? ¿Cómo creen que se siente? ¿Alguna vez les sucedió algo parecido?*

- Discuss how the teacher is helping the girl. Ask: *How could the boy help the girl?* *¿Cómo puede el niño ayudar a la niña?* Point to the boys with the bean bag. Ask: *What could these children do?* *¿Qué pueden hacer estos niños para que la niña se sienta mejor?*

ELL Use the chart illustration to enhance children's vocabulary. Encourage children to use facial expressions to demonstrate the emotions the children illustrated might be feeling.

Learning Goals

Social and Emotional Development
• Child demonstrates positive social behaviors, as modeled by the teacher.

Language and Communication
• Child names and describes actual or pictured people, places, things, actions, attributes, and events.

Science
• Child uses senses to observe, classify, investigate, and collect data.

Vocabulary

collect	juntar	compare	comparar
hand lens	lupa	observe	observar
predict	predecir	tool	herramienta

Differentiated Instruction

 Extra Support

Observe and Investigate
If...children have trouble focusing the hand lens, **then...**show them how to place the hand lens close to the object and pull the lens away slowly until it focuses the object.

 Enrichment

Observe and Investigate
Invite pairs to predict what might happen if they plant the acorns. Have children draw a picture of what might happen.

 Special Needs

Vision Loss
Another way to explore items from nature is to listen to nature sounds, Nature sounds, especially soft ones (rain, birds singing, and so on), have the added benefit of being very calming.

Science Time

Social Emotional Skills Model positive social behaviors by displaying a warm, welcoming attitude toward each child, especially those who seem isolated.

Oral Language and Academic Vocabulary

 Can children work together with a classmate?

Observing Nature Point to the children using a hand lens in the *Math and Science Flip Chart*, page 11. Say: *These children are using a tool to learn about something in nature.* *Estos niños están usando una herramienta para aprender algo sobre la naturaleza.*

● Explain that the hand lens helps them see things clearly. Say: *A hand lens can make something look bigger than it really is. How will that help you observe something better?* *Una lupa sirve para ver las cosas más grandes de lo que realmente son. ¿Creen que eso puede ayudarlos a observar mejor algo? ¿Por qué?* Tell children that you can collect things so you can compare them in the classroom. Observe students to make sure they do not pick up organisms or plants not discussed in class. Be mindful of safety issues, such as allergies and insect bites.

● Ask: *How can the children work together with tools to learn about things in nature?* *¿De qué modo los niños pueden usar herramientas para aprender más sobre la naturaleza?* Discussion should include taking turns.

ELL Help children understand the meaning of *bigger*. Draw a flower. Then draw a bigger one next to it. Say: *This flower is bigger.* Ask children to repeat.

Observe and Investigate

Can children work together to discover something new about items from nature?

Observing Nature Have children work in groups. Display pictures of things from nature. Provide each group with items from nature, such as pea pods, pine cones, acorns, and so on. Also provide a Jumbo Hand Lens. Discuss how you can discover new things by observing and working together. Say: *A hand lens can help you see things more closely so you can learn about them.* *Una lupa puede ayudarlos a ver las cosas más de cerca y a aprender sobre ellas.*

● Tell children to work together to look at the things from nature.

● Encourage pairs to describe what they see with the hand lens as they look at the items.

● Use the Sequence Cards set "Seeds to Flower" to illustrate how items from nature can change.

Math and Science Flip Chart, page 11

Center Time

Center Rotation Center Time includes teacher-guided activities and independent activities. Refer to the **Learning Centers** on pages 138–139 for independent activity ideas.

small group 30 minutes

Math and Science Center

✓ **Can children work together to observe and describe objects?**

✓ **Can children make a prediction based on an observation of objects?**

Materials Jumbo Hand Lenses, cloth texture squares, items from nature

Looking Closely Tell children they will be using a hand lens to continue their observation of the things from nature, along with some new items.

- Encourage pairs to look at the details of two like items, such as an acorn and a seed pod or two types of cloth. Ask: *Is this acorn smooth? Do you think the seed is smooth, too? Observe both items closely. ¿Es suave esta bellota? ¿Creen que la semilla es suave también? Observen ambos elementos con atención.* Talk about whether or not they can see or feel the differences.

- Have children draw a picture of one of the items they observed.

Center Tip

If...children have trouble making a prediction, **then...**ask questions to guide them, such as: *Do the acorn and the seed look like their shells are smooth? ¿Parecen suaves las cáscaras de la bellota y de la semilla?*

Learning Goals

Emergent Literacy: Writing
- Child experiments with and uses some writing conventions when writing or dictating.

Science
- Child uses senses to observe, classify, investigate, and collect data.

Writing

Write this sentence frame on chart paper: *Today I _____.* Encourage children to complete the sentence by recalling things they did during the day. Write their responses. Then read their sentences back, pointing to each word as you read. Display the finished work in the classroom.

Purposeful Play

✓ **Observe children's positive interactions as they work together in centers.**

Children choose an open center for free playtime. Encourage interaction by suggesting that children choose a friend or classmate to work with.

Let's Say Good-Bye

large group 15 minutes

 Read Aloud Revisit "Five Little Monkeys"/"Cinco monitos" for your afternoon Read Aloud. After reading, ask children to retell it in their own words.

 Home Connection Refer to the Home Connections activities listed in the Resources and Materials chart on page 135. Remind children to tell a family member about using a hand lens. Sing the "Good-Bye Song"/"Hora de ir a casa" as children prepare to leave.

Let's Start the Day

Focus Question

How can we play and learn together?

¿Cómo jugamos y aprendemos juntos?

Learning Goals

Language and Communication
• Child uses newly learned vocabulary daily in multiple contexts.
• Child speaks in complete sentences of four or more words including a subject, verb, and object.

Emergent Literacy: Reading
• Child listens for words (for example, hears and separates individual words within a four-word sentence).
• Child asks and answers questions about books read aloud (such as, "Who?" "What?" "Where?").

Vocabulary

classroom	escuela	dance	bailar
draw	dibujar	like	gusta
question	pregunta		

Differentiated Instruction

 Extra Support

Oral Language and Vocabulary
If...children answer questions with a single word or phrase, **then...**offer sentence frames to help them answer in complete sentences, such as: **Amelia likes to _____.** Then have the child repeat the whole sentence.

⭐ **Enrichment**

Oral Language and Vocabulary
Challenge children to think of other verbs. Have them draw a picture that shows the action.

▶ **Opening Routines and Transition Tips**

For **Opening Routines** and **Transition Tips** turn to pages 178–181 and visit **DLMExpressOnline.com** for more ideas.

📖 Read **"The Lion and the Mouse"/"El león y el ratón agradecido"** from the *Teacher's Treasure Book,* page 171, for your morning Read Aloud.

large group · 15 minutes

Language Time

👤👤👤 **Social and Emotional Development** Encourage children to demonstrate positive behavior while playing with a friend or classmate.

Oral Language and Vocabulary

✓ **Can children ask and answer questions about a story?**

✓ **Are children using new vocabulary?**

Amelia's Classroom Display *Amelia's Show-and-Tell Fiesta/Amelia y la fiesta de "muestra y cuenta".* Talk about things children do at school. Ask: **What do you like to do at school?** *¿Qué les gusta hacer en la escuela?* Help children compare Amelia's classroom to their own. Turn to the page where children are sitting at desks in the classroom. Model using a complete sentence to answer a question about the story. Ask: **What do children do at school?** *¿Qué hacen los niños?* Then say: **Some children are drawing.** *Los niños están dibujando.* Ask: **What do you like to draw?** *¿Qué es gusta dibujar?*

Amelia's Show-and-Tell Fiesta
Amelia y la fiesta de "muestra y cuenta"

● Take a picture walk to review the book. Pause to ask questions about what Amelia is doing and thinking. For example, ask: **Does Amelia like to dance? What do the children bring to show-and-tell?** *¿Le gusta bailar a Amelia? ¿Qué llevan los niños a la escuela el día de muestra y cuenta?*

● Guide children to answer each question with a full sentence, such as *Amelia likes to dance.* Encourage them to ask questions of their own.

ELL Use the illustrations in the book to extend children's vocabulary. Display a page and point to a classroom object such as *desk* or *pencil* while you say the word. Have children repeat the word and point to the object.

Phonological Awareness

✓ **Can children isolate words in a sentence?**

Concept of Word Display a Dog Puppet. Say: **I will have the Dog Puppet say a sentence. Stand up when the dog says the word** eats. **Clap when dog says the word** food. *Pónganse de pie cuando el perro diga la palabra come. Y den una palmada cuando escuchen la palabra comida.* As the puppet, say: **A dog eats food.** *El perro come su comida.* Enunciate each word clearly. Invite children to repeat the sentence with you.

Center Time

► **Center Rotation** Center Time includes teacher-guided activities and independent activities. Refer to the **Learning Centers** on pages 138–139 for independent activity ideas.

 small group 60–90 minutes

Construction Center

| **Center Tip** |

✓ **Observe children's ability to stay with an activity until it is complete.**

Materials *Amelia's Show-and-Tell Fiesta*, blocks

Build with Blocks Find the pages in the story where Amelia's dress is illustrated with vegetables. Ask: ***Where do vegetables grow? Do you know what a garden looks like?*** *¿Donde crecen los vegetales? ¿Saben cómo se ve una huerta?*

- Have pairs work together to make a vegetable garden.

- Ask questions about how children have learned to work together. Encourage children to focus on the task at hand.

Center Tip

If...children have difficulty sharing the blocks, **then...**start them off by naming each child's turn at placing a block in the garden.

Library and Listening Center

| **Center Tip** |

✓ **Can children point out individual words in a sentence?**

Materials 4-word sentence strips, word cards, blank cards

Word Puzzle Write a 4-word sentence on a sentence strip. Make each word a different color. Make word cards with words in the corresponding colors. Tell children they will use word cards to create a full sentence.

- Read the sentence strip: ***The boy is reading.*** *Los niños leen libros.* Have children read along with you as you track each word.

- Ask: ***Can you put the sentence together?*** *¿Pueden poner todas las palabras juntas para formar una oración?*

- Have them look at one word at a time on the strip and find the matching card. Have them place each word below the word on the strip. Read the sentence together.

Center Tip

If...children have difficulty reading left to right, **then...**place a star at the beginning of the sentence.

Learning Goals

Social and Emotional Development
- Child shows eagerness, curiosity, and confidence while learning new concepts and trying new things.

Emergent Literacy: Reading
- Child listens for words (for example, hears and separates individual words within a four-word sentence).

Physical Development
- Child develops small-muscle strength and control.

Differentiated Instruction

 Extra Support
Construction Center
If...children have difficulty picturing a garden of blocks, **then...**use play food for the vegetables.

 Enrichment
Library and Listening Center
Challenge partners to cut apart a sentence strip into words and reassemble the strip in order.

 Special Needs
Cognitive Challenges
Make a statement that cues the child to what you are asking. For example, say: *I saw you building with blocks today. What did you build?* *Vi que hoy usaste bloques para construir. ¿Qué construiste?* Wait for a response before repeating the question, since the child may need extra time to process what you are asking.

Focus Question

How can we play and learn together?

¿Cómo jugamos y aprendemos juntos?

 Learning Goals

Emergent Literacy: Reading

• Child names most upper- and lowercase letters of the alphabet.

• Child identifies the letter that stands for a given sound.

• Child describes, relates to, and uses details and information from books read aloud.

• Child asks and answers questions about books read aloud (such as, "Who?" "What?" "Where?").

Vocabulary

fiesta	fiesta
red	rojo
show-and-tell	meustra y cuenta
skirt	vestido
white	blanco
yellow	amarillo

Differentiated Instruction

 Extra Support

Learn About Letters and Sounds

If...children have difficulty saying the /d/ sound, **then...**demonstrate the correct position of the tongue. Say the /d/ sound and words slowly and have children repeat: /d/, /d/, did; /d/, /d/, dad.

 Enrichment

Read Aloud

Encourage children to work with a classmate to act out an illustration from the story. Challenge them to use story vocabulary such as *red, show-and-tell, yellow, skirt,* and *fiesta.*

Literacy Time

large group   15 minutes

📖 Read Aloud

 Do children use prior knowledge to better understand the story?

Build Background Display *Amelia's Show-and-Tell Fiesta.* Tell children you will read a story about a girl who wears a special outfit to school.

● Ask: **What color is your favorite shirt? Do you have a favorite color?** *¿Qué cosas suceden en prekínder?*

Listen for Understanding Display Amelia's Show-and-Tell Fiesta, and read the title and the author.

● Review the story by browsing through the book. Identify the front and back covers. Then read the title.

● Read the book aloud, tracking the text as you read.

● Review the color words and the way the skirt is described in the story. Help children understand the imagery of the peppers, corn, and birds.

Respond to the Story Discuss the story. Draw on children's prior knowledge by asking questions that talk about colors, clothing, and school activities.

TIP As you browse the book, ask children to identify colors.

ELL Enhance children's vocabulary by explaining the meaning of words and phrases from the story, such as *rises before the rooster* for "wakes up early."

● For additional suggestions on how to meet the needs of children at the Beginning, Intermediate, Advanced, and Advanced-High levels of English proficiency, see pages 184–187.

Learn About Letters and Sounds

 Can children identify the sounds for the letters *Mm, Dd, Ss,* and *Aa*?

Review the Letters *Mm, Dd, Ss,* and *Aa* Display the *ABC Big Book* page for *Mm.* Review the letter name and how to form the letters.

● Point to the moon. Ask: **What is this? What sound do you hear at the beginning of the word** moon? *¿Qué es esto? ¿Cor qué sonido empieza la palabra* moon?

● Repeat for the *Dd, Ss,* and *Aa* pages.

Amelia's Show-and-Tell Fiesta

Amelia y la fiesta de "muestra y cuenta"

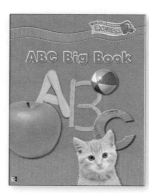

ABC Big Book

Online Math Activity

Introduce Mystery Pictures 1: Match Shapes (online activity). In this activity, children match shapes to outlines in order to construct a mystery picture.

Math Time

Observe and Investigate

 Can children identify circles?

Circle Time! Invite children to explore the circle shape. Tell children that a circle is a shape with no sides or corners. Its shape is round.

- Have children sit in a circle. Say: *Please sit in a circle. Make it the best circle you can! Siéntese en círculo. Formen el mejor círculo posible.*

- Show and name a large, flat circle, such as a hula hoop. As you trace the circle with your finger, discuss how it is round. Say: *See how the circle always curves the same, all around. Observen que el círculo es siempre redondo.*

- Ask children to think of circles they know. Ask: *Does your bicycle have a circle on it? Do any of your toys have circles? ¿Hay algún círculo en sus bicicletas? ¿Alguno de sus juguetes tiene la forma de un círculo?* If possible, distribute circular objects for children to explore by rolling, stacking, and tracing.

- Have children work with partners to make circles with their fingers and arms.

   ELL Point out how the word *circle* is closely related to its Spanish equivalent, *círculo.*

✗✗✗ Social and Emotional Development

Making Good Choices

 Do children offer help when someone is having a problem?

Making New Friends Discuss making new friends. Ask: *Do you have friends at school? How did you make those friends? ¿Tienen amigos en la escuela? ¿Cómo hacen nuevos amigos?* Display the *Making Good Choices Flip Chart,* page 8. Model using a Dog Puppet to review the chart.

- Say: *The girl is sad. Why is she sad? La niña está triste. ¿Por qué está triste?* Have the puppet answer: *She is sad because her puzzle was broken apart. Está triste porque se desarmó su rompecabezas.*

- Ask: *Do you think someone can help her feel better? ¿Crees que alguien puede ayudarla a sentirse mejor?* Have the puppet answer: *A classmate can help her feel better. Sometimes, when people show friendly behaviors to each other, they can begin to like each other and become friends. Un amigo puede ayudarla a sentirse mejor. A veces, cuando alguien se comporta de manera amigable con otra persona, pueden hacerse amigos.*

- Have children take turns using the puppet to role-play the situation.

Making Good Choices Flip Chart, page 8

Focus Question
How can we play and learn together?
¿Cómo jugamos y aprendemos juntos?

Learning Goals

Mathematics
• Child recognizes, names, describes, matches, compares, sorts common two-dimensional shapes (such as circle, square, rectangle, triangle, rhombus).

Vocabulary

color	color	match	igual
rhombus	rombo	trapezoid	trapecio
triangle	triángulo		

Differentiated Instruction

 Extra Support
Math Time
If...children are having difficulty naming the shapes, **then...**review the shape names, one at a time.

 Enrichment
Math Time
Challenge children to describe the shapes in detail, telling about their number of sides (or lack of sides) and other details.

Accommodations for 3's
Math Time
If...children have difficulty matching shapes, **then...**complete the activity as a whole group.

Math Time

Match and Name Shapes Using foam Shape Sets in two colors, play a game where children identify and match shapes. Explain that there are many kinds of shapes. Ask children what shapes they can name.

• Sit in a circle with children. Give each child a shape from one Shape Set.

• Choose a matching shape from the Shape Set of a different color. Say: **Who has a shape that matches my shape?** *¿Quién tiene una figura igual a la mía?*

• Then ask: **How do you know this shape is a match?** *¿Cómo sabes que esta figura es igual?* The child may offer to fit his or her shape on top of your shape to "prove" the match.

• Have children show their shape to a classmate, naming the shape if possible.

• Finally, direct children to the *Math and Science Flip Chart*, page 12. Ask children whether their shape matches a shape on the chart.

Math and Science Flip Chart, page 12

Center Time

Center Rotation Center Time includes teacher-guided activities and independent activities. Refer to the **Learning Centers** on pages 138–139 for independent activity ideas.

small group 30 minutes

Refer to the **Learning Centers** on pages 138–139 for independent activity ideas.

Math and Science Center

✓ **Encourage children to explore different Shape Sets.**

Materials Shape Sets

Explore Shape Sets Prepare two complete Shape Sets for children and observe what children do and say with the shapes as they freely work with them.

- Encourage children to match shapes from one set to the other.

- Say: *Can you match shapes together to make a picture? ¿Pueden colocar las figuras juntas para formar una imagen?*

- Children may also place shapes in order, from largest to smallest.

Center Tip

If...children have difficulty making a picture independently, **then...**encourage them to work together.

Purposeful Play

✓ **Observe children handling shapes.**

Children choose an open center for free playtime. Encourage children to explore the shapes by feeling around them with their fingers, and naming them.

Let's Say Good-Bye

large group 15 minutes

Read Aloud Revisit "The Lion and the Mouse"/"El león y el ratón agradecido" for your afternoon Read Aloud. Remind children to listen for the sounds /m/ and /d/.

Home Connection Refer to the Home Connections activities listed in the Resources and Materials chart on page 135. Encourage children to show their families different things at home that are shaped like circles. Sing the "Good-Bye Song" as children prepare to leave.

✓ Learning Goals

Emergent Literacy: Writing
- Child experiments with and uses some writing conventions when writing or dictating.

Mathematics
- Child recognizes, names, describes, matches, compares, sorts common two-dimensional shapes (such as circle, square, rectangle, triangle, rhombus).

- Child creates two-dimensional shapes; recreates two-dimensional shapes from memory.

Writing

Ask children to draw a picture of themselves helping a classmate. Have them write or dictate a sentence that tells about their picture. Children can use invented spelling or scribble writing for sounds they do not know. Compile the pages into a class book and place it in the classroom library.

DAY 3

Focus Question

How can we play and learn together?

¿Cómo jugamos y aprendemos juntos?

Learning Goals

Social and Emotional Development
• Child learns how to make and keep friends.

Language and Communication
• Child names and describes actual or pictured people, places, things, actions, attributes, and events.

• Child speaks in complete sentences of four or more words including a subject, verb, and object.

Vocabulary

animal	animal	caterpillar	oruga
explore	explorar	nature	árbol
outside	afuera	plants	plantas

Differentiated Instruction

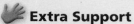 **Extra Support**

Oral Language and Vocabulary
If...children have difficulty using complete sentences when answering questions, **then**...restate the response in a complete sentence and have children echo the sentence.

 Enrichment

Phonological Awareness
Have children draw pictures to represent a word in the song. When they hear that word in the song, ask them to hold up the picture.

Let's Start the Day

 Opening Routines and Transition Tips
For **Opening Routines** and **Transition Tips** turn to pages 178–181 and visit DLMExpressOnline.com for more ideas.

Read **"Opposites"/"Los opuestos"** from the *Teacher's Treasure Book*, page 74, for your morning Read Aloud.

large group   15 minutes

Language Time

Social and Emotional Development Encourage children to get to know more of their classmates by working with children they may not have played with before.

Oral Language and Vocabulary

Can children use varied vocabulary to describe the world outside the classroom?

Outside the Classroom Talk about your school surroundings. Have children look out a window. Ask: *What do you see outside? Can you name something outside the school? ¿Qué ven afuera? ¿Pueden nombrar algo que esté afuera de la escuela?*

● Display *Oral Language Development Card 8*. Discuss what the children are doing. Ask: *Where are the children? What kinds of things do they see outside? ¿Dónde están los niños? ¿Qué clase de cosas pueden ver afuera?* Then review the suggestions on the back of the card.

Oral Language Development Card 8

ELL Use the *Oral Language Development Card* to reinforce children's vocabulary. Point to the grass. Ask: *What is this?* Accept answers in their first languages or in English. Reinforce the English word by repeating it again.

Phonological Awareness

Can children isolate words in a sentence?

Concept of Word Display the *Rhymes and Chants Flip Chart*, page 8. Say: *Listen as I sing "Circle Time." Escuchen mientras canto.* Have children sit in pairs. Assign each pair a word from the song. Then say: *This time, stand when we sing your word. Esta vez presten mucha atención a las palabras. Cuando escuchen la palabra nueva, pónganse de pie.* Then ask pairs to sing the sentence from the song that contains their word. They should stand when they sing their word.

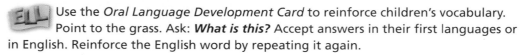

Rhymes and Chants Flip Chart, page 8

Center Time

▶ **Center Rotation** Center Time includes teacher-guided activities and independent activities. Refer to the **Learning Centers** on pages 138–139 for independent activity ideas.

 small group 60–90 minutes

Library and Listening Center | Center Tip

✓ **Listen for the use of a variety of words to describe things outside the classroom.**

Materials books about children playing and learning outside the classroom

Outside the Classroom Have children browse through books to find photos or illustrations of things they might see outside the classroom.

- Have children work in pairs and choose one favorite picture.

- Say: *Point to something you know in the picture. Señalen en la fotografía algo que conozcan.* Ask: *Can you name it? ¿Pueden decir cómo se llama eso?*

- Have children share what they know about the item they named.

Center Tip

If...children have difficulty identifying things in the picture, **then...**give them a clue by asking questions such as: *What grows on the tree? What color is it? ¿Qué crece en el árbol? ¿De qué color es?*

Writer's Center | Center Tip

✓ **Track conventions children use when writing or dictating.**

Materials square sheets of drawing paper, crayons, construction paper for book cover

Make a Book Explain to children that they will make a class book about the ways people can be alike.

- Have children each draw a picture of a person from the classroom or someone from another culture they have seen in a book.

- Write the following four-word frame at the bottom of the drawing: *We are alike because _____.*

- Help children complete the frame as they dictate. Guide them to read each word as you track the print.

Center Tip

If...some children finish before center time is over, **then...** ask them to illustrate the front and back covers of the book.

 Learning Goals

Emergent Literacy: Writing
• Child experiments with and uses some writing conventions when writing or dictating.

Social Studies
• Child respects/appreciates the differing interests, skills, abilities, cultures, languages, and family structures of people.

Differentiated Instruction

 Extra Support
Writer's Center
If...children have difficulty labeling their pictures, **then...**encourage them to write the letters they know, or use scribble writing.

 Enrichment
Writer's Center
Challenge children to share the completed book with a friend by taking a picture walk and talking about the people shown.

♥ **Special Needs**
Speech/Hearing Delays
To help the child develop vocabulary, ask him or her to describe what he or she has drawn. Ask questions that will help the child describe the activity.

Focus Question

How can we play and learn together?

¿Cómo jugamos y aprendemos juntos?

✓ Learning Goals

Social and Emotional Development
• Child shows eagerness, curiosity, and confidence while learning new concepts and trying new things.

Emergent Literacy: Reading
• Child names most upper- and lowercase letters of the alphabet.
• Child identifies the letter that stands for a given sound.
• Child describes, relates to, and uses details and information from books read aloud.

Vocabulary

circle	círculo	exercise	ejercicio
friends	amigos	habits	hábitos
school	escuela	teacher	maestro

Differentiated Instruction

 **Extra Support**

Read Aloud
If...children have difficulty using complete sentences, **then...**model expressing ideas in complete sentences and having children repeat the sentences.

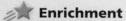 **Enrichment**

Learn About Letters and Sounds
Invite children to have fun with short alliterative phrases that feature /m/ or /d/, such as: *Mark's muddy mittens made a mess* or *Did Dad drop Dee's donuts?*

Literacy Time

large group — 15 minutes

📖 Read Aloud

✓ Do children use prior knowledge when answering questions about a book?

Build Background Remind children that you have already read *Concept Big Book 1: Welcome to School.* Say: **The book was about a preschool that is a lot like our preschool.** *Ese libro hablaba de una escuela muy parecida a la nuestra.*

● Ask: **How is our school like the one in the book? How are you like the children in the book?** *¿En qué se parece nuestra escuela a la del libro? ¿En qué se parecen ustedes a los niños del libro?*

Listen for Understanding Read the title while pointing out that the words in the title are separated by spaces. Say: **Let's count the words—1, 2, 3.** *Vamos a contar las palabras.*

● Read the book. Pause to ask questions that relate to the photographs, such as: **What do we do during circle time? What good habits have you learned?** *¿Qué hacemos en la hora del círculo? ¿Qué buenos hábitos han aprendido?*

Respond to the Book Discuss the book. Revisit several photographs and ask children to use complete sentences to describe what is happening on the page.

TIP Ask children to identify similarities and differences between the classroom activities shown in the book and in their rooms at school.

ELL Build children's understanding of the meaning of the word *exercise*. Use gestures and body movements to demonstrate ways to exercise. Have children show you how they like to exercise.

Learn About Letters and Sounds

✓ Can children recognize the letters *Aa, Dd, Mm,* and *Ss* and identify their sounds?

Name and Write Letters Display the *ABC Picture Cards* for *Aa, Dd, Mm,* and *Ss.*

● Hold up the *Aa* card. Ask: **What is this letter? What sound does it make?** *¿Qué letra es ésta? ¿Qué sonido tiene?*

● Model how to use your finger to write an upper case letter *A* in the air. Have children repeat, using a finger to write the letter in the air, on an interactive whiteboard, or on a partner's back. Say: **Now write lower case a.** *Ahora, escriban la a minúscula.*

● Repeat for the other three letters.

Welcome to School
Bienvenidos a la escuela

ABC Picture Cards

large group 15 minutes

Math Time

Observe and Investigate

Can children identify and match shapes?

Match and Name Shapes Invite children to match and name shapes. Display a complete Shape Set.

- Choose a shape and show the class. Say: ***Which shape in this set matches my shape? How do you know?*** *¿Cuál de estas figuras es igual a mi figura? ¿Cómo lo saben?*
- Ask children to name the shape together. Say: ***What is the name of the shape? How do you know this is a [shape]?*** *¿Cómo se llama esta figura? ¿Cómo saben que es un [nombre de la figura]?* To help them describe shapes, encourage children to feel a shape and its edges while their eyes are shut.
- Repeat with the other shapes. Guide children in describing the shapes, discussing any curves, straight sides, and corners.

ELL Provide visual support by supplying different images with shapes from the Shape Set. Emphasize the names of the shapes as you identify them together.

Building Blocks

Online Math Activity

Children can complete Mystery Pictures 1 during computer time or Center Time.

large group 15 minutes

Social and Emotional Development

Making Good Choices

Do children understand the feelings of others?

A Helpful Classmate Display the *Making Good Choices Flip Chart,* page 8. Point to the girl at the table. Ask: ***How do you think she feels? What might make her feel better?*** *¿Cómo creen que se siente? ¿Cómo podría sentirse mejor?*

- Use the Dog Puppets to act out a scenario based on the chart. For example, have Dog Puppet 1 say: ***I worked hard on this puzzle. Now I have to start all over again!*** *Trabajé mucho en este rompecabezas ¡Ahora tengo que empezar de nuevo!* As Dog Puppet 2, say: ***Would you like some help putting it back together?*** *¿Quieres que te ayude a armarlo de nuevo?*
- Invite children to take turns using the puppets to act out other chart scenarios where classmates feel more or less angry, sad, or happy.

ELL Use the *Making Good Choices Flip Chart* to review basic vocabulary. Point to an object, such as the puzzle. Name the object and have children repeat the word. Then ask them to point to and name other objects.

Making Good Choices Flip Chart, page 8

Learning Goals

Social and Emotional Development

- Child begins to show a greater ability to control intense feelings.
- Child recognizes and manages feelings and impulses; increasingly maintains self-control in difficult situations (can increase or decrease intensity of emotions with guidance).
- Child understands and respects the different ideas, feelings, perspectives, and behaviors of others.

Mathematics

- Child recognizes, names, describes, matches, compares, sorts common two-dimensional shapes (such as circle, square, rectangle, triangle, rhombus).

Vocabulary

puzzle	rompecabezas	play	jugar
rectangle	rectángulo	side	lado
square	cuadrado	work	tarea

Differentiated Instruction

Extra Support

Observe and Investigate

If...children are having difficulty naming the shape, **then...**go over the different shape names with them, pointing out attributes of the shape.

Enrichment

Making Good Choices

Challenge children to identify different emotions the children shown on the chart might be experiencing, such as happiness, worry, or anger.

Accommodations for 3's

Observe and Investigate

If...children have difficulty matching shapes, **then...**limit matching to familiar shapes.

Focus Question
How can we play and learn together?
¿Cómo jugamos y aprendemos juntos?

Learning Goals

Social and Emotional Development
• Child initiates play scenarios with peers that share a common plan and goal.

Language and Communication
• Child names and describes actual or pictured people, places, things, actions, attributes, and events.
• Child uses newly learned vocabulary daily in multiple contexts.

Social Studies
• Child identifies similarities and differences among people.

Vocabulary

different	diferente	explore	explorar
learn	aprender	outside	afuera
same	igual		

Differentiated Instruction

 Extra Support
Oral Language and Academic Vocabulary
If...children have difficulty identifying same and different, **then...**give examples using concrete objects in the classroom.

 Enrichment
Oral Language and Academic Vocabulary
Provide children with magazines. Challenge them to find and cut out pictures of people. Have them work together to make a poster collage. Help children identify how the people are similar and different.

Social Studies Time

  large group · 20 minutes

Social Emotional Skills Model positive ways to handle conflict, such as using words to settle disputes and taking turns using toys and materials.

Oral Language and Academic Vocabulary

Different People Display the *Making Good Choices Flip Chart,* page 8. Talk about ways in which all the children are the same. Say: ***These children all have eyes and noses. They all have ears too. They are the same in many ways.*** *Todos estos niños tiene ojos y narices. También tienen orejas. Son iguales en muchos aspectos.*

● Explain that the children are different in many ways, too. Ask: ***Can you tell me one thing that is different about two of the children in the chart?*** *¿Pueden decirme algo en que dos de los niños del rotafolio sean diferentes?*

● Accept all differences and record the differences children identify.

 Use concrete objects to demonstrate the concept of *same* and *different.*

Making Good Choices Flip Chart, page 8

Understand and Participate

✓ Can children identify similarities and differences among others, and among themselves and others?

✓ Do children increasingly interact and communicate with peers to initiate pretend play scenarios that share a common plan and goal?

Different Interests Discuss how people are different in many ways. Say: ***People are different in how they look. How are they different in other ways?*** *Las personas son diferentes en su aspecto físico. ¿Qué otras diferencias pueden tener?* Display books and pictures of people of many different cultures. Discuss some of the differences shown, such as clothing, food, and skills.

● Hold up two pictures and ask: ***How are the people different? How are they the same?*** *¿En qué se diferencian estas personas? ¿En qué se parecen?*

● Encourage children to name things other than physical differences, such as language, the foods they like to eat, and so on.

Center Time

 Center Rotation Center Time includes teacher-guided activities and independent activities. Refer to the **Learning Centers** on pages 138–139 for independent activity ideas.

 small group   30 minutes

Pretend and Learn Center

✓ **Observe children using varied vocabulary as they role-play exploring.**

Materials dress up items, hair color yarn strips, pictures of people

Time to Explore! Pair children. Have partners choose one picture. Explain that children will pretend to be someone in the picture.

- Say: *Look closely at your picture. Look at the clothing; at the hair color and other things. Dress up like someone in your picture.*
  Observen atentamente su fotografía. Observen la ropa, el color de cabello y otras cosas. Pónganse alguna ropa para parecerse a una de las personas de la fotografía.

- Allow time for children to show their pictures and dress-up clothes for the class.

Center Tip

If...children have difficulty finding appropriate dress-up items on their own, **then**...encourage them to ask their partner for help.

Learning Goals

Emergent Literacy: Reading
- Child identifies the letter that stands for a given sound.

Social Studies
- Child identifies similarities and differences among people.

✏ Writing

Write the letter *s* on chart paper or an interactive whiteboard. Say: **Let's pretend we are exploring our playground. *What might we see that begins with the sound of s, /s/?*** *Imaginen que estamos en el patio de juegos. ¿Qué cosa podemos ver que empiece /s/?* Record children's suggestions. If necessary, give prompts such as, **What playthings might we see?** *¿Qué juegos podemos ver?* (swing, slide, sandbox, seesaw). Read the list aloud, pointing to and reading each word while emphasizing the /s/ sound. Display the finished work in the ABC Center.

Purposeful Play

✓ **Track how often children label differences and how fully they are able to describe them as they work with others.**

Children choose an open center for free playtime. Encourage children to think about the many ways people are alike and different as they work in centers.

Let's Say Good-Bye

  large group   15 minutes

 Read Aloud Revisit "Opposites"/"Los opuestos" for your afternoon Read Aloud. Remind children to listen for the /m/ and /d/ sounds.

Home Connection Refer to the Home Connections activities listed in the Resources and Materials chart on page 135. Remind children to talk with their families about things they learn when they explore outside. Sing the "Good-Bye Song" as children prepare to leave.

DAY 4

Let's Start the Day

Focus Question

How can we play and learn together?

¿Cómo jugamos y aprendemos juntos?

Learning Goals

Language and Communication
- Child demonstrates an understanding of oral language by responding appropriately.
- Child names and describes actual or pictured people, places, things, actions, attributes, and events.

Emergent Literacy: Reading
- Child listens for words (for example, hears and separates individual words within a four-word sentence).

Vocabulary

hike	excursión
make-believe	fantasía
pretend	simular
real	real

Differentiated Instruction

 Extra Support

Oral Language and Vocabulary
If...children have difficulty naming imaginary sights on their hike, **then...**offer prompts such as: *What's crawling on that rock?* or *What splashed into the water? ¿Qué animal se arrastra por la piedra?* o *¿Qué animal se tiró al agua?*

Enrichment

Phonological Awareness
Challenge children to make up a four-word sentence for the puppet to recite. Repeat the class activity with the new sentence.

Opening Routines and Transition Tips

For **Opening Routines** and **Transition Tips** turn to pages 178–181 and visit **DLMExpressOnline.com** for more ideas.

Read **"Let's Pretend to Bake a Cake"/**"Hagamos como que horneamos un pastel" from the *Teacher's Treasure Book*, page 206, for your morning Read Aloud.

Language Time

Social and Emotional Development Model positive behaviors as you show children how to initiate scenarios with peers.

Oral Language and Vocabulary

✓ **Can children distinguish between real and make-believe?**

Let's Make-Believe Ask children when they have heard the words "make-believe" before.

- Ask: *What do you know about what this word means? ¿Saben lo que quiere decir esta palabra?* Explain that when something is make-believe, it is not real. Say: *Let's take a make-believe, or pretend, hike. Hagamos una excursión de fantasía.*

- Lead children on a "hike" around the room. Point and say: *Look! There's a big bird in that tree! ¡Miren! ¡Hay un pájaro enorme en ese árbol!* Invite children to work with others to name things they pretend to see on the hike.

- Conclude the hike and say: *Our hike is over! What did you see? Was the bird real or make-believe? ¡Se terminó la excursión! Vamos a sentarnos. ¿Qué vieron? ¿Era el pájaro real o imaginario?* Repeat for other objects on the hike.

ELL Extend children's understanding of the difference between real and make-believe by browsing through several books of each type. Point to appropriate illustrations and say: *This is real.* or *This is not real. It is make-believe.*

Phonological Awareness

✓ **Can children isolate a word in a sentence?**

Listen and Clap Display a Dog Puppet. Say: *The dog puppet will say a sentence. Listen for each word in the sentence. El perrito dirá una oración. Escuchen cada palabra de la oración.*

- Ask: *Who can find the word* boy? *Clap when you hear the word. ¿Quién puede reconocer la palabra* boy? *Den una palmada cuando escuchen esa palabra.* Have the puppet say, "The boy can run."

- Continue isolating other words in the sentence.

- Repeat with these sentences: "The teacher can write. The girl can play. The dog can jump."

Center Time

▶ **Center Rotation** Center Time includes teacher-guided activities and independent activities. Refer to the Learning Centers on pages 138–139 for independent activity ideas.

 small group 60–90 minutes

Library and Listening Center

✓ **Can children interact and communicate with classmates?**

Materials photo chart of actions for "Wheels on the Bus," tape recorder or CD player (optional), recording of "Wheels on the Bus" (optional)

Get on the Bus! Prepare a photo chart of the actions for "Wheels on the Bus."

- Sing the song with the entire class, demonstrating the motions.

- Have children work in pairs and listen quietly to the song as you sing or play it. Have them use the photo chart as a reference for the motions.

- Tell partners they will pretend to be on stage acting the song out together. Have children decide which one will sing the song and which one will do the hand motions. Switch roles.

- Conclude by having both children sing and use hand motions.

Center Tip

If...children are unfamiliar with the song, **then...**pair them with children who are familiar with the words and motions.

ABC Center

✓ **Observe children's ability to identify objects that begin with the sounds /a/, /d/, /m/ and /s/.**

✓ **Track children's ability to identify individual words within a sentence.**

Materials magazines, scissors, glue or paste, large sheet of construction paper labeled *Aa, Dd, Mm, Ss* at the top

Letter Sounds Display the poster and have children identify the letters. Say: **Think about the sound each letter makes.** *Piensen en el sonido de cada letra.*

- Ask children to cut out pictures of things that start with each sound.

- Have them glue the pictures to the poster.

- Help children write four-word sentences using the item in the picture as one of the words. For example: /s/; sun; *The sun is bright*.

Center Tip

If...children have difficulty finding objects for all four letters and sounds, **then...**have them make a poster for just one letter and sound.

Learning Goals

Emergent Literacy: Reading
- Child names most upper- and lowercase letters of the alphabet.
- Child identifies the letter that stands for a given sound.

Emergent Literacy: Writing
- Child writes some letters or reasonable approximations of letters upon request.

Fine Arts
- Child expresses emotions or ideas through art.
- Child participates in a variety of music activities (such as listening, singing, finger plays, musical games, performances).

Differentiated Instruction

✋ Extra Support
Library and Listening Center
If...children have difficulty focusing for the entire recording, **then...**have them listen to part of the song at a time.

★ Enrichment
ABC Center
Challenge children to use what they know about sounds to label some of the pictures on the ABC charts they make.

Accommodations for 3's
ABC Center
If...children have difficulty writing letters to label beginning sounds, **then...**allow them to use magnetic letters to denote beginning sounds they hear.

Focus Question

How can we play and learn together?

¿Cómo jugamos y aprendemos juntos?

Learning Goals

Language and Communication
• Child demonstrates an understanding of oral language by responding appropriately.
• Child uses newly learned vocabulary daily in multiple contexts.

Emergent Literacy: Reading
• Child names most upper- and lowercase letters of the alphabet.
• Child describes, relates to, and uses details and information from books read aloud.
• Child asks and answers questions about books read aloud (such as "Who?" "What?" "Where?").

Vocabulary

back	espalda	catch	atrapar
gingerbread	jengibre	head	cabeza
man	hombre	nose	hocico
woman	mujer		

Differentiated Instruction

 Extra Support

Learn About Letters and Sounds
If...children have difficulty matching a letter, **then...**have them note the similarities as they trace that letter on the *Alphabet Wall Card* and on each of the cards you prepared.

 Enrichment

Read Aloud
Encourage children to work with a friend to act out the story. Challenge children to use story vocabulary such as *gingerbread, man, woman*, and *catch* as they role-play various characters.

Literacy Time

large group 15 minutes

📖 Read Aloud

✓ Do children use prior knowledge to bring meaning to read-aloud text?

Build Background Review the meaning of the word "make-believe." Say: *Today we'll read a make-believe story about a gingerbread man.* *Hoy leeremos un cuento imaginario sobre un hombrecito de jengibre.*

• Ask: *What is a gingerbread man? ¿Qué es un hombrecito de jengibre?*

• Ask: *What would you do with a real gingerbread man? ¿Qué harían con una galleta real con la forma de un hombrecito de jengibre?*

Listen for Enjoyment Read the title of the story from the *Teacher's Treasure Book*, page 278. Explain that the old woman in the story bakes a gingerbread man. Then the gingerbread man runs away from the old woman.

• Ask: *Why do you think the gingerbread man runs away? ¿Por qué creen que el hombrecito de jengibre se escapa?*

• *Say: Listen to find out who tries to catch the gingerbread man. Escuchen el cuento para descubrir quién intenta atrapar al hombrecito de jengibre.*

• Read the story aloud, using the flannel board characters to act out events. Invite children to join in when you read the repeated text.

Respond to the Story Discuss the story. Help children recall that the gingerbread man ran too fast for anyone to catch him. Ask: *How does the fox trick the gingerbread man? ¿Cómo hace el zorro para engañar al hombrecito de jengibre?*

ELL Enhance children's vocabulary by explaining that the word *gingerbread* is made up of two words: *ginger* and *bread*. Explain that gingerbread isn't really a bread, but it can be eaten like bread. Bring in gingerbread men to demonstrate.

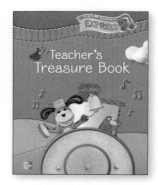

Teacher's Treasure Book, page 278

Learn About Letters and Sounds

✓ Can children match letters by observing similarities and differences?

Alphabet Match Prepare letter cards by printing individual letters *M, m, D,* and *d*. Display the *Alphabet Wall Card* for *Mm*. Say: *This is the letter* M. *Ésta es la letra* M. Have children repeat the letter name. Then have them trace the upper case and lower case letters in the air, on an interactive whiteboard, or on a partner's back. Point out the straight lines in the upper case *M* and the curved lines in the lower case m.

• Repeat with the *Alphabet Wall Card* for *Dd*.

• Display one of the prepared cards. Say: *Look at this letter. Which letter does this match? Miren esta letra. ¿A qué tarjeta corresponde?* Have children match the prepared letter card with the appropriate *Alphabet Wall Card*.

• Repeat with the other letter cards.

Alphabet Wall Cards

Online Math Activity

Child can complete Mystery Pictures 1 during computer time or Center Time.

Math Time

Observe and Investigate

 Can children recognize common shapes?

Match Blocks Have children match various block shapes to objects in the classroom. Tell children that you can see many shapes in the objects around you.

- This lesson repeats the activity introduced on Day 1. Place different block shapes in front of you. Have children sit in a circle around you.

- Show the face of one block. Say: **Look at this block. Now look around the classroom. Can you find another object that has the same shape?** *Observen este bloque. Ahora, miren a su alrededor. ¿Pueden encontrar otro objeto con la misma forma?*

- Repeat with each block shape.

- Take each incorrect answer as an opportunity to politely correct children. Talk children through incorrect responses, such as choosing something to match a square that is actually rectangular.

ELL Provide support by naming the shape for children. Describe the shape for children, telling how many sides it has and other characteristics.

✕✕✕ Social and Emotional Development

Making Good Choices

 Do children understand that different people look at the same situation in different ways?

Classroom Rules Use the Dog Puppets to role-play a classroom conflict situation. Have one puppet say: **It's fun to throw bean bags with friends!** *Es divertido jugar con mis amigos a tirarnos bolsas de frijoles.*

- Have the other puppet say: **But when you threw the bean bag, you knocked over my tower of blocks. That made me mad.** *Pero cuando tiraste la bolsa, derrumbaste mi torre de bloques. Eso me hizo sentir muy triste.*

- Have the first puppet turn to the children and ask: **What should I do**? *¿Qué tengo que hacer?* Elicit responses from the children. Acknowledge and discuss all responses, and then have the first puppet say to the other: **I'm sorry. I will try to follow the rules. I'll play with the bean bags somewhere else.** *Lo lamento. Intentaré seguir las reglas. Jugaré con las bolsas en otro lugar.*

- Have children role-play the situation, asking how each response would make the children feel.

✓ Learning Goals

Social and Emotional Development
- Child begins to show a greater ability to control intense feelings.
- Child begins to be responsible for individual behavior and actions.
- Child understands and respects the different ideas, feelings, perspectives, and behaviors of others.

Mathematics
- Child recognizes, names, describes, matches, compares, sorts common two-dimensional shapes (such as circle, square, rectangle, triangle, rhombus).

Vocabulary

classroom	salón de clases	friends	amigos
help	ayudar	rules	reglas
sad	triste	shapes	figuras
square	cuadrado	triangle	triángulo

Differentiated Instruction

✋ **Extra Support**
Observe and Investigate
If...children are having difficulty finding objects, **then...**demonstrate by placing the block next to a similarly-shaped classroom object.

⭐ **Enrichment**
Making Good Choices
Challenge children to use the puppets to role-play a time when someone needed help remembering to follow classroom rules, such as when someone wanted to keep playing instead of cleaning up.

Accommodations for 3's
Observe and Investigate
If...children have difficulty identifying shapes on their own, **then...**have them look for shapes in the classroom with a partner.

Learning Goals

Mathematics

• Child creates two-dimensional shapes; recreates two-dimensional shapes from memory.

Vocabulary

cans	latas	food	comida
match	corrsponda	round	redondo
trace	trazo		

Differentiated Instruction

👋 **Extra Support**

Math Time

If...children have difficulty matching the can shapes, **then...**help them move the can shape over the various circles to find one that matches.

⭐ **Enrichment**

Math Time

Challenge children to trace other shapes on the paper.

Accommodations for 3's

Math Time

If...children need help holding the can, **then...** hold the can for them as they choose where it goes.

💜 **Special Needs**

Cognitive Challenges

Throughout the week, decide what two shapes and two sizes you want the child to learn about. Then, adapt the math activities to focus only on those two.

Math Time

  large group / 20 minutes

 Can students create shapes and match shapes by size?

Circles and Cans Guide children in a game of matching traced circle shapes with food cans. Explain to children that the term *round* means "circular."

● Display several food cans, and discuss the shape of the flat faces with children. Say: **This is a can. How can you describe the bottom of this can?** *¿Qué forma tiene el fondo de esta lata?*

● Point out to children that the bottom and top of each can is round, or circular.

● Show large sheets of paper and trace one or two cans to demonstrate for children. Have children come up and trace the bottoms of the differently sized food cans. Then shuffle the papers and cans.

● Ask children to match the cans to the traced circles. Ask: **Which circle is the same size as this can?** *¿Qué círculo tiene el mismo tamaño que esta lata?* Say: **I can place this can on the circle to check that it matches.** *Coloquen sus latas en el círculo que corresponda.*

Center Time

Center Rotation Center Time includes teacher-guided activities and independent activities. Refer to the **Learning Centers** on pages 138–139 for independent activity ideas.

 small group 30 minutes

Math and Science Center

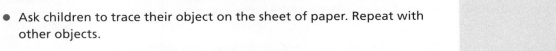

Encourage children to trace different shapes onto sheets of paper.

Materials classroom objects

Tracing Shapes Invite children to find classroom objects and bring them to a table. Provide sheets of paper for children to trace the shapes of their objects.

- Begin by having children name one of their objects. Say: *What is the name of your object? ¿Cuál es el nombre de sus objetos?* Then say: *What is the shape of your object? ¿Cuál es la forma de sus objetos?*

- Ask children to trace their object on the sheet of paper. Repeat with other objects.

- Have children name all the shapes they traced.

Center Tip

If...children have difficulty tracing the shapes, **then**...guide their hands as they trace.

Purposeful Play

Observe children tracing and playing with shapes.

Children choose an open center for free playtime. Encourage children to color in their shapes and draw pictures over them.

Learning Goals

Emergent Literacy: Writing
- Child experiments with and uses some writing conventions when writing or dictating.

Mathematics
- Child recognizes, names, describes, matches, compares, sorts common two-dimensional shapes (such as circle, square, rectangle, triangle, rhombus).
- Child creates two-dimensional shapes; recreates two-dimensional shapes from memory.

Writing

Write this sentence frame on chart paper: *Today I learned about _____.* Encourage children to complete the sentence by recalling something they learned during the day. Track each word as you read it, then track the words as children read it back to you. Display the finished work in the classroom.

Let's Say Good-Bye

 large group 15 minutes

 Read Aloud Revisit "Let's Pretend to Bake a Cake"/"Hagamos como que horneamos un pastel" for your afternoon Read Aloud. Remind children to listen for the sounds of /d/ and /m/.

 Home Connection Refer to the Home Connections activities listed in the Resources and Materials chart on page 135. Remind children to retell the story of "The Gingerbread Man" to their families. Sing the "Good-Bye Song" as children prepare to leave.

DAY 5

Focus Question

How can we play and learn together?

¿Cómo jugamos y aprendemos juntos?

Learning Goals

Social and Emotional Development
• Child demonstrates positive social behaviors, as modeled by the teacher.

Language and Communication
• Child names and describes actual or pictured people, places, things, actions, attributes, and events.

Emergent Literacy: Reading
• Child listens for words (for example, hears and separates individual words within a four-word sentence).

Vocabulary

faces	caras	happy	feliz
places	lugares	quiet	callado
share	compartir		

Differentiated Instruction

 Extra Support

Phonological Awareness
If...children have difficulty counting words, **then...**speak the lines instead of singing them.

⭐ **Enrichment**

Oral Language and Vocabulary
Challenge children to draw and write about what they do during circle time. Encourage them to write the letters they know and use scribble writing for the rest.

Let's Start the Day

 Opening Routines and Transition Tips
For **Opening Routines** and **Transition Tips** turn to pages 178–181 and visit DLMExpressOnline.com for more ideas.

📖 Read **""The Traveling Musicians"/**"Los músicos viajeros" from the *Teacher's Treasure Book,* page 297, for your morning Read Aloud.

Language Time

 large group · 15 minutes

👨‍👩‍👧 **Social and Emotional Development** Encourage children to listen to their classmates as they work and play together.

Oral Language and Vocabulary

✓ **Do children use a variety of words to describe how friends and classmates play and work together?**

Work and Play Discuss different things children do together at school. Ask: *How do we work together? How do we play together?* ¿Cómo trabajamos juntos? ¿Cómo jugamos juntos?

● Display the *Rhymes and Chants Flip Chart,* page 8. Ask: *What are the children doing?* ¿Qué están haciendo los niños?

● Say: *Point to a child who is talking.* Ask: *What are the other children doing?* Señalen al niño que está hablando. ¿Que están haciendo los otros niños? Discuss how taking turns talking and listening helps children learn and play together.

● Provide child-friendly explanations of vocabulary words. Track the words as you sing the song. Then repeat, inviting children to sing along.

ELL Enhance children's vocabulary, describing the difference between talking and listening. Point to your mouth and say: *I am talking.* Cup your hand to your ear. Say: *Now I will listen while you talk.* Take turns talking and listening.

Phonological Awareness

✓ **Can children isolate and count words in a sentence?**

Concept of Word Display the *Rhymes and Chants Flip Chart,* page 8.

● Say: *Listen to the words as I sing the first line of the song. Can you count how many words you hear?* Escuchen las palabras mientras canto la canción. ¿Cuántas palabras escuchan? Sing the first line and have children hold up a finger to as you sing each word. Ask: *How many fingers am you holding up?* ¿Cuándos dedos tengo aquí?

● Continue the activity with other sentences from the song. Have the children hold up their fingers as you sing the song together to isolate words.

Rhymes and Chants Flip Chart, page 8

Center Time

▶ **Center Rotation** Center Time includes teacher-guided activities and independent activities. Refer to the **Learning Centers** on pages 138–139 for independent activity ideas.

 small group 60–90 minutes

Construction Center

	Center Tip

 Observe children remaining focused on a group activities for about 20 minutes.

 Determine if children can follow a pattern to make a block tower.

Materials building blocks in various colors, sample block tower

Building Directions Explain that many people have to work together in their jobs. Sometimes they work together to understand what they have to do. Say: *Builders work together to understand and follow directions when building something. You can work together to build a tower. Los constructores trabajan juntos para saber qué deben hacer y siguen indicaciones cuando construyen algo. Ustedes pueden trabajar juntos para construir una torre.*

● Display a simple tower. Have children work in pairs to select blocks to make a tower like the sample.

● When each pair has copied the tower, have them work to make towers for one another to copy.

Center Tip

If...children have difficulty matching the pattern to build a tower, **then...** help them locate the matching blocks before they start to build.

Creativity Center

	Center Tip

 Observe children following directions to create gingerbread men.

Materials gingerbread man outlines, scissors, crayons, buttons, glue

Make a Gingerbread Man Tell children they will make a gingerbread man. Supply outlined figures of a gingerbread man. Say: *You can work with a partner. You can help each other make a gingerbread man. Pueden trabajar con un compañero. Pueden ayudarse entre ustedes para hacer un hombrecito de jengibre.*

● Have children cut out a gingerbread man figure.

● Ask them to draw a face on their figure.

● Have them glue 3 buttons to the gingerbread man's chest. Display the figures around the room.

Center Tip

If...children have difficulty counting the correct number of buttons, **then...** display three Two-Color Counters. Have them choose buttons to correspond to the number of counters they see.

Learning Goals

Social and Emotional Development
• Child shows eagerness, curiosity, and confidence while learning new concepts and trying new things.

Mathematics
• Child counts 1–10 concrete objects correctly.

Physical Development
• Child completes tasks that require eye-hand coordination and control.

Differentiated Instruction

 Extra Support
Creativity Center
If...a child has difficulty positioning buttons on the gingerbread man figure, **then...**draw a light X in pencil where each button belongs.

Enrichment
Creativity Center
Help children glue their gingerbread man cutouts to craft sticks. Challenge them to use the cutouts as puppets as they retell the story.

Accommodations for 3's
Creativity Center
If...children have difficulty cutting out gingerbread men shapes, **then...**have them decorate the shape without cutting it out.

 Special Needs
Behavioral Social/Emotional
Some children with behavioral/social issues, especially those with autism, may become very good at making and copying patterns. The child might even recognize and extend the pattern. If this is the case, let her or him have some extra time to make the pattern.

Focus Question

How can we play and learn together?

¿Cómo jugamos y aprendemos juntos?

 Learning Goals

Emergent Literacy: Reading

• Child names most upper- and lowercase letters of the alphabet.

• Child identifies the letter that stands for a given sound.

• Child describes, relates to, and uses details and information from books read aloud.

• Child asks and answers questions about books read aloud (such as "Who?" "What?" "Where?").

Vocabulary

fiesta	fiesta	red	rojo
show-and-tell	muestra y cuenta	skirt	vestido
white	blanco	yellow	amarillo

Differentiated Instruction

 Extra Support

Read Aloud

If...children have difficulty answering questions about the book, **then...**turn to the illustration that offers a clue to the answer. Point to the answer.

⭐ **Enrichment**

Read Aloud

Encourage children to work with a friend to act out the story. Challenge them to use story vocabulary as they role-play Amelia and other characters.

Accommodations for 3's

Learn About Letters and Sounds

If...children have difficulty matching certain letters to the sounds they make, **then...**review the letter in the *ABC Big Book*, stressing the beginning sound as you name the objects pictured.

Literacy Time

 large group — 15 minutes

📖 Read Aloud

✓ Can children draw on prior knowledge to answer questions about the story?

Build Background Revisit *Amelia's Show-and-Tell Fiesta*. Say: **We read about Amelia and the skirt she wore to show-and-tell.** *Leímos sobre Amelia y su vestido especial.*

● Help children use their prior knowledge of the story to answer questions. Ask: **What is show-and-tell? What color is Amelia's skirt?** *En una fiesta de "mostrar y contar", traemos a la escuela un objeto especial para mostrar a los demás. ¿Qué traerían ustedes para mostrar a sus amigos?*

Listen for Understanding Display *Amelia's Show-and-Tell Fiesta* and read the title.

● Browse through the book to review the story. Build print awareness by pointing out examples of environmental print.

● Read the book aloud, pausing to discuss the illustrations.

Respond to the Story Ask: **Do you have any questions about this story? What would you like to ask Amelia about her skirt? Do you want to ask her about show-and-tell?** *¿Tienen alguna pregunta sobre el cuento? ¿Qué le preguntarían a Amelia sobre su vestido? ¿Y sobre el día de muestra y cuenta?*

TIP Help children make connections between Amelia's school and their own. Ask them to point out objects and activities in her classroom that they see or do in their own.

ELL Help children understand the meaning of the word *classroom*. Explain that the word is made up of two smaller words: *class* and *room*. Say: **A classroom is a room where a group of children play and learn together.**

Learn About Letters and Sounds

✓ Can children identify the letters that make the sounds /a/, /d/, /m/, and /s/?

Sounds of Aa, Dd, Mm, and Ss Display the *ABC Picture Cards* for *Aa, Dd, Mm,* and *Ss*.

● Ask: **Which letter makes the /s/ sound?** *¿Qué letra tiene el sonido /s/?* Have one child stand up and hold the *Ss* card.

● Repeat until all four cards are held up.

● Say: **I'll say a word. Tell me who has the card for the letter you hear at the beginning of the word. Yo voy a decir una palabra. Digan quién tiene la letra con la que empieza esa palabra. Say: Monkey. Tell me who has the card.** *¿Quién tiene la tarjeta correcta?*

● Repeat with the other sounds and words such as *add, ace, soup,* and *dirt*.

Amelia's Show-and-Tell Fiesta

Amelia y la fiesta de "muestra y cuenta"

ABC Picture Cards

 large group 15 minutes

Math Time

Observe and Investigate

 Can children correctly identify circles?

Circle or Not? Draw circles and other curved shapes with children. Tell them that some shapes that look like circles are not circles.

Online Math Activity
Children can complete Mystery Pictures 1 during computer time or Center Time.

- Draw a true circle on a surface where the entire class can view it. Say: *What shape is this? Why is it a circle? ¿Qué figura es ésta? ¿Por qué es un círculo?* Draw an oval on the same surface. Say: *What does this shape look like? Is it a circle? ¿A qué se parece esta figura? ¿Es un círculo?* Discuss with children why the shape is not a circle.

- Draw several other sized circles and shapes that are somewhat like circles and review their differences. Summarize by reviewing what a circle is. Say: *A circle is round. It has a curved line that always curves the same amount, no matter where you place your finger on it! Un círculo siempre es redondo. ¡No importa por dónde lo mires, los círculos siempre tienen la misma curva!*

ELL Find a circular object in the classroom and have children trace the curved line with their finger as you describe what a circle is.

 **large group** 15 minutes

Social and Emotional Development

Making Good Choices

 Can children identify situations where someone needs help to work or play together?

Making Friends Display the *Making Good Choices Flip Chart*, page 8. Review the concepts from the week by asking children questions based on the flip chart.

- Ask: *Who is working together? What are they doing? ¿Quiénes están trabajando juntos? ¿Qué están haciendo? ¿Quién necesita ayuda?*

- Ask: *Who needs some help? ¿Quién necesita ayuda?* Discuss why the girl needs help and what someone could do to be helpful. Ask: *What would you say to the boys who are throwing the bean bags? How can they work and play with the other children? ¿Qué les dirían a los niños que arrojan los sacos de frijoles? ¿Cómo pueden trabajar y jugar con los otros niños?*

Making Good Choices Flip Chart, page 8

Learning Goals

Social and Emotional Development
- Child understands and respects the different ideas, feelings, perspectives, and behaviors of others.

Mathematics
- Child recognizes, names, describes, matches, compares, sorts common two-dimensional shapes (such as circle, square, rectangle, triangle, rhombus).

Vocabulary

circle círculo	oval óvalo
round redondo	

Differentiated Instruction

Extra Support
Observe and Investigate
If...children need help during the Circle or Not? activity, **then...**make non-circles very obvious, such as long ovals and shapes that are not closed.

Enrichment
Observe and Investigate
Have children identify circles and things that are not circles around the classroom.

Accommodations for 3's
Observe and Investigate
If...children need help with the computer, **then...**complete the activity with a small group while the rest of the class rotates through the centers.

Learning Goals

Social and Emotional Development
• Child is aware of self in terms of abilities, characteristics and preferences, and respects personal boundaries.

Language and Communication
• Child names and describes actual or pictured people, places, things, actions, attributes, and events.

Physical Development
• Child engages in a sequence of movements to perform a task.

Vocabulary

catch	atrapar	fast	rápido
inside	interior	outside	aire libre
run	correr		

Differentiated Instruction

 Extra Support

Oral Language and Academic Vocabulary
If...children have difficulty with the riddle format, **then...**have them respond to questions instead. For example, say: **What can you do outside in the snow?** *¿Qué pueden hacer afuera, en la nieve?*

 Enrichment

Oral Language and Academic Vocabulary
Challenge children to come up with their own outside/inside riddles. Give children the opportunity to ask the class to solve their riddles.

Outside Play Time

large group 20 minutes

Personal Safety and Health Skills Engage children in active play. Have children stand and run in place when you say: *Run, run, as fast as you can!* *¡Corran lo más rápido que puedan!* Explain that when children run inside they have to stay in their own space. When they are outside they can run around. Tell children they will play a running game outside, too.

Oral Language and Academic Vocabulary

✓ **Can children use varied words to describe outside and inside activities?**

Inside or Outside Ask: *What things do we do inside our classroom? What do we do outside?* *¿Qué cosas podemos hacer en el interior del salón de clases? ¿Qué hacemos al aire libre?*

● Say: *Listen to this riddle: I do this outside. I do it in the snow. What am I doing?* *Escuchen este acertijo: Esto lo hago al aire libre. Lo hago en la nieve. ¿Qué estoy haciendo?* (sledding, skiing, making a snowman, and so on)

● Say: *I do this inside. I use a pencil. What am I doing?* *Esto lo hago en el interior. Uso un lápiz. ¿Qué estoy haciendo?* (writing, drawing, and so on)

● Continue with other riddles, using examples such as outside in the water, inside with a book, and so on.

● Encourage children to create riddles on their own.

ELL Enhance children's understanding of the opposites *outside* and *inside*. Show a picture of children on a playground or in a park. Ask: *Are the children inside or outside?* Then show a picture of children in school. Ask: *Are the children inside or outside?*

Move and Learn

✓ **Can children form positive relationships when playing an outside game in a group?**

✓ **Do children display physical coordination as they perform active tasks?**

Run, Run! Take children outside. Say: *We're going to play a game.* *Vamos a jugar a un juego.* Explain that one child will be the cat who baked the gingerbread man and everyone else will be gingerbread people.

● Explain that when the cat says *Run, run, as fast as you can!* the gingerbread people begin running and the cat begins chasing them.

● Explain the boundaries within which children can run. Define the rule as to what constitutes "catching" and ask the children to repeat the rule back to you.

● When the cat catches a gingerbread person, they change places and the game continues. Ask children how they might vary the game, such as by hopping, skipping, and so on.

Center Time

Center Rotation Center Time includes teacher-guided activities and independent activities. Refer to the **Learning Centers** on pages 138–139 for independent activity ideas.

 small group 30 minutes

Writer's Center

✓ **Observe children's ability to use language conventions as they dictate or write.**

Materials drawing paper, crayons

Class Book Say: *Let's make a class book.* *Vamos a crear un libro de clase.*

- Have each child draw an outside activity.

- Ask children to write or dictate a sentence that describes their picture. Remind them to use what they know about sounds and letters and/or scribble writing.

- Collate the drawings to make a class book.

Center Tip

If...some children finish ahead of others, **then...**ask them to illustrate a front and back cover for the book. Add the title *We Go Outside.*

Learning Goals

Social and Emotional Development
• Child demonstrates positive social behaviors, as modeled by the teacher.

Emergent Literacy: Writing
• Child experiments with and uses some writing conventions when writing or dictating.

Writing

On chart paper, write the headings *Inside* and *Outside*. Have children recall what they did throughout the day. Record their ideas, asking children to tell under which heading each idea belongs. Return to the chart to read the sentences under each heading, tracking the words as you read. Display the finished work in the classroom.

Purposeful Play

✓ **Observe children interacting appropriately as they work and play together.**

Children choose an open center for free playtime. Suggest that children work together to have the Dog Puppets act out a game of tag or another outside game.

Let's Say Good-Bye

 large group 15 minutes

 Read Aloud Revisit "The Traveling Musicians"/"Los músicos viajeros" for your afternoon Read Aloud. Ask children to listen to find out how friends work and play together.

Home Connection Refer to the Home Connections activities listed in the Resources and Materials chart on page 135. Remind children to teach their families how to play "Run, Run!" Sing the "Good-Bye Song" as children prepare to leave.

In general, the purpose of assessing young children in the early childhood classroom is to collect information necessary to make important decisions about their developmental and educational needs. Because assessment is crucial to making informed teaching decisions, it is necessarily a vital component of *DLM Early Childhood Express.* The guidelines and forms found online allow the teacher to implement assessment necessary in the pre-kindergarten classroom.

Effective assessment is an ongoing process that always enhances opportunities for optimal growth, development, and learning. The process of determining individual developmental and educational needs tailors early childhood education practices and provides a template for setting individual and program goals.

Pre-kindergarten assessment should be authentic; that is, it should be a natural, environmental extension of the classroom. Assessments should be incorporated into classroom activities whenever possible, not completed as separate, pull-out activities in which the teacher evaluates the student one-on-one. Whenever possible, assessment should evaluate children's real knowledge in the process of completing real activities. For example, observing children as they equally distribute snacks would be a better assessment of their ability to make groups than observing an exercise in which children group counters would be.

It is also important to note that assessments should be administered over time, as environmental influences can greatly impact single outcomes. If a pre-kindergarten child is tired or ill, for example, the child may not demonstrate knowledge of a skill that has actually been mastered. It is also important to consider the length of assessment for children of this age, as attention spans are still developing and can vary greatly based on environmental influences. Most assessments should be completed within half an hour.

If possible, use multiple types of assessment for the same content area when working with pre-kindergarten children. Some children may be able to demonstrate mastery kinesthetically if they are not able to use expressive language well; others may not process auditory instruction adequately, but will be able to complete an assessment after observing someone model the task. It is vital that the assessment process should never make the child anxious or scared.

Informal Assessment

INFORMAL assessments rely heavily on observational and work-sampling techniques that continually focus on child performance, processes, and product over selected periods of time and in a variety of contexts.

ANECDOTAL assessments are written descriptions that provide a short, objective account of an event or an incident. Only the facts are reported—where, what, when, and how. Anecdotal records are especially helpful when trying to understand a child's behavior or use of skills. These recordings can be used to share the progress of individual children and to develop and individualize curriculum.

The Anecdotal Observational Record Form can be used at any time to document an individual child's progress toward a goal or signs indicating the need for developmental or medical evaluation. Observations can reflect the focused skills for the week, but are not limited to those skills. You may pair the form with video or audio recordings of the child to complete an anecdotal record.

Anecdotal Observational Record Form

CHECKLISTS are lists of skills or behaviors arranged into disciplines or developmental domains and are used to determine how a child exhibits the behaviors or skills listed. Teachers can quickly and easily observe groups of children and check the behaviors or skills each child is demonstrating at the moment.

Weekly Assessment

Weekly Assessments measure progress toward specific guidelines that are addressed in the weekly curriculum. The Performance Assessment Checklist measures progress toward the guidelines of the entire curriculum. It is intended to be used three times per year.

Performance Assessment Checklist

When using either type of checklist, it is important to remember that the skills and behaviors on the list are only guidelines. Each child is unique and has his or her own developmental timetable. It is also important to remember that the checklist only documents the presence or absence of a specific skill or behavior during the time of observation. It does not necessarily mean the skill is consistently present or lacking, though consistency may be noted when the skill has been observed over time.

PORTFOLIO assessments are collections of thoughtfully selected work samples, or artifacts, and accompanying reflections indicative of the child's learning experiences, efforts, and progress toward and/ or attainment of established curriculum goals. They are an authentic, performance-based method to allow teachers to analyze progress over time. As children choose work samples for their portfolios, they become involved in their own learning and assessment and begin to develop the concept of evaluating their own work.

Although early childhood activities tend to focus on processes as opposed to products, there are numerous opportunities to collect samples of children's work. Items to collect include drawings, tracings, cuttings, attempts to print their names, and paintings. You may also include informal assessments of a child's ability to recognize letters, shapes, numbers, and rhyming words.

Formal Assessment

FORMAL assessments involve the use of standardized tests. They are administered in a prescribed manner and may require completion within a specified amount of time. Standardized tests result in scores that are usually compared to the scores of a normative group. These tests generally fall into the following categories: achievement tests, readiness tests, developmental screening tests, intelligence tests, and diagnostic tests.

Assessing Children with Special Needs

Children with special needs may require a more thorough initial assessment, more frequent on-going assessments, and continuous adaptation of activities. Assessment is essentially the first task for the teacher or caregiver in developing the individualized instruction program required for children with disabilities.

Assessing Children Who Are English Language Learners

Whenever possible, assessments should be given in both the child's first language and in English.

Essential Question

Why is school important?

Class Play

Perform a Story Re-Enactment for Family

- Before the performance, have children look at pictures in the story *Yellowbelly and Plum Go to School*. Help them choose a character to act out in the play. Multiple children can portray each character.

- Have the children make character masks to wear as they perform. Enlarge the character faces from the story onto cardstock. Cut out large eyes so children can see to move around freely. Have the children paint the masks. When masks are dry, tape a tongue depressor to the back of the mask for students to use to hold the mask in place.

- Choose individual pages for groups of two or three to act out. Have them practice actions from the story, such as playing submarine, playing envelope, playing instruments, painting, and so on.

- A few days before the play, have children paint four large pictures to use as scenery for the performance:

school building	**friends playing**
school classroom	**playground**

- Organize the classroom into the above four areas. Display children's work from the four weeks in each area. Focus each area on one of the weekly themes. After the play, move the backdrop scenery to the four areas of the classroom and attach each week's focus question.

- Allow children to wear their masks as they share their work in different areas.

- Encourage families to read aloud *Yellowbelly and Plum Go to School* with their child.

Evaluate and Inform

 Review the informal observation notes you recorded for each child during the four weeks of the unit. Identify areas in which individual children will need additional support.

 Send a summary of your observation notes home with children. Encourage parents to respond to the summary with questions or comments.

 Review dated samples of children's work in their portfolios. Copy some of these samples to send home to families along with the observation summary.

 Send home the Unit 1 My Library Book, *How Can I Learn at School?*, for children to read with their families.

Celebrar la unidad

Pregunta esencial

¿Por qué es importante la escuela?

Obra de teatro de la clase

Representar la recreación de un cuento para la familia

- Antes de la representación, pida a los niños que observen las imágenes del cuento *Barrigota y Pipón van a la escuela*. Ayúdelos a escoger un personaje para representar en la obra de teatro. Varios niños pueden representar cada personaje.

- Pida a los niños que hagan máscaras de los personajes para usarlas durante la representación. Amplíe las caras de los personajes del cuento en una cartulina. Recorte agujeros grandes para los ojos, así los niños pueden ver y moverse con soltura. Pida a los niños que pinten las máscaras. Cuando las máscaras estén secas, pegue un palito de paleta o un depresor lingual en la parte de atrás de las máscaras, para que los estudiantes puedan sostener la máscara en su lugar.

- Escoja páginas específicas para que las representen grupos de dos o tres niños. Pídales que practiquen las acciones del cuento, como jugar al submarino, jugar al sobre, tocar instrumentos musicales, pintar, etc.

- Unos días antes de la función, pida a los niños que pinten cuatro dibujos grandes para usar como decorado de la obra:

edificio de la escuela	**amigos jugando**
salón de clases de la escuela	**área de juego**

- Organice a la clase en las cuatro áreas mencionadas anteriormente. Exhiba en cada área el trabajo realizado por los niños durante las cuatro semanas. Enfoque cada área en uno de los temas semanales. Después de la obra, traslade el decorado utilizado como telón de fondo a las cuatro áreas del salón de clases y pegue la pregunta de enfoque de cada semana.

- Permita que los niños usen sus máscaras mientras comentan su trabajo en las diferentes áreas.

- Anime a las familias a leer en voz alta *Barrigota y Pipón van a la escuela* con su hijo(a).

Evaluar e informar

- Repase las notas de la observación informal que realizó sobre cada niño durante las cuatro semanas de la unidad. Identifique las áreas en las que algunos niños en particular necesitarán apoyo adicional.

- Envíe a casa con cada niño un resumen de sus notas de observación. Anime a los padres a responderle con preguntas o comentarios.

- Revise las muestras fechadas del trabajo de los niños en sus portafolios. Haga copias de algunas de estas muestras y envíelas a las familias junto con el resumen de sus observaciones.

- Deles a los niños el librito de la Unidad 1, *¿Cómo puedo aprender en la escuela?*, para leer con sus familias.

Appendix

About the Authors

NELL K. DUKE, ED.D., is Professor of Teacher Education and Educational Psychology and Co-Director of the Literacy Achievement Research Center at Michigan State University. Nell Duke's expertise lies in early literacy development, particularly among children living in poverty, and integrating literacy into content instruction. She is the recipient of a number of awards for her research and is co-author of several books including *Literacy and the Youngest Learner: Best Practices for Educators of Children from Birth to 5* and *Beyond Bedtime Stories: A Parent's Guide to Promoting Reading, Writing, and Other Literacy Skills From Birth to 5.*

DOUG CLEMENTS is SUNY Distinguished Professor of Education at the University of Buffalo, SUNY. Previously a preschool and kindergarten teacher, Clements currently researchs the learning and teaching of early mathematics and computer applications. He has published over 100 research studies, 8 books, 50 chapters, and 250 additional publications, including co-authoring the reports of President Bush's National Mathematics Advisory Panel and the National Research Council's book on early mathematics. He has directed twenty projects funded by the National Science Foundation and Department of Education's Institute of Education Sciences.

JULIE SARAMA Associate Professor at the University at Buffalo (SUNY), has taught high school mathematics and computer science, gifted and talented classes, and early childhood mathematics. She directs several projects funded by the National Science Foundation and the Institute of Education Sciences. Author of over 50 refereed articles, 4 books, 30 chapters, 20 computer programs, and more than 70 additional publications, she helped develop the Building Blocks and Investigations curricula and the award-winning Turtle Math. Her latest book is *Early Childhood Mathematics Education Research: Learning Trajectories for Young Children.*

WILLIAM TEALE is Professor of Education at the University of Illinois at Chicago. Author of over one hundred publications on early literacy learning, the intersection of technology and literacy education, and children's literature, he helped pioneer research in emergent literacy. Dr. Teale has worked in the area of early childhood education with schools, libraries, and other organizations across the country and internationally. He has also directed three U.S. Department of Education-funded Early Reading First projects that involve developing model preschool literacy curricula for four-year-old children from urban, low-income settings in Chicago.

Contributing Authors

Kimberly Brenneman, PhD, is an Assistant Research Professor of Psychology at Rutgers University. She is also affiliated with the Rutgers Center for Cognitive Science (RuCCS) and the National Institute for Early Education Research (NIEER). Brenneman is co-author of *Preschool Pathways to Science (PrePS): Facilitating Scientific Ways of Thinking, Talking, Doing, and Understanding* and is an educational advisor for PBS's *Sid the Science Kid* television show and website. Research interests include the development of scientific reasoning and methods to improve instructional practices that support science and mathematics learning in preschool.

Peggy Cerna is an independent Early Childhood Consultant. She was a bilingual teacher for 15 years and then served as principal of the Rosita Valley Literacy Academy, a Pre-Kindergarten through Grade 1 school in Eagle Pass, Texas. Cerna then opened Lucy Read Pre-Kindergarten Demonstration School in Austin, Texas, which had 600 Pre-Kindergarten students. During her principalship at Lucy Read, Cerna built a strong parental community with the collaboration of the University of Texas, AmeriCorps, and Austin Community College. Her passion for early literacy drove her to create book clubs where parents were taught how to read books to their children.

Dan Cieloha is an educator with more than 30 years' experience in creating, implementing, and evaluating experientially based learning materials, experiences, and environments for young children. He believes that all learners must be actively and equitably involved in constructing, evaluating, and sharing what they learn. He has spearheaded the creation and field-testing of a variety of learning materials including *You & Me: Building Social Skills in Young Children*. He is also president of the Partnership for Interactive Learning, a leading nonprofit organization dedicated to the development of children's social and thinking skills.

Paula A. Jones, M.Ed., is an Early Childhood Consultant at the state and national levels. As a former Early Childhood Director for the Lubbock Independent School District, she served as the Head Start Director and co-founded three of their four Early Childhood campuses which also became a model design and Best Practices Program for the Texas Education Agency. She was a contributing author for the first Texas Prekindergarten Guidelines, served as president for the Texas Association of Administrators and Supervisors of Programs for Young Children, and is a 2010 United Way Champions for Children Award winner.

Bobbie Sparks is a retired educator who has taught biology and middle school science as well as being the K-12 district science consultant for a suburban district. At Harris County Department of Education she served as the K-12 science consultant in Professional Development. During her career as K-12 science consultant, Sparks worked with teachers at all grade levels to revamp curriculum to meet the Texas science standards. She served on Texas state committees to develop the TEKS standards as well as committees to develop items for tests for teacher certification in science.

Rita Abrams is a composer, lyricist, educator, and author whose music has won two Emmy Awards, multiple ASCAP Awards, and a variety of others including Parents' Choice, American Education Foundation, and Associated Press. As a teacher she sang her international hit, "Mill Valley," with the Strawberry Point School Third Grade Class. Since then, Abrams has continued to blend her classical music background, special education graduate work, and early childhood teaching experience into a prolific recording career including myriad children's albums, video and film scores. She also creates musical theatre for both children and adults.

Opening Routines

Below are a few suggested routines to use for beginning your day with your class. You can rotate through them, or use one for a while before trying a new approach. You may wish to develop your own routines by mixing and matching ideas from the suggestions given.

1. Days of the Week

Ask children what day of the week it is. When they respond, tell them that you are going to write a sentence that tells everyone what day of the week it is. Print "Today is Monday." on the board. If you have a helper chart, have children assist you in finding the name of the day's helper. Print: "Today's helper is Miguel." Ask the helper to come forward and find the Letter Tiles or ABC Picture Cards that spell his or her name.

As the year progresses, you might want to have the helper find the letters that spell the day of the week. Eventually some children may be able to copy the entire sentence with Letter Tiles or ABC Picture Cards.

2. Calendar Search

Print "Today is _____." on the board. Ask children to help you fill in the blank. Print the day of the week in the blank. Invite children to look at the calendar to determine today's date. Write the date under the sentence that tells what day of the week it is. Invite children to clap out the syllables of both the sentence and the date.

Review the days of the week and the months of the year using the "Days of the Week Song"/"Canción de los dias de la semana" and the "Months of the year"/ "Los meses del año."

Ask children what day of the week it was yesterday. When they respond, ask them what day it is today. Place a seasonal sticker on today's date. Have children follow your lead and recite "Yesterday was Monday, September 12. Today is Tuesday, September 13. Tomorrow will be Wednesday, September 14."

3. Feelings

Make happy- and sad-faced puppets for each child by cutting yellow circles from construction paper and drawing happy and sad faces on them. Laminate the faces, and glue them to tongue depressors. Cover two large coffee cans. On one can glue a happy face, and write the sentence "I feel happy today." Glue the sad face to the second can, and write the sentence "I feel sad today."

Give each child a happy- and a sad-faced puppet. Encourage children to tell how they feel today and to hold up the appropriate puppet. Encourage children to come forward and place their puppets in the can that represents their feelings. Later in the year you can add puppets to represent other emotions.

You can vary this activity by using a graph titled "How I Feel Today"/"Como me siento hoy." Have children place their puppets in the appropriate column on the graph instead of in the cans.

4. Pledge of Allegiance/ Moment of Silence

Have children locate the United States flag. Recite the Pledge of Allegiance to the U.S. flag. Then allow a minute for a moment of silence.

Discuss these activities with children, allowing them to volunteer reasons the Pledge of Allegiance is said and other places they have seen the Pledge recited.

5. Coming to Circle

Talk with children about being part of a class family. Tell children that as part of a class family they will work together, learn together, respect each other, help each other, and play together. Explain that families have rules so that jobs get done and everyone stays safe. Let children know they will learn rules for their classroom. One of those rules is how they will come together for circle. Sing "This is the Way We Come to Circle" (to the tune of "This is the Way We Wash Our Clothes").

This is the way we come to circle.
Come to circle, come to circle.
This is the way we come to circle,
So early in the morning.

This is the way we sit right down,
Sit right down, sit right down.
This is the way we sit right down,
So early in the morning.

This is the way we fold our hands,
Fold our hands, fold our hands.
This is the way we fold our hands,
So early in the morning.

Transition Tips

Sing songs or chants such as those listed below while transitioning between activities:

1. I Am Now in Pre-K

To the tune of "I'm a Little Teapot"

I am now in Pre-K,
I can learn.
I can listen. I can take a turn.
When the teacher says so,
I can play.
Choose a center and together we'll play.

2. Did You Clean Up?

To the tune of "Are You Sleeping, Are You Sleeping, Brother John?"

Did you clean up?
Did you clean up?
Please make sure.
Please make sure.
Everything is picked up.
Everything is picked up.
Please. Thank you!
Please. Thank you!

Chant: Red, Yellow, Green
Red, yellow, green
Stop, change, go
Red, yellow, green
Stop, change, go
Green says yes.
And red says no.
Yellow says everybody wait in a row.
Red, yellow, green
Stop, change, go
Red, yellow, green
Stop, change, go

3. The Five Senses Song

To the tune of "If You're Happy and You Know It"

I can see with my eyes every day (clap clap)
I can see with my eyes every day (clap clap)
I can see with my eyes
I can see with my eyes
I can see with my eyes every day (clap clap)
(Repeat with smell with my nose, hear with my ears, feel with my hands, and taste with my mouth.)

4. Eat More Vegetables

To the tune of "Row, Row, Row Your Boat"

Eat, eat, eat more,
Eat more vegetables.
Carrots, carrots, carrots, carrots
Eat more vegetables.
(Repeat with broccoli, lettuce, celery, and spinach.)

5. Circle Time

To the tune of "Here We Go 'Round the Mulberry Bush"

This is the way we come to circle
Come to circle, come to circle.
This is the way we come to circle
So early in the morning.

This is the way we sit right down,
Sit right down, sit right down.
This is the way we sit right down,
So early in the morning.

Play a short game such as one of the following to focus children's attention:

Name That Fruit!

Say: *It's red on the outside and white on the inside. It rhymes with chapel!*

Children answer, "Apple!" and then repeat twice, "Apple/Chapel."

Repeat with other fruits, such as cherry and banana.

I Spy

Use a flashlight to focus on different letters and words in the classroom. Have children identify them.

Monkey See Monkey Do

Choose one child to be the monkey leader. He or she will act out a motion such as twist, jump, clap, or raise hand, and the rest of the monkeys say the word and copy the motion.

Let's Play Pairs

Distribute one *ABC Picture Card* to each child. Draw letters from an additional set of cards. The child who has the matching letter identifies it and goes to the center of his or her choice.

That's My Friend!

Take children's name cards with their pictures from the wall and distribute making sure no one gets his or her own name. When you call a child's name, she or he has to say something positive about the child on the card and end with "That's my friend!"

Name Game

Say: *If your name begins with ____, you may choose a center.* Have the child say his or her name as he or she gets up. Repeat the child's name, emphasizing the beginning sound.

Center Management

Learning Centers provide children with additional opportunities to practice or extend each lesson's skills and concepts either individually or in small groups. The activities and materials that are explored in the centers not only promote oral language but also help develop children's social skills as they work together. The use of these Learning Centers encourages children to explore their surroundings and make their own choices.

Teacher's Role

The Learning Centers allow time for you to:

- Observe children's exploration of the centers.

- Assess children's understanding of the skills and concepts being taught.

- Provide additional support and encouragement to children who might be having difficulty with specific concepts or skills. If a child is having difficulty, model the correct approach.

Classroom Setup

The materials and activities in the centers should support what children are learning. Multiple experiences are necessary for children's comprehension. The centers should also engage them in learning by providing hands-on experiences. Every time children visit a center and practice skills or extend concepts being taught in the lessons, they are likely to broaden their understanding or discover something new.

In order to support children's learning, the materials and activities in the Learning Centers should change every week. It is important that all the children have a chance to explore every center throughout each week. Be sure they rotate to different centers and do not focus on only one activity. You might also consider adding new materials to the centers as the week progresses. This will encourage children to expand on their past work. Modify or add activities or materials based on your classroom needs.

It is crucial that children know what is expected of them in each center. To help children understand the expectation at each center, display an "I can" statement with an illustration or photograph of a student completing the activity. Discuss these expectations with children in advance, and reinforce them as needed. These discussions might include reviewing your typical classroom rules and talking about the limited number of children allowed in each center. Remind them that they may work individually or in small groups.

Library and Listening Center

Children should feel free throughout the day to explore books and other printed materials. Create a comfortable reading area in the room, and fill it with as many children's books as possible. Include a number of informational books that tell why things happen and books of rhymes, poems, and songs, as well as storybooks and simple alphabet books.

Before beginning each unit in the program, bring in books about the specific concepts or themes in a unit. Encourage children to bring in books they have enjoyed and would like to share with classmates. Even though they may not be actually reading, have children visit the area often. Here they can practice their book handling, apply their growing knowledge of print awareness, and look at pictures and talk about them. Have them read the books to you or to classmates.

Big Book literature selections from the program have been recorded and are available as part of the *Listening Library Audio CDs*. After each literature reading, encourage children to listen to the recordings. Provide CD players that work both with and without earphones. This way, individual children may listen to selections without disturbing the rest of the class. You will also be able to play the recordings for the whole class, if you choose. Encourage children to record their own stories and then share these stories with their classmates.

As you set up the Learning Centers, here are a few ideas you might want to implement in your classroom.

- Create a separate Workshop Center sign-up chart for children to use when choosing a center to explore.

- Provide an area for children who want to be alone to read or to simply reflect on the day's activities.

- Separate loud areas and quiet areas.

- Hang posters or art at eye level for the children.

- Place on shelves materials, such as books or art supplies, that are easily accessible to the children.

English Language Learners

Teaching the English Language Learner

Stages of English-Language Proficiency

An effective learning environment is an important goal of all educators. In a supportive environment, all English learners have the opportunity to participate and to learn. The materials in this guide are designed to support children while they are acquiring English, allowing them to develop English-language reading skills and the fluency they need to achieve in the core content areas as well.

This guide provides direction in supporting children in four stages of English proficiency: Beginning, Intermediate, Advanced, and Advanced-High. While children at a beginning level by definition know little English and will probably have difficulty comprehending English, by the time they progress to the intermediate or early advanced levels of English acquisition, their skills in understanding more complex language structures will have increased. These stages can be described in general terms as follows:

BEGINNING AND INTERMEDIATE Children identified at these levels of English-language proficiency demonstrate dramatic growth. During these stages, children progress from having no receptive or productive English to possessing a basic command of English. They are learning to comprehend and produce one- or two-word responses to questions, are moving to phrases and simple sentences using concrete and immediate topics, and are learning to interact in a limited fashion with text that has been taught. They progress to responding with increasing ease to more varied communication tasks using learned material, comprehending a sequence of information on familiar topics, producing basic statements and asking questions on familiar subjects, and interacting with a variety of print. Some basic errors are found in their use of English syntax and grammar.

ADVANCED Children who have reached the Advanced level of English-language proficiency have good comprehension of overall meaning and are beginning to demonstrate increased comprehension of specific details and concepts. They are learning to respond in expanded sentences, are interacting more independently with a variety of text, and in using newly acquired English vocabulary to communicate ideas orally and in writing. They demonstrate fewer errors in English grammar and syntax than at the beginning and early intermediate levels.

ADVANCED-HIGH Children who are identified at this level of English-language proficiency demonstrate consistent comprehension of meaning, including implied and nuanced meaning, and are learning the use of idiomatic and figurative language. They are increasingly able to respond using detail in compound and complex sentences and sustain conversation in English. They are able to use standard grammar with few errors and show an understanding of conventions of formal and informal usage.

It is important to provide an instructional scaffold for phonemic awareness, phonics, words structure, language structures, comprehension strategies and skills, and grammar, usage, and mechanics so that children can successfully learn to read while advancing along the continuum of English acquisition. For example, at the Beginning level, you might ask children for *yes* or *no* answers when answering questions about selection comprehension or grammar. Children at the Advanced-High level should be asked to provide answers in complete and expanded sentences. By the time children achieve an Advanced level, their knowledge of English will be more sophisticated because they are becoming more adept at comprehending English and using techniques such as making inferences or using persuasive language.

The following charts illustrate how to use sentence stems with children at each level of English-language proficiency:

Teaching Sentence Stems

- Write the sentence stems on the board, chart paper, or sentence strips. Choose stems that are appropriate for the four general levels of English proficiency.

- Model using the sentence stem(s) for the comprehension strategy or skill.

- Read each phrase as you insert the appropriate words to express an idea. Have children repeat the sentences after you. For Beginning and Intermediate children, use the stems within the questions you ask them.

Linguistic Pattern: *I predict that* _____.

Beginning	Intermediate	Advanced	Advanced-High
Simple questions about the text. Yes-or-no responses or responses that allow children to point to an object or picture.	Simple questions about the text which allow for one- or two-word responses or give children two options for a response to select from.	Questions that elicit a short response or a complete simple sentence using the linguistic pattern.	Have children make predictions on their own. Children should use the linguistic pattern and respond with a complete complex sentence.

Practicing Sentence Stems

- To give children multiple opportunities to generate the language they have just been taught, have them work in pairs or small groups and utilize cooperative learning participation strategies to facilitate this communicative practice.

- Pair children one level of proficiency above or below the other. For example, have Beginning children work with Intermediate level children.

- Use differentiated prompts to elicit the responses that incorporate the linguistic patterns and structures for the different proficiency levels. See the following sample of prompts and responses.

Beginning	Intermediate	Advanced	Advanced-High
Do you predict _____? *Yes/No*	Do you predict _____ or _____? *I predict* _____	What do you predict _____? *I predict* _____	Give a prediction about _____. *I predict* _____.

- Select some common cooperative learning participation strategies to teach to children. Once they have learned some language practice activities, they can move quickly into the various routines. See the examples on the next page.

English Language Learners

My Turn, Your Turn

Children work in pairs.

1. The teacher models a sentence and the whole group repeats, or echoes it.

2. One child generates an oral phrase, and the partner echoes it.

3. Partners switch and alternate roles so that each child has a chance to both generate and repeat phrases.

Talking Stick

Children work in small groups. This strategy allows every child to have an opportunity to speak several times and encourages more reflective or reticent participants to take a turn. Children can "pass" only one time.

1. The teacher charts sentence graphic organizers and linguistic patterns children will use in their responses.

2. The teacher models use of linguistic patterns from the lesson.

3. The teacher asks a question or gives a prompt, and then passes a stick, eraser, stuffed animal, or any other designated object to one child.

4. A child speaks, everyone listens, and then the child passes the object on to the person next to him or her.

5. The next child speaks, everyone listens, and the process continues until the teacher or facilitator gives a signal to return the object.

Think-Pair-Share

This strategy allows children time for processing ideas by building in sufficient wait time to process the question and frame an answer. It is an appropriate strategy to use during small- or large-group discussions or lessons, giving all children a chance to organize their thoughts and have a turn sharing their responses with a partner. It also allows for small group verbal interaction to practice language before sharing with the larger group.

1. After reading or listening to a section of text, the teacher presents a question or task. It is helpful to guide with a specific prompt, modeling the language to be used in the response.

2. Children think about their responses for a brief, designated amount of time.

3. Partners share and discuss their responses with each other.

4. An adaptation can be to have each child share his or her partner's response within a small group to promote active listening.

Teaching Vocabulary

Building the background knowledge and a context for children to learn new words is critical in helping children understand new vocabulary. Primary language can be a valuable tool for preteaching, concept development, and vocabulary. Cognates, or words similar in English counterparts, often provide an opportunity for bridging the primary language and English. Also, children who have background knowledge about a topic can more easily connect the new information they are learning with what they already know than children without a similar context from which to work. Therefore, giving children background information and encouraging them to make as many connections as possible with the new vocabulary word they encounter will help them better understand the selection they are about to read.

In addition to building background knowledge, visual displays such as pictures, graphs, charts, maps, models, or other strategies offer unambiguous access to new content. They provide a clear and parallel correspondence between the visual objects and the new vocabulary to be learned. Thus, because the correlation is clear, the negotiation of meaning is established. Additionally, this process must be constant and reciprocal between you and each child if the child is to succeed in effectively interacting with language.

Included in this guide is a routine for teaching vocabulary words. In addition to this routine, more detailed explanations of the ways to teach vocabulary are as follows:

REAL OBJECTS AND REALIA: Because of the immediate result visuals have on learning language, when explaining a word such as *car,* the best approach is simply to show a real car. As an alternative to the real object, you can show realia. Realia are toy versions of real things, such as plastic eggs to substitute for real eggs, or in this case, a toy car to signify a real car. A large, clear picture of an automobile can also work if it is absolutely recognizable.

If, however, the child has had no experience with the item in the picture, more explanation might be needed. For example, if the word you are explaining is a zoo animal such as an *ocelot,* and children are not familiar with this animal, one picture might be insufficient. They might confuse this animal with a cat or any one of the feline species. Seeing several clear pictures, then, of each individual type of common feline and comparing their similarities and differences might help clarify meaning in this particular instance. When children make a connection between their prior knowledge of the word *cat* with the new word *ocelot,* it validates their newly acquired knowledge, and thus they process learning more quickly.

PICTURES: Supplement story illustrations with visuals such as those found in the ***Photo Library CD, ABC Picture Cards,*** magazine pictures, and picture dictionaries. Videos, especially those that demonstrate an entire setting such as a farm or zoo, or videos where different animals are highlighted in the natural habitat, for instance, might be helpful. You might also wish to turn off the soundtrack to avoid a flood of language that children might not be able to understand. This way children can concentrate on the visual-word meaning correlation.

PANTOMIME: Language is learned through modeling within a communicative context. Pantomiming is one example of such a framework of communication. Some words, such as *run* and *jump,* are appropriate for pantomiming. Throughout this guide, you will find suggestions for pantomiming words like *sick* by coughing, sneezing, and holding your stomach. If children understand what you are trying to pantomime, they will more easily engage in the task of learning.

Letter Formation Guide

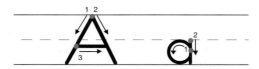  

A Starting point, slanting down left
Starting point, slanting down right
Starting point, across the middle: capital *A*

a Starting point, around left all the way
Starting point, straight down,
touching the circle: small *a*

B Starting point, straight down
Starting point, around right and in
at the middle, around right and in
at the bottom: capital *B*

b Starting point, straight down, back
up, around right all the way: small *b*

C Starting point, around left to
stopping place: capital *C*

C Starting point, around left to
stopping place: small *c*

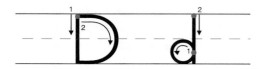 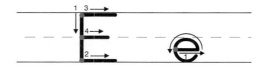 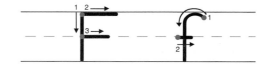

D Starting point, straight down
Starting point, around right and in
at the bottom: capital *D*

d Starting point, around left all the way
Starting point, straight down, touching
the circle: small *d*

E Starting point, straight down
Starting point, straight out
Starting point, straight out
Starting point, straight out: capital *E*

e Starting point, straight out, up and
around to the left, curving down
and around to the right: small *e*

F Starting point, straight down
Starting point, straight out
Starting point, straight out: capital *F*

f Starting point, around left and straight down
Starting point, straight across: small *f*

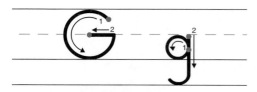 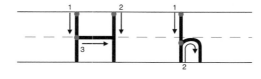 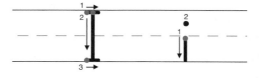

G Starting point, around left, curving up and
around
Straight in: capital *G*

g Starting point, around left all the way
Starting point, straight down, touching the
circle, around left to stopping place: small *g*

H Starting point, straight down
Starting point, straight down
Starting point, across the middle: capital *H*

h Starting point, straight down, back
up, around right, and straight down: small *h*

I Starting point, across
Starting point, straight down
Starting point, across: capital *I*

i Starting point, straight down
Dot exactly above: small *i*

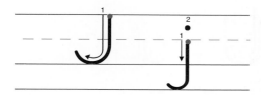

J Starting point, straight down, around left to stopping place: capital J

j Starting point, straight down, around left to stopping place
Dot exactly above: small j

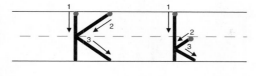

K Starting point, straight down
Starting point, slanting down left, touching the line, slanting down right: capital K

k Starting point, straight down
Starting point, slanting down left, touching the line, slanting down right: small k

L Starting point, straight down, straight out: capital L

l Starting point, straight down: small l

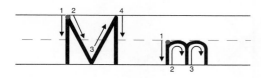

M Starting point, straight down
Starting point, slanting down right to the point, slanting back up to the right, straight down: capital M

m Starting point, straight down, back up, around right, straight down, back up, around right, straight down: small m

N Starting point, straight down
Starting point, slanting down right, straight back up: capital N

n Starting point, straight down, back up, around right, straight down: small n

O Starting point, around left all the way: capital O

o Starting point, around left all the way: small o

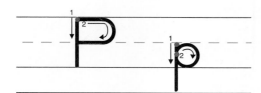

P Starting point, straight down
Starting point, around right and in at the middle: capital P

p Starting point, straight down
Starting point, around right all the way, touching the line: small p

Q Starting point, around left all the way
Starting point, slanting down right: capital Q

q Starting point, around left all the way
Starting point, straight down, touching the circle, curving up right to stopping place: small q

R Starting point, straight down
Starting point, around right and in at the middle, touching the line, slanting down right: capital R

r Starting point, straight down, back up, curving around right to stopping place: small r

Letter Formation Guide

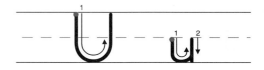

S Starting point, around left, curving right and down around right, curving left and up: capital *S*

s Starting point, around left, curving right and down around right, curving left and up to stopping place: small *s*

T Starting point, straight across
Starting point, straight down: capital *T*

t Starting point, straight down
Starting point, across short: small *t*

U Starting point, straight down, curving around right and up, straight up: capital *U*

u Starting point, straight down, curving around right and up, straight up, straight back down: small *u*

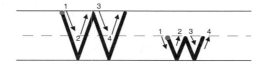

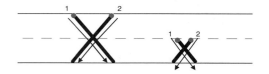

V Starting point, slanting down right, slanting up right: capital *V*

v Starting point, slanting down right, slanting up right: small *v*

W Starting point, slanting down right, slanting up right, slanting down right, slanting up right: capital *W*

W Starting point, slanting down right, slanting up right, slanting down right, slanting up right: small *w*

X Starting point, slanting down right
Starting point, slanting down left: capital *X*

x Starting point, slanting down right
Starting point, slanting down left: small *x*

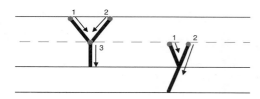

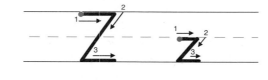

Y Starting point, slanting down right, stop
Starting point, slanting down left, stop
Starting point, straight down: capital *Y*

y Starting point, slanting down right
Starting point, slanting down left, connecting the lines: small *y*

Z Starting point, straight across, slanting down left, straight across: capital *Z*

z Starting point, straight across, slanting down left, straight across: small *z*

Number Formation Guide

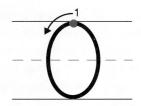

0 Starting point, curving left all the way around to starting point: *0*

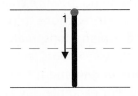

1 Starting point, straight down: *1*

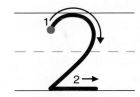

2 Starting point, around right, slanting left and straight across right: *2*

3 Starting point, around right, in at the middle, around right: *3*

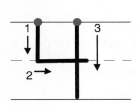

4 Starting point, straight down
Straight across right
Starting point, straight down, crossing line: *4*

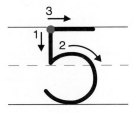

5 Starting point, straight down, curving around right and up
Starting point, straight across right: *5*

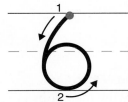

6 Starting point, slanting left, around the bottom curving up, around right and into the curve: *6*

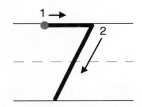

7 Starting point, straight across right, slanting down left: *7*

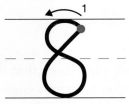

8 Starting point, curving left, curving down and around right, slanting up right to starting point: *8*

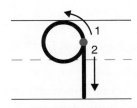

9 Starting point, curving around left all the way, straight down: *9*

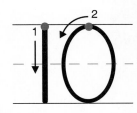

10 Starting point, straight down
Starting point, curving left all the way around to starting point: *10*

Vocabulary Development

Vocabulary development is a key part of *The DLM Early Childhood Express*. Children learn new words through exposure during reading and class discussion. They build language and vocabulary through activities using key words and phrases and by exploring selected vocabulary. After vocabulary words have been introduced, encourage children to use the words in sentences. Again, providing linguistic structures gives children a context for using new vocabulary and building oral language and gives you the opportunity to assess children's understanding of new words. For example, use sentence patterns such as the following:

- A _____ can _____.

- A _____ is a _____.
  (Use this for classification activities. *A tulip is a flower. A rabbit is an animal.*)

- The _____ is _____.
  (Use for describing. *The rabbit is soft.*)

Define words in ways children in your class can understand. When possible, show pictures of objects or actions to help clarify the meanings of words. Provide examples or comparisons to help reinforce the meanings of words and to connect new words to previously learned words. For example, say *The rabbit's FUR is soft like COTTON.* Connect words to categories. For example, say: *Pears are fruits. Are apples fruits? What else is a fruit?* Demonstrate the meaning of words when possible.

During reading, be sure children feel comfortable asking questions and sharing their reactions to what you are reading. Encourage children to share explanations, make predictions, compare and contrast ideas, sequence story events, and describe what you are reading. Encourage children's engagement by modeling reactions and responses while reading. For example, say *I like the part where _____ did _____.* or *This story is about _____.* Support children who are reluctant to speak by using linguistic structures that encourage them to talk about stories and use vocabulary words. You might use the following linguistic structures:

- This story is about _____.

- First _____.

- Next _____.

- Last _____. (Use this for retelling stories.)

- The _____ is the same as _____.

- The _____ is different from _____.

- We read about _____.

Model asking questions before, during, and after reading:

- I wonder what this story is going to be about.

- Who is _____?

- What is _____?

- What did _____ do?

- Why did _____ do _____?

- What happened first? Middle? Last?

Be sure to ask open-ended questions. Unlike questions that simply require a *yes* or *no* or one-word answer, open-ended questions encourage children to think about responses and use new vocabulary in sentences.

Throughout the day, create opportunities for children to talk to each other as they share daily experiences, discuss and explain what they are doing, and talk about what they are learning.

Vocabulary Words by Topic

Animals

alligator/caimán
ant/hormiga
anteater/oso hormiguero
bat/murciélago
bear/oso
beaver/castor
bee/abeja
beetle/escarabajo
bobcat/lince
butterfly/mariposa
camel/camello
cat/gato
chicken/gallina/pollo
chipmunk/ardilla
cow/vaca
crab/cangrejo
deer/venado/ciervo
dog/perro
dolphin/delfín
donkey/burro
dragonfly/libélula
duck/pato
eagle/águila
elephant/elefante
flamingo/flamingo
fly/mosca
fox/zorro
frog/rana
giraffe/jirafa
goat/cabra
gorilla/gorila
grasshopper/saltamontes
hamster/hámster
hippopotamus/hipopótamo
horse/caballo
kangaroo/canguro
koala/coala

ladybug/catarina
leopard/leopardo
lion/león
llama/llama
lobster/langosta
monkey/mono
moose/alce
mosquito/mosquito
mouse/ratón
octopus/pulpo
opossum/zarigüeya
owl/búho
panda/oso panda
parakeet/periquito
peacock/pavo real
pelican/pelicano
penguin/pingüino
pig/cerdo
polar bear/oso polar
porcupine/puerco espín
rabbit/conejo
raccoon/mapache
rhinoceros/rinoceronte
robin/petirrojo
salamander/salamandra
sea horse/caballo de mar
shark/tiburón
sheep/oveja
skunk/mofeta/zorrillo
snake/serpiente
squirrel/ardilla
starfish/estrella de mar
swan/cisne
tiger/tigre
toad/sapo
turkey/pavo
turtle/tortuga
walrus/morsa

whale/ballena
zebra/cebra

Colors and Shapes

blue/azul
green/verde
red/rojo
yellow/amarillo
circle/círculo
diamond/diamante
oval/óvalo
rectangle/rectángulo
square/cuadrado
triangle/triángulo

Signs

deer crossing/cruce de venado
handicapped parking/
    estacionamiento para inválidos
railroad crossing/paso del tren
school crossing/cruce escolar
speed limit/limite de velocidad
stop sign/señal de alto
traffic light/semáforo
yield sign/señal de ceder el paso

Earth

beach/playa
blizzard/tormenta de nieve
cloud/nube
coral reef/arrecife de coral
desert/desierto
dry season/temporada seca
fall/otoño
fog/niebla
forest/bosque
geyser/géiser
glacier/glaciar

hail/granizo
hurricane/huracán
ice/hielo
island/isla
lake/lago
lightning/relámpago
mountain/montaña
ocean/océano
plain/llano
rain/lluvia
rain forest/selva tropical
rainy season/temporada de lluvias
rapids/rápidos
river/río
snow/nieve
spring/primavera
stream/arroyo
summer/verano
sun/sol
tornado/tornado
tundra/tundra
volcano/volcán
waterfall/cascada
wind/viento
winter/invierno

Human Body

ankle/tobillo
arm/brazo
body/cuerpo
ear/oreja
elbow/codo
eyes/ojos
feet/pies
fingers/dedos
hair/pelo
hands/manos

Vocabulary Words by Topic

head/cabeza
hearing/oído
heel/talón
hips/caderas
knee/rodilla
legs/piernas
mouth/boca
nose/nariz
sense/sentido
shoulders/hombros
sight/vista
smell/olfato
taste/gusto
teeth/dientes
toes/dedos de los pies
touch/ tacto

Plants

cactus/cactus
carrot/zanahoria
clover/trébol
cornstalk/planta de maíz
dandelion/diente de león
fern/helecho
grapevine/parra
grass/hierba
lettuce/lechuga
lilac bush/lila de monte
marigold/caléndula
moss/musgo
oak tree/árbol de roble
onion/cebolla
orange tree/naranjo
palm tree/palma
pine tree/pino
poison ivy/hiedra venenosa
rice/arroz
rose/rosa

seaweed/alga marina
sunflower/girasol
tomato/tomate
tulip/tulipán
water lily/nenúfar
wheat/trigo

Clothing

belt/cinturón
blouse/blusa
boots/botas
boy's swimsuit/traje de baño para
    niños
coat/abrigo
dress/vestido
earmuffs/orejeras
girl's swimsuit/traje de baño para
    niñas
gloves/guantes
hat/sombrero
jacket/chaqueta
jeans/pantalones vaqueros
mittens/manoplas
pajamas/pijama
pants/pantalones
raincoat/impermeable
robe/bata
scarf/bufanda
shirt/camisa
shoes/zapatos
shorts/pantalones cortos
skirt/falda
slippers/pantuflas
socks/calcetines
sweat suit/chandal
sweater/suéter
tie/corbata
vest/chaleco

Food

apples/manzanas
bacon/tocino
bagels/roscas de pan
bananas/plátanos
beans/frijoles
beef/carne
beets/betabel
blueberries/arándanos
bread/pan
broccoli/brécol
butter/mantequilla
cake/pastel
cantaloupe/cantalupo
carrots/zanahoria
cauliflower/coliflor
celery/apio
cereal/cereal
cheese/queso
cherries/cerezas
chicken/pollo
clams/almejas
cookies/galletas
corn/maíz
cottage cheese/requesón
crackers/galletas saladas
cream cheese/queso crema
cucumbers/pepinos
eggs/huevos
figs/higos
fish/pescado
grapefruit/toronja
grapes/uvas
green peppers/pimientos verdes
ham/jamón
ice-cream cone/cono de helado
jelly/gelatina
lemons/limones

lettuce/lechuga
limes/limas
macaroni/macarrones
milk/leche
mushrooms/champiñones
nuts/nueces
onions/cebollas
orange juice/jugo de naranja
oranges/naranjas
peaches/duraznos
peanut butter/crema de cacahuete
pears/peras
peas/guisantes
pie/tarta
pineapples/piñas
plums/ciruelas
pork chop/chuleta de puerco
potatoes/papas
radishes/rábanos
raisins/pasas
rice/arroz
rolls/panecillos
salad/ensalada
sausage/salchicha
shrimp/camarón
soup/sopa
spaghetti/espaguetis
squash/calabaza
strawberries/fresas
sweet potatoes/camotes
tomatoes/tomates
watermelon/sandía
yogurt/yogur

Recreation

archery/tiro el arco
badminton/bádminton
baseball/béisbol
basketball/baloncesto
biking/ciclismo
boating/paseo en bote
bowling/boliche
canoeing/piragüismo
climbing/montañismo
croquet/croquet
discus/disco
diving/buceo
fishing/pesca
football/fútbol
golf/golf
gymnastics/gimnasia
hiking/excursionismo
hockey/hockey
horseback riding/equitación
ice-skating/patinaje sobre hielo
in-line skating/patines en línea
lacrosse/lacrosse
pole-vaulting/salto con pértiga
running/atletismo
scuba diving/buceo
shot put/lanzamiento de peso
skiing/esquí
soccer/fútbol
surfing/surfing
swimming/natación
T-ball/T-ball
tennis/tenis
volleyball/voleibol
walking/caminar
waterskiing/esquí acuático
weight lifting/levantamiento

School

auditorium/auditorio
book/libro
cafeteria/cafetería
cafeteria table/mesa de cafetería
calculator/calculadora
chair/silla
chalk/tiza
chalkboard/pizarrón
chart paper/rotafolio
classroom/aula
computer/computadora
construction paper/papel para
    construir
crayons/crayones
desk/escritorio
easel/caballete
eraser/borrador
globe/globo
glue/pegamento
gym/gimnasio
hallway/vestíbulo
janitor's room/conserjería
learning center/centro de
    aprendizaje
library/biblioteca
markers/marcadores
music room/salón de música
notebook paper/papel de cuaderno
nurse's office/enfermería
paint/pintura
paintbrush/pincel
pen/pluma
pencil/lápiz
pencil sharpener/sacapuntas
playground/patio de recreo
principal's office/oficina del
    director

ruler/regla
science room/salón de ciencias
scissors/tijeras
stairs/escaleras
stapler/grapadora
supply room/almacén
tape/cinta adhesiva

Toys

ball/pelota
balloons/globos
bike/bicicleta
blocks/cubos
clay/arcilla
coloring book/libro para colorear
doll/muñeca
doll carriage/careola de muñecas
dollhouse/casa de muñecas
farm set/juego de la granja
game/juego
grocery cart/carro de compras
hats/sombreros
in-line skates/patines
instruments/instrumentos
jump rope/cuerda para saltar
kite/cometa
magnets/imanes
marbles/canicas
puppet/títere
puzzle/rompecabezas
scooter/motoneta
skateboard/patineta
slide/tobogán
stuffed animals/peluches
tape recorder/grabadora
top/trompo
toy cars/carro de juguete
toy trucks/camión de juguete

train set/juego de tren
tricycle/triciclo
wagon/vagón
yo-yo/yó-yó

Equipment

baggage cart/carro para equipaje
baseball/béisbol
bat/bate
mitt/manopla
basketball/pelota de baloncesto
basketball net/canasta
blueprints/planos
computer/computadora
drafting tools/borradores
bow/arco
arrow/flecha
bowling ball/pelota de boliche
bowling pin/bolos de boliche
bridle/freno
saddle/silla de montar
saddle pad/montura
broom/escoba
bulldozer/aplanadora
canoe/canoa
paddle/paleta
cash register/caja registradora
computer/computadora
crane/grúa
dishwasher/lavaplatos
drill/taladro
drum/tambor
drumsticks/palillos
dryer/secadora
dustpan/recogedor
figure skates/patinaje artistico

Vocabulary Words by Topic

football/balón
shoulder pads/hombreras
football helmet/casco
goggles/gafas
golf ball/pelota de golf
golf clubs/palo de golf
tee/tee
hammer/martillo
handcuffs/esposas
badge/placa
hat/gorra
hockey stick/palo de hockey
hockey puck/disco de hockey
ice skates/patines
hoe/azadón
hose/manguera
coat/chaqueta
hat/sombrero
sprinkler/rociador
iron/plancha
ironing board/tabla de planchar
lawn mower/cortacéspedes
mail pouch/bolsa de correo
mirror/espejo
probe/sonda
pick/pico
mop/estropajo
paintbrush/brocha de pintar
piano/piano
pliers/alicates
rake/rastrillo
roller skates/patines
saw/sierra
screwdriver/desarmador
scuba tank/tanque de buceo
mask/máscara
flippers/aletas
shovel/pala

sketch pad/cuaderno para dibujo
palette/paleta
skis/esquís
ski boots/botas para esquiar
poles/palos
soccer ball/balón de fútbol
shoes/zapatos de tenis
stepladder/escalera doble
stethoscope/estetoscopio
surfboard/tabla de surf
tennis ball/pelota de tenis
tennis racket/raqueta de tenis
tractor/tractor
vacuum cleaner/aspiradora
washer/lavadora
water skis/esquís acuáticos
rope/cuerda
life jacket/chaleco salvavidas
watering can/regadera
wheelbarrow/carretilla
wrench/llave inglesa

Home

basement/sótano
bathroom/baño
bathroom sink/lavabo
bathtub/bañera
bed/cama
bedroom/recámara/habitación
blanket/cobija/manta
chair/silla
circuit breaker/cortocircuito
dresser/cómoda
electrical outlet/enchufe
end table/mesa auxiliar
fireplace/chimenea
furnace/horno
kitchen/cocina

kitchen chair/silla de cocina
kitchen sink/fregadero
kitchen table/mesa de cocina
lamp/lámpara
light switch/interruptor de la luz
living room/sala
medicine cabinet/botiquín
nightstand/mesilla de noche
pillow/almohada
refrigerator/refrigerador
shower/ducha
smoke alarm/alarma de incendios
sofa/sofá
stove/estufa
thermostat/termostato
toilet/el baño
water heater/calentador de agua

Occupations

administrative assistant/asistente
    administrativo
air traffic controller/controlador
    aéreo
airline pilot/piloto
architect/arquitecto
artist/artista
astronaut/astronauta
athlete/atleta
author/autor
ballerina/bailarina
banker/banquero
bus driver/conductor de autobús
camera operator/operador de
    cámara
carpenter/carpintero
cashier/cajero
chef/jefe de cocina
computer technician/técnico en

    computación
cosmetologist/cosmetólogo
dancer/bailarín
dentist/dentista
doctor/doctor
electrician/electricista
engineer/ingeniero
farmer/granjero
firefighter/bombero
forest ranger/guardabosques
lawyer/abogado
manicurist/manicurista
musician/músico
nurse/enfermera
paramedic/paramédico
photographer/fotógrafo
police officer/policía
postal worker/empleado postal
real estate agent/corridor de
    bienes raíces
refuse collector/recolector de
    basura
reporter/reportero
school crossing guard/guarda
    escolar
server/mesero
ship captain/capitán de barco
singer/cantante
skater/patinador
teacher/maestro
truck driver/conductor de camión
veterinarian/veterinario
weaver/tejedora

Structures

adobe/casa de adobe
airplane hangar/hangar de avión
airport/aeropuerto
apartment building/edificio de
    departamentos/edificio de pisos
arena/arena
art museum/museo de arte
bakery/panadería
bank/banco
barn/granero
bridge/peunte
bus shelter/parada cubierta
city hall/ayuntamiento
clothing store/tienda de ropa
condominium/condominio
courthouse/tribunal
covered bridge/puente cubierto
dam/presa
dock/muelle
drawbridge/puente levadizo
duplex/dúplex
fire station/estación de bomberos
flower shop/floristeria
garage/garaje
gas station/gasolinera
gazebo/mirador
grain elevator/elevador de granos
grocery store/supermercado
hospital/hospital
house/casa
library/biblioteca
log cabin/cabaña de madera
marina/marina
monument/monumento
movie theater/cine
opera house/teatro de la ópera
palace/palacio

parking garage/estacionamiento
pizza shop/pizzaría
police station/estación de policía
power plant/central eléctrica
pyramid/pirámide
restaurant/restaurante
school/escuela
shelter house/albergue
shopping mall/centro comercial
skyscraper/rascacielos
stadium/estadio
swimming pool/alberca/piscina
tent/tienda
toy store/juguetería
train station/estación del tren
windmills/molino de viento

Transportation

airplane/avión
bicycle/bicicleta
bus/autobús
canoe/canoa
car/coche
four-wheel-drive vehicle/coche con
    doble tracción
helicopter/helicóptero
hot air balloon/globo de aire
    caliente
kayak/kayac
moped/ciclomotor
motor home/casa motora
motorboat/lancha motora
motorcycle/motocicleta
pickup truck/camioneta
rowboat/bote de remos
sailboat/velero
school bus/camión escolar

semitrailer truck/camión con semi-
    remolque
ship/barco
submarine/submarino
subway/metro
taxi/taxi
train/tren
van/furgoneta

Learning Trajectories for Math

Children follow natural developmental progressions in learning. Curriculum research has revealed sequences of activities that are effective in guiding children through these levels of thinking. These developmental paths are the basis for *Building Blocks* learning trajectories.

Learning Trajectories for Primary Grades Mathematics

Learning trajectories have three parts: a mathematical goal, a developmental path along which children develop to reach that goal, and a set of activities matched to each of the levels of thinking in that path that help children develop the next higher level of thinking. The **Building Blocks** learning trajectories give simple labels, descriptions, and examples of each level. Complete learning trajectories describe the goals of learning, the thinking and learning processes of children at various levels, and the learning activities in which they might engage. This document provides only the developmental levels.

The following provides the developmental levels from the first signs of development in different strands of mathematics through approximately age 8. Research shows that when teachers understand how children develop mathematics understanding, they are more effective in questioning, analyzing, and providing activities that further children's development than teachers who are unaware of the development process. Consequently, children have a much richer and more successful math experience in the primary grades.

Each of the following tables, such as "Counting," represents a main developmental progression that underlies the learning trajectory for that topic.

For some topics, there are "subtrajectories"—strands within the topic. In most cases, the names make this clear. For example, in Comparing and Ordering, some levels are "Composer" levels and others involve building a "Mental Number Line." Similarly, the related subtrajectories of "Composition" and "Decomposition" are easy to distinguish. Sometimes, for clarification, subtrajectories are indicated with a note in italics after the title. For example, Parts and Representing are subtrajectories within the Shape Trajectory.

Frequently Asked Questions (FAQ)

1. Why use learning trajectories? Learning trajectories allow teachers to build the mathematics of children—the thinking of children as it develops naturally. So, we know that all the goals and activities are within the developmental capacities of children. Finally, we know that the activities provide the mathematical building blocks for success.

2. When are children "at" a level? Children are at a certain level when most of their behaviors reflect the thinking—ideas and skills—of that level. Most levels are levels of thinking. However, some are merely "levels of attainment" and indicate a child has gained knowledge. For example, children must learn to name or write more numerals, but knowing more numerals does not require more complex thinking.

3. Can children work at more than one level at the same time? Yes, although most children work mainly at one level or in transition between two levels. Levels are not "absolute stages." They are "benchmarks" of complex growth that represent distinct ways of thinking.

4. Can children jump ahead? Yes, especially if there are separate subtopics. For example, we have combined many counting competencies into one "Counting" sequence with subtopics, such as verbal counting skills. Some children learn to count to 100 at age 6 after learning to count objects to 10 or more, some may learn that verbal skill earlier. The subtopic of verbal counting skills would still be followed.

5. How do these developmental levels support teaching and learning? The levels help teachers, as well as curriculum developers, assess, teach, and sequence activities. Through planned teaching and encouraging informal, incidental mathematics, teachers help children learn at an appropriate and deep level.

6. Should I plan to help children develop just the levels that correspond to my children's ages? No! The ages in the table are typical ages children develop these ideas. (These are rough guides only.) These are "starting levels" not goals. We have found that children who are provided high-quality mathematics experiences are capable of developing to levels one or more years beyond their peers.

Developmental Levels for Counting

The ability to count with confidence develops over the course of several years. Beginning in infancy, children show signs of understanding numbers. With instruction and number experience, most children can count fluently by age 8, with much progress in counting occurring in kindergarten and first grade. Most children follow a natural developmental progression in learning to count with recognizable stages or levels. This developmental path can be described as part of a learning trajectory.

Age Range	Level Name	Level	Description
1–2	Precounter	1	At the earliest level a child shows no verbal counting. The child may name some number words with no sequence.
1–2	Chanter	2	At this level, a child may sing-song or chant indistinguishable number words.
2	Reciter	3	At this level, the child may verbally count with separate words, but not necessarily in the correct order.
3	Reciter (10)	4	A child at this level may verbally count to 10 with some correspondence with objects. He or she may point to objects to count a few items, but then lose track.
3	Corresponder	5	At this level, a child may keep one-to-one correspondence between counting words and objects—at least for small groups of objects laid in a line. A corresponder may answer "how many" by recounting the objects.
4	Counter (Small Numbers)	6	At around 4 years of age, the child may begin to count meaningfully. He or she may accurately count objects in a line to 5 and answer the "how many" question with the last number counted. When objects are visible, and especially with small numbers, the child begins to understand cardinality (that numbers tell how many).
4	Producer (Small Numbers)	7	The next level after counting small numbers is to count out objects to 5. When asked to show four of something, for example, this child may give four objects.
4	Counter (10)	8	This child may count structured arrangements of objects to 10. He or she may be able to write or draw to represent 1–10. A child at this level may be able to tell the number just after or just before another number, but only by counting up from 1.
5	Counter and Producer—Counter to (10+)	9	Around 5 years of age, a child may begin to count out objects accurately to 10 and then beyond to 30. He or she has explicit understanding of cardinality (that numbers tell how many). The child may keep track of objects that have and have not been counted, even in different arrangements. He or she may write or draw to represent 1 to 10 and then 20 and 30, and may give the next number to 20 or 30. The child also begins to recognize errors in others' counting and is able to eliminate most errors in his or her own counting.
5	Counter Backward from 10	10	Another milestone at about age 5 is being able to count backward from 10 to 1, verbally, or when removing objects from a group.
6	Counter from N (N+1, N–1)	11	Around 6 years of age, the child may begin to count on, counting verbally and with objects from numbers other than 1. Another noticeable accomplishment is that a child may determine the number immediately before or after another number without having to start back at 1.
6	Skip Counting by 10s to 100	12	A child at this level may count by 10s to 100 or beyond with understanding.
6	Counter to 100	13	A child at this level may count by 1s to 100. He or she can make decade transitions (for example, from 29 to 30) starting at any number.
6	Counter On Using Patterns	14	At this level, a child may keep track of a few counting acts by using numerical patterns, such as tapping as he or she counts.
6	Skip Counter	15	At this level, the child can count by 5s and 2s with understanding.
6	Counter of Imagined Items	16	At this level, a child may count mental images of hidden objects to answer, for example, "how many" when 5 objects are visible and 3 are hidden.
6	Counter On Keeping Track	17	A child at this level may keep track of counting acts numerically, first with objects, then by counting counts. He or she counts up one to four more from a given number.
6	Counter of Quantitative Units	18	At this level, a child can count unusual units, such as "wholes" when shown combinations of wholes and parts. For example, when shown three whole plastic eggs and four halves, a child at this level will say there are five whole eggs.
6	Counter to 200	19	At this level, a child may count accurately to 200 and beyond, recognizing the patterns of ones, tens, and hundreds.
7	Number Conserver	20	A major milestone around age 7 is the ability to conserve number. A child who conserves number understands that a number is unchanged even if a group of objects is rearranged. For example, if there is a row of ten buttons, the child understands there are still ten without recounting, even if they are rearranged in a long row or a circle.
7	Counter Forward and Back	21	A child at this level may count in either direction and recognize that sequence of decades mirrors single-digit sequence.

Learning Trajectories for Math

Developmental Levels for Comparing and Ordering Numbers

Comparing and ordering sets is a critical skill for children as they determine whether one set is larger than another in order to make sure sets are equal and "fair." Prekindergartners can learn to use matching to compare collections or to create equivalent collections. Finding out how many more or fewer in one collection is more demanding than simply comparing two collections. The ability to compare and order sets with fluency develops over the course of several years. With instruction and number experience, most children develop foundational understanding of number relationships and place value at ages four and five. Most children follow a natural developmental progression in learning to compare and order numbers with recognizable stages or levels. This developmental path can be described as part of a learning trajectory.

Age Range	Level Name	Level	Description
2	Object Corresponder	1	At this early level, a child puts objects into one-to-one correspondence, but may not fully understand that this creates equal groups. For example, a child may know that each carton has a straw, but does not necessarily know there are the same numbers of straws and cartons.
2	Perceptual Comparer	2	At this level, a child can compare collections that are quite different in size (for example, one is at least twice the other) and know that one has more than the other. If the collections are similar, the child can compare very small collections.
3	First-Second Ordinal Counter	3	At this level the child can identify the "first" and often "second" object in a sequence.
3	Nonverbal Comparer of Similar Items	4	At this level, a child can identify that different organizations of the same number are equal and different from other sets (1–4 items). For example, a child can identify ••• and •‚• as equal and different from •• or •‚.
4	Nonverbal Comparer of Dissimilar Items	5	At this level, a child can match small, equal collections of dissimilar items, such as shells and dots, and show that they are the same number.
4	Matching Comparer	6	As children progress, they begin to compare groups of 1–6 by matching. For example, a child gives one toy bone to every dog and says there are the same number of dogs and bones.

Age Range	Level Name	Level	Description
4	Knows-to-Count Comparer	7	A significant step occurs when the child begins to count collections to compare. At the early levels, children are not always accurate when a larger collection's objects are smaller in size than the objects in the smaller collection. For example, a child at this level may accurately count two equal collections, but when asked, says the collection of larger blocks has more.
4	Counting Comparer (Same Size)	8	At this level, children make accurate comparisons via counting, but only when objects are about the same size and groups are small (about 1–5 items).
5	Counting Comparer (5)	9	As children develop their ability to compare sets, they compare accurately by counting, even when a larger collection's objects are smaller. A child at this level can figure out how many more or less.
5	Ordinal Counter	10	At this level, a child identifies and uses ordinal numbers from "first" to "tenth." For example, the child can identify who is "third in line."
6	Counting Comparer (10)	11	This level can be observed when the child compares sets by counting, even when a larger collection's objects are smaller, up to 10. A child at this level can accurately count two collections of 9 items each, and says they have the same number, even if one collection has larger blocks.
6	Mental Number Line to 10	12	As children move into this level, they begin to use mental images and knowledge of number relationships to determine relative size and position. For example, a child at this level can answer which number is closer to 6, 4 or 9 without counting physical objects.
6	Serial Orderer to 61	13	At this level, the child orders lengths marked into units (1–6, then beyond). For example, given towers of cubes, this child can put them in order, 1 to 6.
7	Place Value Comparer	14	Further development is made when a child begins to compare numbers with place value understanding. For example, a child at this level can explain that "63 is more than 59 because six tens is more than five tens, even if there are more than three ones."
7	Mental Number Line to 100	15	Children demonstrate the next level when they can use mental images and knowledge of number relationships, including ones embedded in tens, to determine relative size and position. For example, when asked, "Which is closer to 45, 30 or 50?" a child at this level may say "45 is right next to 50, but 30 isn't."
8+	Mental Number Line to 1,000s	16	At about age 8, children may begin to use mental images of numbers up to 1,000 and knowledge of number relationships, including place value, to determine relative size and position. For example, when asked, "Which is closer to 3,500—2,000 or 7,000?" a child at this level may say "70 is double 35, but 20 is only fifteen from 35, so twenty hundreds, 2,000, is closer."

Developmental Levels for Recognizing Number and Subitizing (Instantly Recognizing)

The ability to recognize number values develops over the course of several years and is a foundational part of number sense. Beginning at about age two, children begin to name groups of objects. The ability to instantly know how many are in a group, called *subitizing,* begins at about age three. By age eight, with instruction and number experience, most children can identify groups of items and use place values and multiplication skills to count them. Most children follow a natural developmental progression in learning to count with recognizable stages or levels. This developmental path can be described as part of a learning trajectory.

Age Range	Level Name	Level	Description
2	Small Collection Namer	1	The first sign occurs when the child can name groups of 1 to 2, sometimes 3. For example, when shown a pair of shoes, this young child says, "two shoes."
3	Maker of Small Collections	2	At this level, a child can nonverbally make a small collection (no more than 4, usually 1 to 3) with the same number as another collection. For example, when shown a collection of 3, the child makes another collection of 3.
4	Perceptual Subitizer to 4	3	Progress is made when a child instantly recognizes collections up to 4 and verbally names the number of items. For example, when shown 4 objects briefly, the child says "4."
5	Perceptual Subitizer to 5	4	This level is the ability to instantly recognize collections up to 5 and verbally name the number of items. For example, when shown 5 objects briefly, the child says "5."
5	Conceptual Subitizer to 5	5	At this level, the child can verbally label all arrangements to about 5, when shown only briefly. For example, a child at this level might say, "I saw 2 and 2, and so I saw 4."
5	Conceptual Subitizer to 10	6	This step is when the child can verbally label most arrangements to 6 shown briefly, then up to 10, using groups. For example, a child at this level might say, "In my mind, I made 2 groups of 3 and 1 more, so 7."
6	Conceptual Subitizer to 20	7	Next, a child can verbally label structured arrangements up to 20 shown briefly, using groups. For example, the child may say, "I saw 3 fives, so 5, 10, 15."
7	Conceptual Subitizer with Place Value and Skip Counting	8	At this level, a child is able to use groups, skip counting, and place value to verbally label structured arrangements shown briefly. For example, the child may say, "I saw groups of tens and twos, so 10, 20, 30, 40, 42, 44, 46…46!"
8+	Conceptual Subitizer with Place Value and Multiplication	9	As children develop their ability to subitize, they use groups, multiplication, and place value to verbally label structured arrangements shown briefly. At this level, a child may say, "I saw groups of tens and threes, so I thought, 5 tens is 50 and 4 threes is 12, so 62 in all."

Learning Trajectories for Math

Developmental Levels for Composing (Knowing Combinations of Numbers)

Composing and decomposing are combining and separating operations that allow children to build concepts of "parts" and "wholes." Most prekindergartners can "see" that two items and one item make three items. Later, children learn to separate a group into parts in various ways and then to count to produce all of the number "partners" of a given number. Eventually children think of a number and know the different addition facts that make that number. Most children follow a natural developmental progression in learning to compose and decompose numbers with recognizable stages or levels. This developmental path can be described as part of a learning trajectory.

Age Range	Level Name	Level	Description
4	Pre-Part-Whole Recognizer	1	At the earliest levels of composing, a child only nonverbally recognizes parts and wholes. For example, when shown 4 red blocks and 2 blue blocks, a young child may intuitively appreciate that "all the blocks" includes the red and blue blocks, but when asked how many there are in all, the child may name a small number, such as 1.
5	Inexact Part-Whole Recognizer	2	A sign of development is that the child knows a whole is bigger than parts, but does not accurately quantify. For example, when shown 4 red blocks and 2 blue blocks and asked how many there are in all, the child may name a "large number," such as 5 or 10.
5	Composer to 4, then 5	3	At this level, a child knows number combinations. A child at this level quickly names parts of any whole, or the whole given the parts. For example, when shown 4, then 1 is secretly hidden, and then shown the 3 remaining, the child may quickly say "1" is hidden.
6	Composer to 7	4	The next sign of development is when a child knows number combinations to totals of 7. A child at this level quickly names parts of any whole, or the whole when given parts, and can double numbers to 10. For example, when shown 6, then 4 are secretly hidden, and then shown the 2 remaining, the child may quickly say "4" are hidden.
6	Composer to 10	5	This level is when a child knows number combinations to totals of 10. A child at this level may quickly name parts of any whole, or the whole when given parts, and can double numbers to 20. For example, this child would be able to say "9 and 9 is 18."
7	Composer with Tens and Ones	6	At this level, the child understands two-digit numbers as tens and ones, can count with dimes and pennies, and can perform two-digit addition with regrouping. For example, a child at this level may explain, "17 and 36 is like 17 and 3, which is 20, and 33, which is 53."

Developmental Levels for Adding and Subtracting

Single-digit addition and subtraction are generally characterized as "math facts." It is assumed children must memorize these facts, yet research has shown that addition and subtraction have their roots in counting, counting on, number sense, the ability to compose and decompose numbers, and place value. Research has also shown that learning methods for addition and subtraction with understanding is much more effective than rote memorization of seemingly isolated facts. Most children follow an observable developmental progression in learning to add and subtract numbers with recognizable stages or levels. This developmental path can be described as part of a learning trajectory.

Age Range	Level Name	Level	Description
1	Pre +/–	1	At the earliest level, a child shows no sign of being able to add or subtract.
3	Nonverbal +/–	2	The first sign is when a child can add and subtract very small collections nonverbally. For example, when shown 2 objects, then 1 object being hidden under a napkin, the child identifies or makes a set of 3 objects to "match."
4	Small Number +/–	3	This level is when a child can find sums for joining problems up to 3 + 2 by counting with objects. For example, when asked, "You have 2 balls and get 1 more. How many in all?" the child may count out 2, then count out 1 more, then count all 3: "1, 2, 3, 3!"
5	Find Result +/–	4	**Addition** Evidence of this level in addition is when a child can find sums for joining (you had 3 apples and get 3 more; how many do you have in all?) and part-part-whole (there are 6 girls and 5 boys on the playground; how many children are there in all?) problems by direct modeling, counting all, with objects. For example, when asked, "You have 2 red balls and 3 blue balls. How many in all?" the child may count out 2 red, then count out 3 blue, then count all 5. **Subtraction** In subtraction, a child can also solve take-away problems by separating with objects. For example, when asked, "You have 5 balls and give 2 to Tom. How many do you have left?" the child may count out 5 balls, then take away 2, and then count the remaining 3.

Age Range	Level Name	Level	Description
5	Find Change +/−	5	**Addition** At this level, a child can find the missing addend (5 + _ =7) by adding on objects. For example, when asked, "You have 5 balls and then get some more. Now you have 7 in all. How many did you get?" The child may count out 5, then count those 5 again starting at 1, then add more, counting "6, 7," then count the balls added to find the answer, 2. **Subtraction** A child can compare by matching in simple situations. For example, when asked, "Here are 6 dogs and 4 balls. If we give a ball to each dog, how many dogs will not get a ball?" a child at this level may count out 6 dogs, match 4 balls to 4 of them, then count the 2 dogs that have no ball.
5	Make It +/−	6	A significant advancement occurs when a child is able to count on. This child can add on objects to make one number into another without counting from 1. For example, when told, "This puppet has 4 balls, but she should have 6. Make it 6," the child may put up 4 fingers on one hand, immediately count up from 4 while putting up 2 fingers on the other hand, saying, "5, 6," and then count or recognize the 2 fingers.
6	Counting Strategies +/−	7	This level occurs when a child can find sums for joining (you had 8 apples and get 3 more…) and part-part-whole (6 girls and 5 boys…) problems with finger patterns or by adding on objects or counting on. For example, when asked "How much is 4 and 3 more?" the child may answer "4…5, 6, 7. 7!" Children at this level can also solve missing addend (3 + _ = 7) or compare problems by counting on. When asked, for example, "You have 6 balls. How many more would you need to have 8?" the child may say, "6, 7 [puts up first finger], 8 [puts up second finger]. 2!"
6	Part-Whole +/−	8	Further development has occurred when the child has part-whole understanding. This child can solve problems using flexible strategies and some derived facts (for example, "5 + 5 is 10, so 5 + 6 is 11"), can sometimes do start-unknown problems (_ + 6 = 11), but only by trial and error. When asked, "You had some balls. Then you get 6 more. Now you have 11 balls. How many did you start with?" this child may lay out 6, then 3, count, and get 9. The child may put 1 more, say 10, then put 1 more. The child may count up from 6 to 11, then recount the group added, and say, "5!"

Age Range	Level Name	Level	Description
6	Numbers-in-Numbers +/−	9	Evidence of this level is when a child recognizes that a number is part of a whole and can solve problems when the start is unknown (_ + 4 = 9) with counting strategies. For example, when asked, "You have some balls, then you get 4 more balls, now you have 9. How many did you have to start with?" this child may count, putting up fingers, "5, 6, 7, 8, 9." The child may then look at his or her fingers and say, "5!"
7	Deriver +/−	10	At this level, a child can use flexible strategies and derived combinations (for example, "7 + 7 is 14, so 7 + 8 is 15") to solve all types of problems. For example, when asked, "What's 7 plus 8?" this child thinks: 7 + 8 = 7 [7 + 1] = [7 +7] + 1 = 14 + 1 = 15. The child can also solve multidigit problems by incrementing or combining 10s and 1s. For example, when asked "What's 28 + 35?" this child may think: 20 + 30 = 50; + 8 = 58; 2 more is 60, and 3 more is 63. He or she can also combine 10s and 1s: 20 + 30 = 50. 8 + 5 is like 8 plus 2 and 3 more, so it is 13. 50 and 13 is 63.
8+	Problem Solver +/−	11	As children develop their addition and subtraction abilities, they can solve by using flexible strategies and many known combinations. For example, when asked, "If I have 13 and you have 9, how could we have the same number?" this child may say, "9 and 1 is 10, then 3 more makes 13. 1 and 3 is 4. I need 4 more!"
8+	Multidigit +/−	12	Further development is shown when children can use composition of 10s and all previous strategies to solve multidigit +/− problems. For example, when asked, "What's 37 − 18?" this child may say, "Take 1 ten off the 3 tens; that's 2 tens. Take 7 off the 7. That's 2 tens and 0…20. I have one more to take off. That's 19." Or, when asked, "What's 28 + 35?" this child may think, 30 + 35 would be 65. But it's 28, so it's 2 less…63.

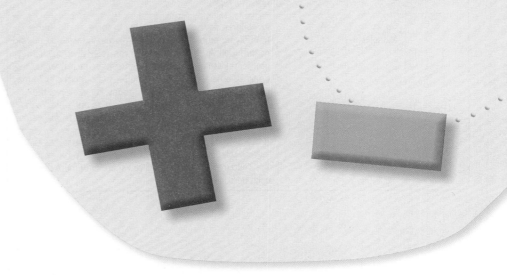

Learning Trajectories for Math

Developmental Levels for Multiplying and Dividing

Multiplication and division build on addition and subtraction understanding and are dependent upon counting and place-value concepts. As children begin to learn to multiply, they make equal groups and count them all. They then learn skip counting and derive related products from products they know. Finding and using patterns aid in learning multiplication and division facts with understanding. Children typically follow an observable developmental progression in learning to multiply and divide numbers with recognizable stages or levels. This developmental path can be described as part of a learning trajectory.

Age Range	Level Name	Level	Description
2	Non-quantitative Sharer "Dumper"	1	Multiplication and division concepts begin very early with the problem of sharing. Early evidence of these concepts can be observed when a child dumps out blocks and gives some (not an equal number) to each person.
3	Beginning Grouper and Distributive Sharer	2	Progression to this level can be observed when a child is able to make small groups (fewer than 5). This child can share by "dealing out," but often only between 2 people, although he or she may not appreciate the numerical result. For example, to share 4 blocks, this child may give each person a block, check that each person has one, and repeat this.
4	Grouper and Distributive Sharer	3	The next level occurs when a child makes small equal groups (fewer than 6). This child can deal out equally between 2 or more recipients, but may not understand that equal quantities are produced. For example, the child may share 6 blocks by dealing out blocks to herself and a friend one at a time.
5	Concrete Modeler ×/÷	4	As children develop, they are able to solve small-number multiplying problems by grouping—making each group and counting all. At this level, a child can solve division/sharing problems with informal strategies, using concrete objects—up to 20 objects and 2 to 5 people—although the child may not understand equivalence of groups. For example, the child may distribute 20 objects by dealing out 2 blocks to each of 5 people, then 1 to each, until the blocks are gone.
6	Parts and Wholes ×/÷	5	A new level is evidenced when the child understands the inverse relation between divisor and quotient. For example, this child may understand "If you share with more people, each person gets fewer."
7	Skip Counter ×/÷	6	As children develop understanding in multiplication and division, they begin to use skip counting for multiplication and for measurement division (finding out how many groups). For example, given 20 blocks, 4 to each person, and asked how many people, the children may skip count by 4, holding up 1 finger for each count of 4. A child at this level may also use trial and error for partitive division (finding out how many in each group). For example, given 20 blocks, 5 people, and asked how many each should get, this child may give 3 to each, and then 1 more.
8+	Deriver ×/÷	7	At this level, children use strategies and derived combinations to solve multidigit problems by operating on tens and ones separately. For example, a child at this level may explain "7 × 6, five 7s is 35, so 7 more is 42."
8+	Array Quantifier	8	Further development can be observed when a child begins to work with arrays. For example, given 7 × 4 with most of 5 × 4 covered, a child at this level may say, "There are 8 in these 2 rows, and 5 rows of 4 is 20, so 28 in all."
8+	Partitive Divisor	9	This level can be observed when a child is able to figure out how many are in each group. For example, given 20 blocks, 5 people, and asked how many each should get, a child at this level may say, "4, because 5 groups of 4 is 20."
8+	Multidigit ×/÷	10	As children progress, they begin to use multiple strategies for multiplication and division, from compensating to paper-and-pencil procedures. For example, a child becoming fluent in multiplication might explain that "19 times 5 is 95, because 20 fives is 100, and 1 less five is 95."

Developmental Levels for Measuring

Measurement is one of the main real-world applications of mathematics. Counting is a type of measurement which determines how many items are in a collection. Measurement also involves assigning a number to attributes of length, area, and weight. Prekindergarten children know that mass, weight, and length exist, but they do not know how to reason about these or to accurately measure them. As children develop their understanding of measurement, they begin to use tools to measure and understand the need for standard units of measure. Children typically follow an observable developmental progression in learning to measure with recognizable stages or levels. This developmental path can be described as part of a learning trajectory.

Age Range	Level Name	Level	Description
3	Length Quantity Recognizer	1	At the earliest level, children can identify length as an attribute. For example, they might say, "I'm tall, see?"
4	Length Direct Comparer	2	In this level, children can physically align 2 objects to determine which is longer or if they are the same length. For example, they can stand 2 sticks up next to each other on a table and say, "This one's bigger."
5	Indirect Length Comparer	3	A sign of further development is when a child can compare the length of 2 objects by representing them with a third object. For example, a child might compare the length of 2 objects with a piece of string. Additional evidence of this level is that when asked to measure, the child may assign a length by guessing or moving along a length while counting (without equal-length units). For example, the child may move a finger along a line segment, saying 10, 20, 30, 31, 32.
6	Serial Orderer to 6+	4	At this level, a child can order lengths, marked in 1 to 6 units. For example, given towers of cubes, a child at this level may put them in order, 1 to 6.
6	End-to-End Length Measurer	5	At this level, the child can lay units end-to-end, although he or she may not see the need for equal-length units. For example, a child might lay 9-inch cubes in a line beside a book to measure how long it is.
7	Length Unit Iterater	6	A significant change occurs when a child iterates a single unit to measure. He or she sees the need for identical units. The child uses rulers with help.
7	Length Unit Relater	7	At this level, a child can relate size and number of units. For example, the child may explain, "If you measure with centimeters instead of inches, you'll need more of them because each one is smaller."
8+	Length Measurer	8	As a child develops measurement ability, they begin to measure, knowing the need for identical units, the relationships between different units, partitions of unit, and the zero point on rulers. At this level, the child also begins to estimate. The children may explain, "I used a meterstick 3 times, then there was a little left over. So, I lined it up from 0 and found 14 centimeters. So, it's 3 meters, 14 centimeters in all."
8+	Conceptual Ruler Measurer	9	Further development in measurement is evidenced when a child possesses an "internal" measurement tool. At this level, the child mentally moves along an object, segmenting it, and counting the segments. This child also uses arithmetic to measure and estimates with accuracy. For example, a child at this level may explain, "I imagine one meterstick after another along the edge of the room. That's how I estimated the room's length to be 9 meters."

Developmental Levels for Recognizing Geometric Shapes

Geometric shapes can be used to represent and understand objects. Analyzing, comparing, and classifying shapes help create new knowledge of shapes and their relationships. Shapes can be decomposed or composed into other shapes. Through their everyday activities, children build both intuitive and explicit knowledge of geometric figures. Most children can recognize and name basic two-dimensional shapes at four years of age. However, young children can learn richer concepts about shape if they have varied examples and nonexamples of shape, discussions about shapes and their characteristics, a wide variety of shape classes, and interesting tasks. Children typically follow an observable developmental progression in learning about shapes with recognizable stages or levels. This developmental path can be described as part of a learning trajectory.

Age Range	Level Name	Level	Description
2	Shape Matcher— Identical	1	The earliest sign of understanding shape is when a child can match basic shapes (circle, square, typical triangle) with the same size and orientation.
2	Shape Matcher— Sizes	2	A sign of development is when a child can match basic shapes with different sizes.
2	Shape Matcher— Orientations	3	This level of development is when a child can match basic shapes with different orientations.
3	Shape Recognizer— Typical	4	A sign of development is when a child can recognize and name a prototypical circle, square, and, less often, a typical triangle. For example, the child names this a square. Some children may name different sizes, shapes, and orientations of rectangles, but also accept some shapes that look rectangular but are not rectangles. Children name these shapes "rectangles" (including the nonrectangular parallelogram).
3	Shape Matcher— More Shapes	5	As children develop understanding of shape, they can match a wider variety of shapes with the same size and orientation.
3	Shape Matcher— Sizes and Orientations	6	The child matches a wider variety of shapes with different sizes and orientations.
3	Shape Matcher— Combinations	7	The child matches combinations of shapes to each other.
4	Shape Recognizer— Circles, Squares, and Triangles	8	This sign of development is when a child can recognize some nonprototypical squares and triangles and may recognize some rectangles, but usually not rhombi (diamonds). Often, the child does not differentiate sides/corners. The child at this level may name these as triangles.
4	Constructor of Shapes from Parts— Looks Like *Representing*	9	A significant sign of development is when a child represents a shape by making a shape "look like" a goal shape. For example, when asked to make a triangle with sticks, the child may create the following: △ .

Age Range	Level Name	Level	Description
5	Shape Recognizer—All Rectangles	10	As children develop understanding of shape, they recognize more rectangle sizes, shapes, and orientations of rectangles. For example, a child at this level may correctly name these shapes "rectangles."
5	Side Recognizer *Parts*	11	A sign of development is when a child recognizes parts of shapes and identifies sides as distinct geometric objects. For example, when asked what this shape is, the child may say it is a quadrilateral (or has 4 sides) after counting and running a finger along the length of each side.
5	Angle Recognizer *Parts*	12	At this level, a child can recognize angles as separate geometric objects. For example, when asked, "Why is this a triangle," the child may say, "It has three angles" and count them, pointing clearly to each vertex (point at the corner).
5	Shape Recognizer—More Shapes	13	As children develop, they are able to recognize most basic shapes and prototypical examples of other shapes, such as hexagon, rhombus (diamond), and trapezoid. For example, a child can correctly identify and name all the following shapes:
6	Shape Identifier	14	At this level, the child can name most common shapes, including rhombi, without making mistakes such as calling ovals circles. A child at this level implicitly recognizes right angles, so distinguishes between a rectangle and a parallelogram without right angles. A child may correctly name all the following shapes:
6	Angle Matcher *Parts*	15	A sign of development is when the child can match angles concretely. For example, given several triangles, the child may find two with the same angles by laying the angles on top of one another.

Age Range	Level Name	Level	Description
7	Parts of Shapes Identifier	16	At this level, the child can identify shapes in terms of their components. For example, the child may say, "No matter how skinny it looks, that's a triangle because it has 3 sides and 3 angles."
7	Constructor of Shapes from Parts—Exact Representing	17	A significant step is when the child can represent a shape with completely correct construction, based on knowledge of components and relationships. For example, when asked to make a triangle with sticks, the child may create the following:
8	Shape Class Identifier	18	As children develop, they begin to use class membership (for example, to sort) not explicitly based on properties. For example, a child at this level may say, "I put the triangles over here, and the quadrilaterals, including squares, rectangles, rhombi, and trapezoids, over there."
8	Shape Property Identifier	19	At this level, a child can use properties explicitly. For example, a child may say, "I put the shapes with opposite sides that are parallel over here, and those with 4 sides but not both pairs of sides parallel over there."
8	Angle Size Comparer	20	The next sign of development is when a child can separate and compare angle sizes. For example, the child may say, "I put all the shapes that have right angles here, and all the ones that have bigger or smaller angles over there."
8	Angle Measurer	21	A significant step in development is when a child can use a protractor to measure angles.
8	Property Class Identifier	22	The next sign of development is when a child can use class membership for shapes (for example, to sort or consider shapes "similar") explicitly based on properties, including angle measure. For example, the child may say, "I put the equilateral triangles over here, and the right triangles over here."
8	Angle Synthesizer	23	As children develop understanding of shape, they can combine various meanings of angle (turn, corner, slant). For example, a child at this level could explain, "This ramp is at a 45° angle to the ground."

Developmental Levels for Composing Geometric Shapes

Children move through levels in the composition and decomposition of two-dimensional figures. Very young children cannot compose shapes but then gain ability to combine shapes into pictures, synthesize combinations of shapes into new shapes, and eventually substitute and build different kinds of shapes. Children typically follow an observable developmental progression in learning to compose shapes with recognizable stages or levels. This developmental path can be described as part of a learning trajectory.

Age Range	Level Name	Level	Description
2	Pre-Composer	1	The earliest sign of development is when a child can manipulate shapes as individuals, but is unable to combine them to compose a larger shape.
3	Pre-Decomposer	2	At this level, a child can decompose shapes, but only by trial and error.
4	Piece Assembler	3	Around age 4, a child can begin to make pictures in which each shape represents a unique role (for example, one shape for each body part) and shapes touch. A child at this level can fill simple outline puzzles using trial and error.
5	Picture Maker	4	As children develop, they are able to put several shapes together to make one part of a picture (for example, 2 shapes for 1 arm). A child at this level uses trial and error and does not anticipate creation of the new geometric shape. The children can choose shapes using "general shape" or side length, and fill "easy" outline puzzles that suggest the placement of each shape (but note that the child is trying to put a square in the puzzle where its right angles will not fit).
5	Simple Decomposer	5	A significant step occurs when the child is able to decompose ("take apart" into smaller shapes) simple shapes that have obvious clues as to their decomposition.

Age Range	Level Name	Level	Description
5	Shape Composer	6	A sign of development is when a child composes shapes with anticipation ("I know what will fit!"). A child at this level chooses shapes using angles as well as side lengths. Rotation and flipping are used intentionally to select and place shapes.
6	Substitution Composer	7	A sign of development is when a child is able to make new shapes out of smaller shapes and uses trial and error to substitute groups of shapes for other shapes in order to create new shapes in different ways. For example, the child can substitute shapes to fill outline puzzles in different ways.
6	Shape Decomposer (with Help)	8	As children develop, they can decompose shapes by using imagery that is suggested and supported by the task or environment.
7	Shape Composite Repeater	9	This level is demonstrated when the child can construct and duplicate units of units (shapes made from other shapes) intentionally, and understands each as being both multiple, small shapes and one larger shape. For example, the child may continue a pattern of shapes that leads to tiling.
7	Shape Decomposer with Imagery	10	A significant sign of development is when a child is able to decompose shapes flexibly by using independently generated imagery.
8	Shape Composer—Units of Units	11	Children demonstrate further understanding when they are able to build and apply units of units (shapes made from other shapes). For example, in constructing spatial patterns, the child can extend patterning activity to create a tiling with a new unit shape—a unit of unit shapes that he or she recognizes and consciously constructs. For example, the child may build Ts out of 4 squares, use 4 Ts to build squares, and use squares to tile a rectangle.
8	Shape Decomposer — Units of Units	12	As children develop understanding of shape, they can decompose shapes flexibly by using independently generated imagery and planned decompositions of shapes that themselves are decompositions.

Developmental Levels for Comparing Geometric Shapes

As early as four years of age, children can create and use strategies, such as moving shapes to compare their parts or to place one on top of the other, for judging whether two figures are the same shape. From Pre-K to Grade 2, they can develop sophisticated and accurate mathematical procedures for comparing geometric shapes. Children typically follow an observable developmental progression in learning about how shapes are the same and different with recognizable stages or levels. This developmental path can be described as part of a learning trajectory.

Age Range	Level Name	Level	Description
3	"Same Thing" Comparer	1	The first sign of understanding is when the child can compare real-world objects. For example, the children may say two pictures of houses are the same or different.
4	"Similar" Comparer	2	This sign of development occurs when the child judges two shapes to be the same if they are more visually similar than different. For example, the child may say, "These are the same. They are pointy at the top."
4	Part Comparer	3	At this level, a child can say that two shapes are the same after matching one side on each. For example, a child may say, "These are the same" (matching the two sides).
4	Some Attributes Comparer	4	As children develop, they look for differences in attributes, but may examine only part of a shape. For example, a child at this level may say, "These are the same" (indicating the top halves of the shapes are similar by laying them on top of each other).
5	Most Attributes Comparer	5	At this level, the child looks for differences in attributes, examining full shapes, but may ignore some spatial relationships. For example, a child may say, "These are the same."
7	Congruence Determiner	6	A sign of development is when a child determines congruence by comparing all attributes and all spatial relationships. For example, a child at this level may say that two shapes are the same shape and the same size after comparing every one of their sides and angles.
7	Congruence Superposer	7	As children develop understanding, they can move and place objects on top of each other to determine congruence. For example, a child at this level may say that two shapes are the same shape and the same size after laying them on top of each other.
8+	Congruence Representer	8	Continued development is evidenced as children refer to geometric properties and explain with transformations. For example, a child at this level may say, "These must be congruent because they have equal sides, all square corners, and I can move them on top of each other exactly."

Developmental Levels for Spatial Sense and Motions

Infants and toddlers spend a great deal of time learning about the properties and relations of objects in space. Very young children know and use the shape of their environment in navigation activities. With guidance they can learn to "mathematize" this knowledge. They can learn about direction, perspective, distance, symbolization, location, and coordinates. Children typically follow an observable developmental progression in developing spatial sense with recognizable stages or levels. This developmental path can be described as part of a learning trajectory.

Age Range	Level Name	Level	Description
4	Simple Turner	1	An early sign of spatial sense is when a child mentally turns an object to perform easy tasks. For example, given a shape with the top marked with color, the child may correctly identify which of three shapes it would look like if it were turned "like this" (90 degree turn demonstrated), before physically moving the shape.
5	Beginning Slider, Flipper, Turner	2	This sign of development occurs when a child can use the correct motions, but is not always accurate in direction and amount. For example, a child at this level may know a shape has to be flipped to match another shape, but flips it in the wrong direction.
6	Slider, Flipper, Turner	3	As children develop spatial sense, they can perform slides and flips, often only horizontal and vertical, by using manipulatives. For example, a child at this level may perform turns of 45, 90, and 180 degrees. For example, a child knows a shape must be turned 90 degrees to the right to fit into a puzzle.
7	Diagonal Mover	4	A sign of development is when a child can perform diagonal slides and flips. For example, children at this level may know a shape must be turned or flipped over an oblique line (45 degree orientation) to fit into a puzzle.
8	Mental Mover	5	Further signs of development occur when a child can predict results of moving shapes using mental images. A child at this level may say, "If you turned this 120 degrees, it would be just like this one."

Developmental Levels for Patterning and Early Algebra

Algebra begins with a search for patterns. Identifying patterns helps bring order, cohesion, and predictability to seemingly unorganized situations and allows one to make generalizations beyond the information directly available. The recognition and analysis of patterns are important components of young children's intellectual development because they provide a foundation for the development of algebraic thinking. Although prekindergarten children engage in pattern-related activities and recognize patterns in their everyday environment, research has revealed that an abstract understanding of patterns develops gradually during the early childhood years. Children typically follow an observable developmental progression in learning about patterns with recognizable stages or levels. This developmental path can be described as part of a learning trajectory.

Age Range	Level Name	Level	Description
2	Pre-Patterner	1	A child at the earliest level does not recognize patterns. For example, a child may name a striped shirt with no repeating unit a "pattern."
3	Pattern Recognizer	2	At this level, the child can recognize a simple pattern. For example, a child at this level may say, "I'm wearing a pattern" about a shirt with black and white stripes.
4	Pattern Fixer	3	At this level the child fills in missing elements of a pattern, first with ABABAB patterns. When given items in a row with an item missing, such as ABAB_BAB, the child identifies and fills in the missing element (A).
4	Pattern Duplicator AB	4	A sign of development is when the child can duplicate an ABABAB pattern, although the children may have to work alongside the model pattern. For example, given objects in a row, ABABAB, the child may make his or her own ABABAB row in a different location.
4	Pattern Extender AB	5	At this level the child extends AB repeating patterns. For example, given items in a row—ABABAB—the child adds ABAB to the end of the row.
4	Pattern Duplicator	6	At this level, the child is able to duplicate simple patterns (not just alongside the model pattern). For example, given objects in a row, ABBABBABB, the child may make his or her own ABBABBABB row in a different location.
5	Pattern Extender	7	A sign of development is when the child can extend simple patterns. For example, given objects in a row, ABBABBABB, he or she may add ABBABB to the end of the row.
7	Pattern Unit Recognizer	8	At this level, a child can identify the smallest unit of a pattern. For example, given objects in a row with one missing, ABBAB_ABB, he or she may identify and fill in the missing element.

Developmental Levels for Classifying and Analyzing Data

Data analysis contains one big idea: classifying, organizing, representing, and using information to ask and answer questions. The developmental continuum for data analysis includes growth in classifying and counting to sort objects and quantify their groups. Children eventually become capable of simultaneously classifying and counting; for example, counting the number of colors in a group of objects. Children typically follow an observable developmental progression in learning about patterns with recognizable stages or levels. This developmental path can be described as part of a learning trajectory.

Age Range	Level Name	Level	Description
2	Similarity Recognizer	1	The first sign that a child can classify is when he or she recognizes, intuitively, two or more objects as "similar" in some way. For example, "that's another doggie."
2	Informal Sorter	2	A sign of development is when a child places objects that are alike in some attribute together, but switches criteria and may use functional relationships as the basis for sorting. A child at this level might stack blocks of the same shape or put a cup with its saucer.
3	Attribute Identifier	3	The next level is when the child names attributes of objects and places objects together with a given attribute, but cannot then move to sorting by a new rule. For example, the child may say, "These are both red."
4	Attribute Sorter	4	At the next level the child sorts objects according to given attributes, forming categories, but may switch attributes during the sorting. A child at this stage can switch rules for sorting if guided. For example, the child might start putting red beads on a string, but switches to spheres of different colors.
5	Consistent Sorter	5	A sign of development is when the child can sort consistently by a given attribute. For example, the child might put several identical blocks together.
6	Exhaustive Sorter	6	At the next level, the child can sort consistently and exhaustively by an attribute, given or created. This child can use terms "some" and "all" meaningfully. For example, a child at this stage would be able to find all the attribute blocks of a certain size and color.

Age Range	Level Name	Level	Description
6	Multiple Attribute Sorter	7	A sign of development is when the child can sort consistently and exhaustively by more than one attribute, sequentially. For example, a child at this level can put all the attribute blocks together by color, then by shape.
7	Classifier and Counter	8	At the next level, the child is capable of simultaneously classifying and counting. For example, the child counts the number of colors in a group of objects.
7	List Grapher	9	In the early stage of graphing, the child graphs by simply listing all cases. For example, the child may list each child in the class and each child's response to a question.
8+	Multiple Attribute Classifier	10	A sign of development is when the child can intentionally sort according to multiple attributes, naming and relating the attributes. This child understands that objects could belong to more than one group. For example, the child can complete a two-dimensional classification matrix or form subgroups within groups.
8+	Classifying Grapher	11	At the next level the child can graph by classifying data (e.g., responses) and represent it according to categories. For example, the child can take a survey, classify the responses, and graph the result.
8+	Classifier	12	A sign of development is when the child creates complete, conscious classifications logically connected to a specific property. For example, a child at this level gives a definition of a class in terms of a more general class and one or more specific differences and begins to understand the inclusion relation.
8+	Hierarchical Classifier	13	At the next level, the child can perform hierarchical classifications. For example, the child recognizes that all squares are rectangles, but not all rectangles are squares.
8+	Data Representer	14	Signs of development are when the child organizes and displays data through both simple numerical summaries such as counts, tables, and tallies, and graphical displays, including picture graphs, line plots, and bar graphs. At this level the child creates graphs and tables, compares parts of the data, makes statements about the data as a whole, and determines whether the graphs answer the questions posed initially.